Developing a Universal Religion

David Hockey

Developing a Universal Religion

Why one is Needed
and
How it might be Derived

David Hockey

Stephenson-Hockey Publishing

Stephenson-Hockey Publishing
Portland, Ontario
Canada

Copyright © 2003, by David Hockey

All rights reserved. No part of this book may be reproduced or transmitted in any form or by any means, electronic, mechanical or otherwise, without written permission from the author, except for the inclusion of brief quotations in a review.

Copies of this book may be purchased from most local bookstores. Quantity discounts are available on bulk purchases and may be obtained from the publisher. Call 613 272-3119, fax 613 272-8712, visit our website at www.S-HPub.com, or e-mail office@s-hpub.com for details.

National Library of Canada Cataloguing in Publication

Hockey, David, 1932-
   Developing a universal religion : why one is needed and how it might be derived / David Hockey.

Includes bibliographical references and index.
ISBN 0-9731156-1-0

   1. Religions (Proposed, universal, etc.) 2. Religion—Philosophy. 3. Religion—Moral and ethical aspects. I. Title.

BL390.H62 2004   210   C2003-905343-1

Cover photograph of the Tarantula Nebula.
High-speed ejecta from exploded stars (lower right-hand corner) create luminous filaments seen throughout. New stars are being formed in the central region.
Photograph created by The Hubble Heritage Team (AURA/STScI/NASA).

Printed and bound in Canada by Hignell Book Printing

Contents

CONTENTS V
ACKNOWLEDGEMENTS VII
INTRODUCTION 9

PART ONE: THINKING AND MORAL PROBLEMS 13
    INTRODUCTION TO PART ONE 15
    CHAPTER ONE: THINKING 17
    CHAPTER TWO: SOLVING PROBLEMS 35
    CHAPTER THREE: MAKING DECISIONS 47
    CONCLUSION TO PART ONE 53

PART TWO: RELIGIONS AND THEIR SOURCE 55
    INTRODUCTION TO PART TWO 57
    CHAPTER FOUR: RELIGIONS' ORIGINS 59
    CHAPTER FIVE: REVELATIONS AND CONVERSIONS 69
    CHAPTER SIX: PRESENT DAY RELIGIONS 83
    CONCLUSION TO PART TWO 101

PART THREE: PURPOSE 103
    INTRODUCTION TO PART THREE 105
    CHAPTER SEVEN: THE UNIVERSE 107
    CHAPTER EIGHT: LIFE 119
    CHAPTER NINE: LOOKING FOR A PURPOSE 133
    CHAPTER TEN: LIFE AND EXPLOITING 145
    CONCLUSION TO PART THREE 155

PART FOUR: DEVELOPING A UNIVERSAL RELIGION ... 157
    INTRODUCTION TO PART FOUR 159
    CHAPTER ELEVEN: WHY BOTHER? 161
    CHAPTER TWELVE: POSSIBLE APPLICATIONS 173
    CHAPTER THIRTEEN: DETERMINING MORAL BEHAVIOURS 187
    CHAPTER FOURTEEN: A UNIVERSAL RELIGION 203
    CONCLUSION TO PART FOUR 211

CHAPTER POSTSCRIPTS 213
    CONSCIOUSNESS AND CONSCIENCE 215
    PURPOSE AND MEANING 218
    RATIONALITY IN SCIENCE AND RELIGION 220
    CREATIVITY, FREE WILL, AND A REVELATION 223
    GÖDEL'S THEOREM, GENERAL SYSTEMS THEORY, AND THE
    CONSERVATION LAWS 229
    ORIGIN THEORY MODIFICATIONS 233
    MULTI-YEAR TARGETS 234

CHAPTER AND POSTSCRIPT ENDNOTES 236

SELECTED BIBLIOGRAPHY 307

INDEX 311

Acknowledgements

I wish to thank my readers. David Mess, who valiantly ploughed through several early attempts to write this book and so often helped me rethink what I wanted to say. John Radley, who emailed corrections and many helpful suggestions from the other side of the world. Phil Brady and Rob Preston, both of whom stressed the need to simplify, then showed how this might be done; they might still see the need for more. And my daughter, Mandy Brady, who somehow managed to find time in her very busy family and professional life to copy edit; I owe her so much. Where I have gone amiss is entirely my fault, not theirs.

This book is dedicated to my wife and children (because I would like them to have a record of what I have spent so much time thinking about), and to my grandchildren (because I would like them to have an easier time than I had, should they ever start looking for something rational to believe in). It is also offered to readers who like to think for themselves. May they all find something of value within its covers.

David Hockey

Introduction

*Our understanding of reality predisposes what we choose to value—
a place in heaven after death, or a heaven on earth while alive.*

What is a "universal" religion?

A universal religion is one intended to accompany, not replace, existing religions. One that might act as an "umbrella," covering the gaps between existing religions and providing moral guidance when none seems otherwise available or suggesting alternatives when religious differences seem insurmountable. One that looks far into the future and whose focus is on guiding civilizations, nations and communities rather than individuals. One that all beings, of any or no religion, might feel worth adopting, because it complements and enhances their current thinking and beliefs. One that any and all life forms would recognize as relevant to them, be they simple cave dwellers or advanced aliens living far away in other galaxies. One that might guide moral behaviour for as long as life exists.

Could such a religion exist?

You might best answer this question yourself, but please wait until you have read this book.

Why develop a universal religion?

Because, in short, humanity lacks the means to make moral decisions recognizable by all as universally applicable. Without the common purpose that a universal religion could provide, international discussions become quagmires of national interests, organizations owe allegiance to no greater ideal than a hotchpotch of those held by their executives and stockholders, and terrorists deem their warped illusions to be beyond anyone's reproach. Other, and perhaps more compelling reasons to develop a universal religion, are presented and discussed in the second half of the book.

Furthermore, the need for some kind of universal religion and for the purpose that would have to be placed at its head, may already have made itself known to some of us. The first appears as a vague pull toward some kind of spirituality; the second as the brutal recognition that life can seem meaningless. Both urge us to respond.

Is it possible to develop a universal religion?

Again, you might be the best judge of this, once you have reviewed some of the issues discussed in this book.

The book's design

To properly understand the need for a universal religion, we must first understand *why* religions are needed. Part One of this book examines the neurological and environmental conditions that create the mental need for a religion. Essentially, our minds are problem-solving and decision-making entities, handling practical situations proficiently but often finding moral ones difficult. Religions help by shaping the background "environment" that defines the moral problem that confronts us.

Unfortunately, none of our existing religions could become the basis for a universal religion. The rationale for stating so is developed in Part Two.

Part Three searches for a purpose that is significant enough to be used when universally applicable moral decisions have to be made. It gives reasons for stating that life's behaviour itself may provide such a purpose. Part Four presents some philosophical and practical reasons for using such a purpose then illustrates how it might be used to develop a rational code of "moral" behaviour. Part Four ends with a few suggestions about religion building.

The emphasis throughout this book is on the importance of choosing a suitable (i.e., universal, timeless and rational) purpose and using it to make decisions that impact upon civilization's progress. In that such a purpose will generate moral solutions, it may eventually head a "universal religion." However, this book explores only the reasons why such a religion is needed and how one might be derived; the possible development of one is a task that others might like to think about undertaking.

A few chapters may present too much scientific information for some readers. This amount of detail has been included because science has much to tell us about life and the universe, knowledge that must not be ignored when seeking the foundation for a new religion (just as knowledge of prevailing circumstances was used—albeit possibly with no conscious consideration—by the developers of our existing religions). Introductions are used to mitigate the possible problem of information overload and to help the reader stay focused. Summaries vary; where thought helpful, they provide point-form notes, otherwise they might simply broaden a point of view as a conclusion might. Endnotes and postscripts embellish but also separate the less essential from the main body of text. Almost all of the references are to be found in readily available books or journals. However, if some sections occasionally seem too much to digest, or if what is being explained is already understood, then by all means skim to find just the parts of interest. Reading each chapter's introduction and summary (then perhaps pausing for reflection) before reading (or skipping) the chapter itself, might be the best way to proceed.

Part One

Thinking and Moral Problems

Introduction to Part One

Why do humans have beliefs and religions? This question puzzled me for many years. The answer, "to help us solve moral problems and make moral decisions," only introduces other questions. Why do we have moral problems anyway? Clearly, everyday living requires us to solve many practical problems, but where do moral problems come from?

To understand why humans need beliefs and religions we must first investigate how we think—particularly how we solve practical problems and make practical decisions. Understanding these matters explains why solving abstract problems of morality requires us to invoke beliefs and construct religions. And this, in turn, equips us to examine, with some impartiality, the religions we now employ (we attempt to do this in Part Two).

Chapter One tackles the first task. It discusses the brain, moves to the idea of a mind, and ends by exploring what we usually mean when we say we are thinking. We will find that a great deal of our thinking has to do with solving problems.

Chapter Two shows that all problems originate in, and are structured by, the various environments that we inhabit; practical problems devolve from the practical environment, social problems from the social environment, and so on. But moral problems, issues of "right" or "wrong," originate entirely within our minds, and it is the mind's lack of an environment (other than the one each of us constructs—more about this in Part Two) that makes these difficult to solve.

Chapter Three discusses decision-making. It points out that the desire to attain a purpose is basic to making any decision, be it practical or moral. Moral judgements are metaphysical judgements, so we must have some metaphysical purpose in mind (and also want to attain it) before we can make moral decisions. Religions provide such purposes. They also provide various metaphysical environments; these create and structure our moral problems, as we shall see.

In short, Part One demonstrates that we cannot solve moral problems or make moral decisions without valuing the attainment of some kind of purpose (which can be spiritual or secular). We do not do this because there is (or is not) a god. We do not do this because we follow a religion. We do this, as we will shortly discover, because we try to think rationally when solving important problems and when making important decisions.

Chapter One

Thinking

A discussion about thinking must begin by saying a little about the brain and the mind. The first exists in concrete form: it is pinkish-grey in colour, weighs about three pounds, and has the consistency of jelly. It contains about a hundred billion neural cells supported within some thousand billion neuroglial cells, consumes about twenty percent of the body's energy, and can be dissected and examined microscopically. But the mind is quite a different kettle of fish. In fact, some neuroscientists refute its very existence. They prefer the simpler explanation that thoughts occur in the brain, and claim that what we call the "mind" does not exist. However, it is simpler to discuss the two separately, and this is how they will be treated in this book.

1. The brain

The brain's chief job is to store and operate the controls that command many inherited (or instinctive) body functions. This section discusses a little of what happens during this process, so that the difference between what the brain does and what is involved when thinking can be made clearer.

Instinctive behaviours are transmitted from one generation to the next through gene codings, as has been demonstrated many times. For instance, fruit flies normally wake up with daylight, nap in the afternoon, then fall asleep at dusk. This behaviour is controlled by a gene, the so-called "period gene." If this gene is removed from male and female flies which then mate, their descendants sleep at random times. If the gene is then returned to these time-less progeny, they and their offspring will resume regular sleep patterns. The first, tiny part of this instinctive behaviour started as the result of a mutation[1] eons ago that caused one fly to sleep during the dark, with the concomitant reduced danger of being eaten compared to flies that were sleeping during the day. Surviving and passing this mutation to its descendants, this fly became the progenitor of successive generations that also fell asleep at dusk, so surviving in greater numbers than those lacking this trait.[2]

Jonathan Weiner provides an example[3] that nicely illustrates the value of instinctive behaviour in animals larger than fruit flies. He describes an experiment that uses a blackened piece of cardboard or wood cut into a bird-like shape. When this shape is moved in one direction across a light sky or ceiling it appears to be the silhouette of a goose flying; if it is moved in the other direction it resembles a hawk. When newly hatched goslings, raised in an incubator and having had no contact whatsoever with any adult goose, are shown the cut-out moving in the goose-resembling direction, they pay no attention. When the same cut-out is moved in the opposite direction, they scatter and attempt to hide.

Instinctive behaviours, like all others, depend upon the brain recognizing the significance of signals received from body sensors, or from the presence or absence of chemicals in body fluids. The question slowly being answered[4] is, "how does the brain know what to do when it receives such signals?" Neurons in the brain (Hercule Poirot's "little grey cells") hold the answer.

Most human neural cells (neurons) resemble minute, spiky blobs with tails. The blob, or body, is called the soma. The tail, a long, thin, branching, tube-like extension, is called the axon. The hundreds of short, spiky structures fringing the soma are called dendrites. When activated, electrical signals in the form of electrically charged chemical ions travel from the dendrites, through the soma, along the axon and its branches (the fanout[5]), to a number of bubble-like terminating vesicles. Ions arriving at the vesicles cause the discharge of neurotransmitter chemicals into the minute gaps that separate one neuron from another. These chemicals are detected by so-called synaptic knobs on dendrites belonging to neighbouring neurons, where they may start new ion flows within receptive neurons.

Neural networks store information for later use. This is done in a two-step process. First, flows of chemical ions circulating in tiny closed networks of neurons hold data temporarily. Much information from eyes, ears and other sense organs is temporarily stored in such neural loops while being screened for significance. Since the majority of incoming information is of little interest, most of it is discarded. (Cutting off the energizing nutrients prevents the loops from becoming significant.) Second, information having a relationship to other pre-stored or incoming data that is deemed significant can be kept active by constantly re-energizing the loops. This induces the growth of synaptic knobs on dendrites.[6] Additional synaptic knobs facilitate the transmission of neurochemicals across the dendritic gaps and thus build pathways of lowered electro-chemical resistance connecting one neuron to another. These pathways form neural networks that can retain the bytes of information that induced their formation for many years. Millions and millions of neural networks, each storing tiny bits of information, are to be found within everyone's brain (most laid down during our first few years of life).[7]

The brain analyzes and interprets information coming from the senses[8] by routing it through earlier-formed neural networks. These respond (think "resonate") to the presence of specific, tiny, chunks of information that match the chunks that earlier caused the network to form. This can be illustrated by electronically tracing what happens to information received by the eye, a well-explored example that helps us to understand what the brain does with data from other body sense organs. Light, reflected from the object we are looking at, enters the eye and falls upon the light-sensitive rods and cones in the eye's retina. This creates millions of tiny signals, and these travel along the optic nerve to the brain. Key aspects of the component signal, such as information bytes denoting vertical edges, excite existing neural patterns (i.e., tiny memories) of the kinds of objects that have vertical edges. The same "analysis" is done for horizontal edges, relative sizes, colours, shapes (for instance, the vertices of any triangular aspects the object may possess), and so on.[9] This process continues until the brain excites a pattern that matches stored patterns of objects similar to the one being viewed and the object is "recognized." "Recognition" is complete when additional characteristics, retrieved from other neural networks storing "memories," can be added.[10]

Memories of objects and events are built up by a reverse process. Early in life, a toddler, staring at a fir tree, for example, would have stored information in his or her brain about its general shape, colour, branch pattern, leaf shape and other characteristics. Each aspect would have been broken into smaller bytes, temporarily then permanently stored and linked by neural pathways to other related bytes (including, but added much later, bytes representing the name of the tree). If more fir trees were noted, neurotransmitting chemicals would continue to induce the formation of synaptic knobs linking and reinforcing stored memories of tree parts and whole trees. Eventually, neural networks storing relatively detailed memories of fir trees would be built. Information received upon seeing a maple tree, having many similar features, would connect into many of the same neural patterns used by the fir tree memory, but would, of course, connect into other quite different ones. (At least, it would for those who had learned the difference between a fir and a maple. Those who had not discovered the similarities and differences would have to make do with a generic tree-memory.)

Whether or not any of this knowledge affects survival would be a matter of circumstance, but it is clear that memories built up through experience do greatly affect what we know,[11] as well as what we come to believe and how we behave. Much more about this later.

Information that depicts frequently seen objects travels along, and reinforces, the same neural pathways, making them evident by the thousands of synaptic knobs (as many as 10,000 or more) that form on the dendrites of neurons along these routes. Such large numbers of synaptic links vastly increase the brain's sensitivity to similar stimuli,[12] thereby decreasing response time—an important survival feature in potentially dangerous environments. Conversely, seldom-seen objects take more mental effort and may be only slowly recognized. Because our brains can carry out many functions simultaneously, we experience signal analysis and recognition as though it happens instantaneously. However, information flow along neural axons and across synaptic gaps is slow compared to information flow in computers.

Of course, recognizing the significance of incoming stimuli involves a lot more than described above. To better appreciate how information from our senses is used within our brains, consider what must be happening if, for example, we suddenly notice that we are about to walk into the branch of a tree. Before the brain can induce any action, it must, at the very least, understand the following. First, it must understand the nature of the tree's relationship to us (e.g., that the tree will do nothing to us if we do not bump into it). Second, the brain—as well as the mind—must have access to, and be able to use, memories of what actions have succeeded in the past (e.g., that we can avoid trouble by simply ducking our head or by stepping sideways). Third, the brain needs to be constantly aware of the body's abilities and limitations (e.g., it must know that we can't jump out of the way if, for example, we walk with a cane). All these things, and many more, must be known to the brain just so that it can cause the body to act in a suitable manner.

It is important to note that most of what has been described above is not thinking, for even simple life forms perform many of the same functions. They react to stimuli, and show evidence of possessing memories by using the information stored in these memories when reacting. Amoebae move away from acidic areas. Earthworms sense the void of large holes in the ground and move around them. Spiders feel their web trembling and emerge to envelop prey, and so on. All living entities respond to changes in their environment by sensing stimuli of one kind or another, then acting upon what these stimuli represent to them.[13] These sensing, analyzing and danger-avoiding activities are continually being carried out, even by primitive animals. Advanced animals have inherited these same abilities, most of which occur within the brain. But almost all of these are programmed activities which take place without any thought.[14] They form what may be considered to be a lower level of neural functioning. Although collecting, storing and recognizing signals are important and necessary functions significant to thinking (just as buying and storing tools and materials are important functions in a factory's operation), they are not "thinking" per se. They are simply operations that trigger the release of action-inducing chemicals. In as much, these functions are similar to many others that support and maintain the body's welfare. Section three of this chapter clarifies this distinction.

2. The Mind

We will have much to say about the mind, memories and thinking, so these terms should first be defined. It is reasonable, for our purposes, to say that the myriad of neural networks of stored information that we call memories, when considered together, form what we might call a "quiescent" mind—a mind that is ready to handle information, but is not actually doing so. (A person with such a mind would be called "brain dead," and the kind and amount of information that such a "mind" might be reactivated to handle would vary greatly with circumstances.) An "active" mind would be one where chemical ion flows are carrying information from place to place. All living minds are constantly active.

The term "memories" includes all of an individual's mentally stored facts, theories, opinions, personal experiences, recallable emotions, past thoughts, ideas, etc. "Thinking," for most of our purposes, can be defined as the act of seeking relationships between these memories, or between memories and current stimulations being received from body sensors. (What occurs during thinking is examined more thoroughly in the next section.)

Animal behaviour studies suggest that many animals possess rudimentary thinking abilities. Tool making is considered to be evidence of the ability to think and many creatures make and use tools. Racoons pick up and use stones to break open clams. Beavers not infrequently shape wood as they construct dams to hold water to store and preserve food they need during winter. Chimpanzees use rocks or heavy sticks to crack open hard-shelled fruit and nuts; they also fashion drinking cups and rain-sheltering umbrellas from banana leaves, and use sticks to extract insects and grubs from small holes.[15] Birds also make and use tools.[16]

Many animal behaviourists contend that their studies demonstrate animals can think. Hausser declares that animals think,[17] but simply lack the ability to express their many thoughts and emotions to others.[18] Calvin states that animals can assess their environment, consider alternative actions and make decisions—all necessitating the ability to think.[19] That animals can think implies that thinking, like every other biological feature and process, has evolved over the ages. Thinking certainly did not suddenly spring, fully formed, into existence in humans.

The specific content of any mind (animal or human) is currently hidden to investigators because the mind functions only when neural networks are biochemically or electrically activated, and, to date, scientists have no technique precise enough to find out just which memories of the multitude locked in the brain's neural patterns are being activated at any particular instant.[20] Nevertheless, neural networks are real; they can be seen (and photographed as they develop) increasing in complexity as infants age and learn. (The increasing complexity of an adult's learning brain is hidden within, and masked by, its multitude of existing neural pathways.) The biochemical flows that retrieve and carry information stored within these neural patterns is also real. In short, neural networks whose paths store memories within the brain constitute the mind, and thinking depends upon biochemical flows activating some or many of these networks, so releasing (and making available for potential use) the information they hold.

3. First- and Second-level Thinking

Just what does the human mind do when it thinks? Here I must conjecture a little.

Thinking seems to occur on several levels. (The term "level" will be used to distinguish one kind of mental activity from another.[21] These thinking activities overlap, and are not actually separate and distinct. They could be described as different "modes of thought," but separating the process into three "levels" aids explanation.) Before we begin, let us discount what happens purely autonomically—the brain's control of body functions mentioned in section one. As has been stated, what the brain does reflexively is not considered thinking; we will mostly ignore this kind of activity from here on.

3.1. First-level Thinking—Awareness

In what will be called the "first level" of thinking, the brain simply absorbs information from its sensors (predominantly the eyes for humans). First-level thought amounts to little more than a general awareness of one's surroundings. Cassirer writes about this mental activity as follows. "In the realm of mythic conception" . . . (which preceded the use of words and language) . . . "thought does not confront its data in an attitude of free contemplation, seeking to understand their structure and their systematic connections, and analyzing them according to their parts and functions, but is simply captivated by a total impression. Such thinking does not develop the given content of experience; it does not reach backward or forward from that vantage point to find 'causes' and 'effects,' but rests content with taking in the sheer existent."[22]

Animals, certainly, have this ability. Most mammals mainly comprehend their environment visually, as we do, but many obtain the same kind of awareness predominantly through a different sense—that which has become their most highly developed one. Bats, we know, rely upon their ears, much more than their eyes, to build instantaneous mental pattern-pictures of their surroundings. Dogs are likely to develop odour maps of their territory.

First-level thinking is restricted to this kind of activity; the mental equivalent of simply displaying information within the brain. It exists only as temporary neural ion flows that form patterns, none of which become associated with previously stored patterns, for memories are not needed to generate this kind of awareness. These experiences never (unless linked to other memories during subsequent second-level thinking activities and recalled as an impression of some kind) form part of any permanent memory.[23] "First level" might be defined as the direct and continual subconscious mapping of one's awareness of surroundings. It is the mental equivalent of images forming on a screen at the back of a pin-hole camera, or on a table-top placed beneath a camera obscura. The images are clear and colourful, active and information rich, but transient.

3.2. Second-level Thinking—Association

Second-level thinking occurs in two forms, subconscious and conscious. It is defined to be occurring when the mind discovers meaningful associations between stored memories (i.e., earlier-formed, data-storing, neural networks) and incoming information, between two or more sets of incoming data, or between stored memories.[24] Second-level thinking happens continuously at the subconscious level and intermittently at the conscious level. (This implies that subconscious thought precedes conscious thought, a phenomenon that brain-scanning has verified. We will refer to this again, in Chapter Five.)

Scanning incoming data for relevancy and significance is second-level thinking's most important function. A living entity's most relevant and important concern is almost always survival (resulting in a constant search for active threats or potential danger,[25] and for food and water). Its second most relevant and important concern is the possible opportunity to reproduce. The nature of this kind of thinking means that information is almost always stored in conjunction with emotional overtones.[26]

Almost all subconscious second-level thinking is immediately discarded (as most habitat environments are benign and otherwise not of much significance). When meaningful relationships between incoming data and stored memories are found, they may trigger body reactions (such as danger-avoiding activity) and may break through from the subconscious into the conscious mind, where they are further considered.[27]

Again, animals make these associations and comparisons (continually at the subconscious level, and periodically, with varying degrees of ability, at the conscious level). Animals generally ignore non-threatening events but react to potential danger situations, demonstrating that they know from past experience or instinct (remembering the gosling experiment) how to distinguish one from the other.

(Animals can do more than simply react to situations; they can plan ahead, using a knowledge of prevailing circumstances—social as well as situational. Dunbar [after describing how an old, ousted, male chimpanzee used rewards and punishments to manipulate an alliance with a weak young chimpanzee and so regain and retain control of a harem from its new, stronger leader] concluded that the behaviour of monkeys and apes showed that they can predict the outcome of their actions.[28])

Associating memories and/or stimuli in meaningful ways forms the basis of second-level thinking; language is certainly not needed to make such neural network linkages. Infants demonstrate that they can make associations and comparisons long before they can speak; for example, they react with surprise if some aspect of a frequently observed image has been changed.

The critical aspects that distinguish second-level thinking from first-level thinking are that, during second-level thinking, two or more sets of information are compared, differences are noted, and the relevance of any found variance is sought. The degree to which any detected difference is understood depends upon the sophistication of the animal—its evolutionary level, past experiences, education and intelligence. Simple animals may understand little about any discovered differences; humans may understand much.

The discovered relationship may, as previously noted, be immediately discounted and forgotten. However, those deemed to be significant may become stored as part of a new neural network if one or more links are forged between pre-existing patterns. The simple example that follows might clarify this important process.

Imagine that I want to drill a hole through a block of wood, and that I have the required drill but the drill bits are too short. What would I do? Well, I would look around to see what I had that might be long enough. When this first happened to me, it took a little while to think of cutting the head from a long nail then using the nail. However, the second time this occurred, I quickly remembered my previous solution.

The first situation above entailed second-level thought, the second occurrence did not. In the first situation, my mind had to mentally list the properties a useful bit must possess (strength, hardness, rigidity, length and so on) then cause me to seek something that possessed such properties. The two data sets (the neural network patterns that stored information about what was required, and the streams of data coming from my eyes as I looked over my workshop) were compared, and matches that denoted relevance to the problem induced temporary ion-flow loops between corresponding aspects. Once a solution was found, once I had spotted a nail and realized that it would serve my purpose, the temporary links[29] that were significant were retained long enough to be made permanent through the growth of synaptic knobs, thus becoming available for future use as part of my neural network complex. Linking and learning turn out to be the same thing.

Simply remembering something done, heard, seen or read about is not second-level thinking, it is merely reactivating previously formed neural paths. No new links are made, and nothing new is learned during simple recall.[30] In other words, recalling memories to mind is similar to looking at a picture or running a movie in one's head, whereas second-level thinking is more akin to looking at two pictures or running two movies side-by-side, while constantly comparing and contrasting the two.

Infants, with brains containing well over 100 billion neurons, make neural links continuously as they attempt to join sensory stimuli with information that is stored in memory.[31] Infants and young children learn quickly and easily, because stimuli are being stored and linked on a more-or-less "tabula rasa" (a term meaning "blank slate," first used by John Locke in 1690 in his *Essay Concerning Human Understanding* to describe the mind of a newborn). That many of these associations will turn out to be incorrect and unusable is inconsequential; the links that matter are the ones that are subsequently reinforced through use. Billions of early made connections remain unused throughout all our lives, slowly atrophying. Christian de Duve pointed out[32] that neurons initially make many loose connections; these are strengthened only if useful, and are discarded if not. The associations that are used, of course, are those connecting memories that, by being linked, provide useful understandings: the name of a toy, object or a sibling; the idea that certain results always follow certain activities (things fall to the ground when released, for instance); how to call for food, etc.[33] Adults learn more slowly, because their minds first attempt to fit new stimuli into previously existing networks, and only when this can't be done do they progress to looking for, then forming, completely new links. In other words, adults do not immediately think when reacting to a stimulus; they first search, very rapidly and almost entirely subconsciously, for past associations and use them, whenever the fit seems close enough.

Realizing that second-level thinking is little more than electrochemically comparing memories with incoming data (or comparing memories already in storage), recognizing relationships of significance between them, then making new neural links, tells us again that this kind of thinking cannot be unique to humankind. The brains of many animals do this.[34] In fact, we should expect linkages to form between memories and incoming sensory stimulations in all animate entities, because sense receptor cells and neurons exist to provide information so that similarities and differences between incoming and stored memories can be detected. Animals and humans learn what these variations may imply and use this knowledge to survive and to mate.[35] In short, humans are not the only life forms that think—animals do too.

However, thinking did not become what we generally understand it to be today until early humans discovered the use of words and languages. The next section shows how this ability led to a more comprehensive level of thought, one that we will be calling third-level thinking. Third-level thinking is, primarily, a human activity.

4. Third-level Thinking and Language

The advances brought about by human thought have made modern life so different from the way it was just a few hundred years ago, that folks of those days might rightly have called us sorcerers or magicians, were we and a few of our many technologies to suddenly have appeared among them. People of such times would never have been able to understand how others many kilometres away can be heard, how their image can be projected upon a screen, how heavy machines can fly through the air, how joints and body organs can be replaced, or how pest- and disease-resistant plants can be developed. Today most of us take these developments for granted.

How has it been possible for humans to discover and accomplish so much in just a few thousand years? Many other species have existed for tens of millions of years; why have none ever attained anything even remotely approaching human achievements?

Why did their cognitive ability not develop as it has for humans? The answer, we know, is two-fold: humans possess opposable thumbs (whose manipulative capacity has been enhanced by bipedalism—allowing unrestricted hand usage and maximizing latent abilities to build and use tools) and, even more importantly, we have developed and use languages.

Language development probably began when sounds were used to express emotions. This practice is widespread among animals and birds who can be heard declaring their feelings when they grunt, cry, bark or sing. Such sounds sum their current emotional state and declare it to the world, conveying meaning to other sentient species around them. Intentional sounds—those that are not just involuntary reactions to a stimuli—are commonly expressed to improve the survival chances of the originator and its species.

There is an important difference between publicizing one emotion and vocalizing a series of them. A cry of pain can be an instinctive reaction, requiring no thinking ability—a behaviour discussed previously. A cry of pain followed by one of anger, then one of threat, may well be demonstrating the use of something like a language because the animal is attempting to make others understand and respond to its mental or emotional state.

The development of any language, like most evolutionary change, would doubtlessly have taken place sporadically, in dribbles and spurts. Significant advances were likely only made whenever a particular kind of vocalization could be repeatedly used to convey some special meaning to another, or when an exchange of sounds enabled an exchange of intentions, and such an interchange was reiterated with some consistency.[36]

Animals can, and do, use languages with some proficiency. Gerbils have developed a fairly complex language to warn one another of the presence of predators. Dolphins, like whales, exchange complex information sonically; they can also recognize, and respond appropriately to, the meaning hidden within the grammatical structure of human hand signals. Chimpanzees use primitive language forms, and many have been trained to select symbols that convey their desires for food, drink, or toys. They are also able to express a whole range of other reactions in response to questioning. Several have been trained to use sign language, and one such chimp subsequently taught others this communication method.[37]

Primitive language usage would have emerged a great many times as species developed,[38] but it has never developed to any significant extent (as far as we know) in any species other than our own. Two evolutionary developments contributed to our ability: a deep-set larynx (which forms a large, resonating chamber, possibly helped into position as we began walking upright) and vocal chords (which can vibrate and are controllable). These features allow us to form and vocalize an almost unlimited number of distinctly different sounds.[39]

Thinking by using word equivalents became possible as soon as words began to be used. A simple proto-language (employing nouns, verbs, subjects, objects, and simple sentence structures) would have begun to take shape from the outset.

Language use would have improved our species' ability to recall memories (the first step in discovering links or relationships between them and incoming stimuli). Once relationships had been found and named, early humans would have used this knowledge within their clans to enhance their group's survival. Third-level thinking and language development would now continue forever hand-in-hand, because an improvement in one concomitantly produces an improvement in the other.

Cassirer, discussing these early phases of language development, stated: "Before the intellectual work of conceiving and understanding of phenomena can set in, the work of naming must have preceded it, and have reached a certain point of elaboration. For it is this process which transforms the world of sense impression, which animals also possess, into a mental world, a world of ideas and meanings. All theoretical cognition takes its departure from a world already preformed by language."[40]

Word arrangements, syntax and sentence structures are essential components of all languages.[41] Thus the ability to sequence thoughts must have developed before language could have evolved. Calvin suggests[42] that this skill first arose as our ancestors learned how to throw rocks and sticks accurately, an ability which requires the careful sequencing of vision, arm, and finger movements to be successful.[43] This is likely to have happened about two million y.a. (years ago), when *Homo erectus* descended from trees to live on the African plains, and throwing from an upright posture became a common occurrence. Sequencing (of data) is a necessary part of comparing memories and incoming stimuli; it simplifies the discovery of meaningful relationships between mental data, and, as earlier noted, relationship-discovering is the quintessential feature of second-level thinking.

Various kinds of evidence exist indicating *Homo*'s early use of language. Rudgley, in *The Lost Civilizations of the Stone Age*,[44] refers to work done by Dietrich and Ursula Mania, on findings that date to between 350,000 and 300,000 y.a. from the Bilzingsleben Lower Palaeolithic site near Halle in former East Germany. This site contains evidence of workshop areas, complete with anvil stones (where tools were made) and stone, wood and bone remnants (all showing tool markings). Four artifacts with a series of parallel-cut incisions were also found. It is thought that a clan of considerable dexterity lived and worked in this area, one which very likely used some rudimentary form of language, and that the parallel lines probably conveyed some specific meaning.

Rhulen, a linguist, by investigating word origins, has found evidence that supports the theory that all languages originate from one, proto-sapiens, language, which existed some 100,000 y.a.[45] Nichols has examined syntax and other structural mechanisms used in languages, and dates their origins even further back, to at least 132,000 y.a.[46]

Words and language are central to what we are calling third-level thinking. We may not always select and use actual words when thinking consciously, but a few moment's reflection about how attention is being directed from one aspect to another within our mind when thinking consciously makes it apparent that we use sentence-structure equivalents. (Tattersall and Matternes go as far as to say that we could not even conceive the idea of thought if we did not use a language.[47])

Third-level thinking manifests itself as if we were talking to ourselves. For instance, when we are preparing to express a point of view we fabricate sentences, developing and rejecting trains of thought within our minds. We usually attempt to follow one main track when thinking, but our central theme is always surrounded by a plethora of other, loosely associated, thoughts and images, each offering more data for potential inclusion. Our thoughts wend their way among these submissions, and only finally crystallize when we mouth or write a statement, or act upon a thought. Cassirer again: "only symbolic expression can yield the possibility of prospect and retrospect, because it is only by symbols that distinctions are not merely made, but fixed in consciousness. What the mind has once created, what has been culled from the total sphere of consciousness, does not fade away again when the spoken word has set its seal upon it and given it definite form."[48]

Third-level thinking is slow compared to the speed of second-level thinking because word selection and arrangement takes time. Moreover, third-level thinking is always preceded by second-level thinking. Although we may feel that our conscious thoughts occur immediately, experiments (particularly those with people who have sustained brain damage[49]) show that unconscious emotional signals—a component of subconscious thinking, alluded to earlier—always precede conscious thinking, and certainly affect decision making.[50]

The consequences of prior subconscious second-level thinking have been often noted by novelists. They, not infrequently, state that their characters "took over" and wrote the story. Actually, their subconscious second-level thinking would have continuously explored and developed associations between memories of characters, and the results of this activity would have been fed to their conscious second and third level of thinking, giving rise to the feeling that their characters were in control.[51]

Language development facilitated huge improvements in *Homo sapiens'* ability to problem solve,[52] and this significantly increased their survival ability. Language use allowed early men and women to teach weapon construction, organize group hunting, deploy themselves to previously determined purposes, and so on, considerably enhancing their chances of obtaining food, killing animals or besting enemies. Greater skill and efficiency in these areas left more time for other activities—in animal and plant domestication, artistry and creativity, pottery and ornament production, culture and recreation, to provide just a few examples. Thinking, language use, problem solving, and the practical application of what has been learned form a spiral of constant and accelerating improvement that continues in humans today. (But only as long as the whole is reality-based: introducing fanciful assumptions about the nature of things warps and obstructs the whole process. More about this in later chapters.)

5. Language and Uniqueness

This might be a good time to note that, although we use words as though they mean to others exactly what they mean to us, this is never the case. The precise meaning or nuance of every word differs from one person to another for several reasons.

We learn a language by linking mental images of objects and events to words and phrases that we memorize. But the library of mental images we each must have before we can begin to learn a language is built from life experiences, and these are unique to each possessor. Every word a speaker or writer uses is defined for that person by the bank of memories carried within their mind. But, each person hearing or reading these words interprets their meaning using their own memory set. (A couple of crude examples: one person says "tree," thinking of a small fir tree in a garden; the other person hears "tree," and thinks of a large maple tree in a forest. Or, one person says "look at that car," admiring its colour; the other says "yes," seeing its model and thinking of the engine that powers it.) We can never convey precisely what we have in mind to another person. Furthermore, each of us defines what we consider to be true by referring to what we know about ourselves and our universe (i.e., by referring to the memories of reality that life has delivered to our minds since infancy) and this is constantly changing, as our knowledge about objects and events keeps changing.[53] Thus, even our personal definition of the "truth" will change as we ourselves age and mature.[54]

The fact that word meanings change over time and become more precise as we understand more, can be readily illustrated by considering the word "atom." Two thousand years ago there was debate about whether such a thing even existed. Two hundred years ago a few believed that atoms existed, but no one knew anything about their structure. Twenty five years ago physicists wondered about the possibility of quarks existing within atoms; today we know that quark trios make up the protons and neutrons that are nuclear components of every atom, and that quarks are possibly composed of dimensionally bound energy fields.

Now, not everyone knows such details, but some do. And the images that the word "atom" conjures up in the minds of those who do, are clearly more meaningful, precise, potentially useful and valuable than the mind images of those who do not know about such things.

Remove language, and third-level thinking will disappear, mental consciousness[55] will degenerate, and what we have been calling second-level thinking will be all that remains. Uninhibited feelings and emotions may then dominate behaviour as they once must have done in dinosaur days.

6. Thinking and the Universe

Linking sensory data together, as second-level thinking does, can produce meaningful results precisely because everything in the universe is linked to every other thing through causality. Causality simply means that nothing in the universe happens without some preceding cause. This more-or-less obvious fact (known to René Descartes over three hundred years ago) actually reveals several other important details about the universe.

Causality states that everything that happens has been caused by some previous event or events, and it means that everything that exists today was created from some thing or things that existed in another form at an earlier time. In other words, events and things don't just appear out of thin air, something causes them to appear.

It is easy to understand that everything is made from smaller pieces, and that these are, in turn, made from even smaller fragments. Also we can readily understand that the properties of any structure depends upon the properties of its components. For example, we don't build railway bridges out of wood these days; it's not strong enough. We use steel made mostly from iron, because iron atoms are tightly bound together by an electromagnetic force. (Wood is made from larger, widely spaced, carbon-based molecules that are only weakly held together.) The properties and behaviour of everything can be similarly explained in terms of more fundamental properties, once we know enough. The point is, we wouldn't discover any such relationship through second-level thinking, nor develop any such explanation with all its useful predictions, if the universe was not causal.

Causality affects everything about us; it allows us to learn and it allows us to make things that work. Consequently (although not consciously) we have built this concept deep into the roots of the languages we use and the thinking we do.[56] However, we don't usually go around saying that the universe is causal; we just expect it to behave rationally or logically. Rational behaviour has been defined as behaviour that is consistent with, or based upon, reason or logic, and neither is possible without the existence of limitless causal relationships. One single break in this chain of causality would negate every one of the explanations and predictions we so much rely upon in all aspects of life.

The fact that the universe is causal has a number of very interesting linguistic consequences. One is that the very words and languages we use must grow out of, and conform to, the reality that surrounds us. This cannot be otherwise. We might try to invent a language not limited by the nature of the universe, but what could it possibly be? Existing words could not be used, for each one carries some of our understanding about the nature of things. Words would have to be invented, but none of these could refer to anything within the universe, by definition of what we are trying to do. We would end up with gibberish, not a language. It would convey no meaning and bring about no understanding. In fact we could not even invent such a language, because we are unable to think without being affected and constrained by the logic and rationality of the knowledge about the universe that we carry within our brains.

Steven Pinker[57] argues that a "Universal Grammar" underlies and constrains all languages. He further claims that the existence of a Universal Grammar is evidence that culture is not just a matter of nature and nurture, as the standard social science model would have us believe. This, he suggests, means that morality cannot be relative to time or situation, but must be universal and becomes built into our minds by our use of a language. I would amend his claim and state that all languages are constrained by the physical cause-and-effect rationality of the universe. It is this causality and rationality that underpins and structures language's "Universal Grammar."

As for morality; we devise our moral statements using words whose definitions vary from one language to another, and that change from time to time and from person to person, as previously noted. Thus, no humanly stated moral law or ethical principle can be universal or permanent.

7. Thinking and Intelligence

Webster[58] defines intelligence as follows.

> *the power or act of understanding; mental acuteness or sagacity; the power of meeting any situation, esp. a novel situation, successfully by proper behavior adjustments; the ability to apprehend the interrelationships of presented facts in such a way as to guide action towards a desired goal.*

Any of these definitions may be applied to second-level thinking. Third-level thinking enhances and continues this process; it amplifies "mental acuteness or sagacity." Thus, thinking and intelligence amount to much the same thing. Chapter Two investigates this connection a little more fully by discussing the mental gymnastics of problem solving.

Summary

The following points are important to this book.

- The brain receives, stores (in temporary as well as permanent locations), and uses information to direct activities that support the body's welfare. These responses are mostly "hardwired," the result of millions of years of evolution, and do not involve what we call "thinking."
- The mind develops as meaningful relationships between stored information (memories) and incoming sensory perceptions are discovered. Mental activities include becoming aware (first-level thinking), noting relationships (second-level thinking), and consciously manipulating information using words and a language.
- Sentient species think (to the extent that this is possible for their species) and act rationally most of the time. To do otherwise reduces the species' chances of survival because their home (the universe) is rationally (i.e., causally) constructed.

A dropped larynx, vocal chords, time, imagination, and much practice, have changed grunts into sonnets, and caves into space stations. Languages have allowed us to name, record and even tell friends on the other side of the world about the neural-link-forming relationships we discover everywhere we bother to look.

The universe's causality binds thinking, language and intelligence together. Applying what we have discovered through investigating causality's consequences enables us to solve problems and make decisions proficiently. Rational thought helps us to survive; it gifts us with understanding and confers a degree of control over objects and events.

Additional layers of mental ability will doubtless accrue as life continues to evolve: heightened empathy, intuitive-like jumps in comprehension, telepathy perhaps; capabilities unimaginable today, as some of our current capabilities would have been unimaginable a few thousand years ago. Life's rise from bacteria to cephalopod to humankind—as we can trace on this planet alone—provides reason enough to expect more intellectual aptitude to come in the future.

The future of humans as a species is much less predictable. It depends so much on our willingness to think and act rationally. Solving problems and making decisions, both practical and moral, in a manner that respects the universe's causality, are the activities that will determine humanity's future.

It is time to examine how we actually perform these tasks.

(A postscript to this chapter titled "Consciousness and Conscience" is to be found commencing page 215.)

Chapter Two

Solving Problems

Humans excel at solving problems. (Pinker actually states that the mind has evolved simply to outsmart the competition by being able to solve problems.[1]) Humans living and working in space is possibly one of the best examples of how successful we have become in problem solving, but examples can be found in all fields of endeavour, from discovering how genes work, to creating an emotional demand for a new product.

Problems come in two flavours, tangible and abstract. Or, if you like, practical and metaphysical. The difference between these two types can be illustrated by discussing the kinds of problems that interest mathematicians and scientists. Chapter Two provides some examples, then explores how we all typically go about solving everyday problems. This approach will show why moral problems are often difficult to solve, what humans have done to reduce this difficulty, and prepares the way for later suggesting what might be done to facilitate moral problem solving in the future.

1. Mathematical Problems

Mathematics is an edifice, built from the ground up, assembled, definition by definition, from scratch. Those of you who studied geometry in school will remember its never-ending series of theorem proofs. Geometry, we were told, is one of the oldest branches of mathematics, taught by Pythagoras in the sixth century BCE, and used by the Pharaohs' surveyors to restore field boundaries each time the Nile flooded. Geometry starts with the very simplest statement, a definition of a point, a line or a circle, then looks for the extensions and connections that are logically implicit within these definitions. The whole process is repeated each time a new definition (that of a parallelogram, for instance) is introduced.

Mathematicians have been adding new definitions to geometry for centuries. At the same time, they have been busy constructing other branches of mathematics: algebra, calculus, trigonometry, topology, set theory, and so on. Each function, each definition, and each statement in every branch has to be very carefully assessed for logical consistency when introduced, then again every time it is used to link to something newly added, and once more whenever it is put to theoretical or practical use. This is done, because each newly added feature introduces more relationships, and it is these relationships that determine if the whole assembly makes sense. Mathematics, then, is held together just as precisely as the universe itself seems to be held together.[2]

Through these means, mathematics is created to be internally sound and rational, self sufficient to the extent of possessing its own reality, dependent upon the real world only in as much as it is built from a language defined in the real world, and connected to the real world in meaning only if we choose to make such a connection. By itself, mathematics is abstract, pure and complete; it does not need to be given any link to the universe (other than that necessarily implicit in its nomenclature). In fact, it is not uncommon for mathematicians to explore the properties of creations such as multidimensional space or imaginary numbers—fancies which no one has experienced first hand.

However, we can, and very often do, link our mathematical understandings to the real world. We do this, for instance, when demonstrating to children that three fingers plus two fingers equals five fingers. Remarkably, it is becoming more and more certain that the mentally constructed world of abstract mathematics contains the ability to describe, explain and predict the very concrete behaviour of the real universe we inhabit.[3] Pythagoras showed this over two and a half thousand years ago, when he described mathematically a property of two dimensional space (the relationship between squares formed on the sides of a right-angled triangle). Newton demonstrated the same connection between mathematics and reality over four hundred years ago, when he showed mathematically that the force holding planets in orbit is related to the involved masses and distances between them. Einstein confirmed this connection when he discovered and proved, again mathematically, that the properties of the four (space-plus-time) dimensions prohibit matter from moving faster than the speed of light. Mathematicians continually push the boundaries and today routinely use complex number theories to define the properties of multidimensional space, a reality which some think may actually exist (perhaps within black holes, or defining fundamental "superstring"[4] properties, or building a universe external to our own).

Because mathematics has been rigorously and logically constructed to be an abstract entity, mathematicians think that its various domains will be considered to be as true in a million years time as they would have been a million years ago, long before they could have been understood by any sentient being living upon this planet. (Moreover, because scientists can use mathematics to predict and explain events occurring billions of light-years distant,[5] they also consider that these mathematical statements hold true in other galaxies, and are therefore discoverable by life forms living upon planets in those regions.) To pure mathematicians, it is often a subsequent (and, possibly, less important) finding that the mathematical properties they uncover have meaning in the real world. They prefer to solve problems within the bounded beauty of a fully discoverable, self-consistent, abstract world. Be this as it may, the many connections between abstract mathematics and the practical realities of the real world have allowed us to solve countless complex problems, and have led to a multitude of discoveries in arenas as diverse as economics, sociology, epidemiology, space flight, nuclear physics, genetics, cosmology and medicine, to name just a few.

That logically generated mathematics describes and defines the universe so accurately reinforces a fact that has already been stated: the universe must be causal and rational, for, if it were not, the intrinsic fit between mathematics and the universe's functioning would not exist.

2. Scientific Problems

Scientists are a similar breed of specialists to mathematicians. They also deduce relationships, but their work typically starts from, and is grounded in, the concrete world (for example, in the field or in the laboratory), rather than the abstract world.[6] Scientists aim to uncover the causal and connective relationships that exist between "real" events and "real" things. They strive to explain and understand reality.

We might say that science began when humans started to wonder about the nature of their surroundings in some kind of organized manner; when individuals first asked what might be causing the sun and stars to appear to move, or thunder to deafen, or animals to be so similar inside yet so outwardly different. Middleton, in his 1963 discourse on the scientific revolution, realized that this occurred many centuries ago. He noted that Thales of Miletus (who lived from 640-546 BCE) wanted to *explain* the universe. In other words, Thales understood that there is a causal reason for each tiny piece of the universe to be the way it is. This, stated Middleton, marked the birth of science.[7]

Slowly, by careful observation, control of variables, measurement, accurate records, repetition and a great deal of thought, scientists began to understand why nature behaves as it does. Understanding grew in leaps and bounds once scientists learned to extend their senses' abilities by building instruments: first measuring sticks, balances and graduated containers, then micrometers, microscopes and telescopes. They found that precision and knowledge go hand-in-hand.[8] Accurate measurements allowed Copernicus and Galileo to place the sun, rather than the Earth, at the centre of our collection of planets.[9] Newton carefully observed moving objects (some say a falling apple), then wrote the gravitational formula that explains how the universe is held together. Wallace and Darwin recorded fine details of life's species, then deduced the mechanism of evolution. Einstein employed acutely crafted thought-experiments about relativity, then extended the significance and value of Newton's work.

Scientists and mathematicians follow similar methodologies; they seek and uncover facts, then try to discover any relationships that may exist between these facts, or between these and other known facts or theories. Both professions are delving deeper and deeper into the nature of the universe, and the two, seemingly distinct, knowledge domains are converging. Scientists routinely use mathematics to obtain precision and to extend their discipline's utility. Mathematicians use their skills to describe what is happening in the centre of stars, and to reconstruct what must have happened moments after the universe began. The abstract explains the concrete; the concrete adds flesh to the abstract.

3. Problem Environments

Of course we all, scientists, mathematicians or laypersons, solve many problems every day. While most of these are addressed and resolved routinely and efficiently, the speed and accuracy of our problem solving depends almost entirely upon one factor—how well we understand the background situation, i.e., the "environment" (examples discussed below will shortly clarify and extend this term) that contains and presents the problem we are trying to solve. Everyday problems are solved very quickly, often without realizing a problem is being addressed, because we generally know a lot about the various environments we inhabit. On the other hand, scientific and mathematical problems not infrequently take a long time to solve; this is usually because those working on the problem do not yet have sufficient information about their problem's environment.

To correctly solve any problem then, we must correctly understand its "environment." This is because a problem is only properly solved when its solution can be used within (or is accepted by) the relevant environment, without causing additional problems. Luckily, each problem's environment also invariably contains the criteria which the problem's solution must satisfy.

It is important to understand the meaning of the term "environment" when used in the current context. The word is used here to identify the physical, social, occupational, political, economic, religious, cultural, or other context (or an often complex combination of several such contexts) that contain the problem that confronts us. Recognizing that problems exist within one or more environments is key to understanding how problems (particularly moral ones) are solved.

Thinking about a few everyday situations may help to clarify this discussion. Consider dressing, cutting the lawn, and cooking a meal. The choices to be made in each case can be thought of as being minor problems to be solved, and we'll review each in turn.

When we select something to wear from a choice of clothes, we refer to the occasion or situation for which we are dressing in order to decide what to wear. This is so whether we are dressing for work, to go on a trip, climb a mountain, or just lounge in the house. We choose clothes by considering what's available (e.g., clean, comfortable, appropriate, etc.) and the circumstances pertaining when wearing the clothes (e.g., temperature, weather, others present, etc.), although for routine occasions this may happen so quickly that we don't notice that we are solving little problems. The criteria or standards that determine the success of the eventual choice made is clearly located in the environment that presents the problem—in some of the situations just mentioned, the work, social, local, or home environments. (Furthermore, note that the environment also determines what kind of goal can be achieved successfully; for instance, it is not possible to receive praise for being fashionably dressed if no one else will be present when lounging in the house. More about this in Chapter Three.)

Consider the second example. I look out of the window and notice that the grass needs cutting, perhaps just a small problem now but one that will grow if neglected. So I make the decision to mow the grass later in the afternoon. In this case, note that I appear to be driven to meet some standard of lawn appearance, and that this standard has been set by my external environment—the society and culture in which I live. If I had earlier decided to ignore society's conventions, or if I lived in a place where people did not bother about such matters, then long grass would not be seen as a problem, and I may not even notice how tall the grass had become. Note, again, that when there is a problem, it is an external environment that both thrusts the problem upon me, and that holds the standards or criteria to be met when correcting the problem. Living in town, I would probably have to mow the grass weekly; living in the country, once or twice a month might suffice.

Now the third example: imagine preparing a meal. When I am in this situation I find that before I can choose a menu or select a method of cooking I must first think about who will be eating the meal, what food is available, where I might have to go to buy missing ingredients, what might be nice to eat today, what has been recently eaten by those attending, other goals I might want to achieve with these particular guests, and so on. All of these thoughts relate to my environment (the physical, social, nutritional and emotional elements mostly, in this case) and this environment limits what I can do if I want to cook and serve a successful meal.

Note that, besides referring to external environments we also refer to what's inside our minds, our "internal environment," because a great deal of relevant information has been stored there and some of it is used in making any decision. For example, our mind tells us what cooking skills we have, whether or not the lawn mower is in working condition, when a particular suit was last worn, etc. But, in all cases, our mind is only providing previously acquired information relevant to the situation we are in, and this information always comes from some knowledge of external environments of one kind or another.

Sometimes, our own bodies may present a problem to the mind (a craving for salty food, for instance), in which case it is our body's feelings or standards of well-being that have to be included in the problem-solving process. This is still an example of a problem stemming from an environment external to the mind (the organs or systems that are calling for salt are external to the mind. Problems that arise solely within the mind are special situations, and will be discussed in section four.)

We should mention here that dressing or cooking to suit nothing other than our own current feelings is also, like the salt-craving example, an attempt to satisfy a mood biochemically caused by some agent (dopamine or serotonin, perhaps) within our body or brain, i.e., it emanates from a source that is again external to our mind. We choose the solution that best satisfies our desires. In cases like these, we might say we "go with the flow." (A few of us may try to do this much of the time—living in the "here and now" was popular a few decades ago and is still a desired behaviour for some.) However, simply responding to biochemical desires is an emotional, not reasoned, response to a situation, and not of much pertinence to the current discussion.

To recapitulate and summarize this section: problems can never be solved without reference to the particular environment that presents them. This will always be true, for several reasons. First, we have to know, understand and explore the properties of a problem's environment to determine what is causing a problem. Second, each environment contains the criteria that must be met if a problem is to be solved without causing additional problems. And, third, we must know what the environment will permit us to achieve before we can select an achievement to strive for. Only once we understand what is causing the problem, what can or can't be done about it, what end-results are achievable (and desirable to us—more about this in

Chapter Three), can we then solve the problem. In short; to succeed, we must know what we want and can do.

Well, that is probably enough about how we solve practical problems; now we are ready to investigate what we do to solve moral problems.

4. Moral Problems

Moral problems can emerge from any environment—home, family, business, social, medical, and so on, and many may look just like any other kind of problem. None come with a flag that states, "Beware—Moral Problem!" So, the mind cranks up the same problem-solving routine it has been using since second-level thinking began. It gathers details about the situation that presents the problem and quickly formulates several solutions. It then has to decide which solution is the most appropriate. And this is where difficulties may arise, as a simple example might illustrate.

Imagine that someone in a store takes an item to the checkout counter and the clerk rings up the wrong price. If the checkout price is higher than it should be, most people would question it and ask for a correction. But, if it were lower, some might speak up while others might say nothing. This kind of situation, most would say, is a moral one, and the action taken would be the result of making a moral decision. The problem of which choice to make (speak up and pay more, or say nothing and save) can be simple for some. Many might invariably be "honest" and speak up; others might always choose to maximize their personal gain and would say nothing. People in either of these categories might not even notice that there is a choice; for them there is no problem to be solved, their mind-set automatically provides just one solution and they act upon the decision their mind presents without questioning it.

However, some would see that they are being asked to make a moral decision, and this is where difficulties can arise. To understand why, we have to discuss what's happening in a little more detail.

Moral problems are actually very similar to mathematical problems. Like math problems (which have their origins in the abstract mathematical environment that defines them), moral problems arise from their own abstract moral environment. And we must understand the true nature of this environment in order to find satisfactory solutions. Moreover, the more difficult the problem is, the more we have to understand about its environment.

Moral problems ask the mind to decide which solutions are "right" rather than "wrong," and which behaviours might be deemed to be "good" rather than "bad." Now, as we have seen, the criteria needed to select the right answers for practical problems are found by examining the environment that presents the problem. But what environment actually presents moral problems? From where do they stem? This would be the rightful place to find the criteria sought, but this presents a dilemma: the universe contains no practical, concrete, "real" or verifiable moral environment waiting to be found and consulted.

Moral problems arise solely within the mind, and it is therefore the mind itself that both defines the moral environment and contains the criteria that solutions must meet to be deemed satisfactory. Everything that makes some particular concern a "moral problem" to a person is contained wholly within that person's mind. Thus, it is the mind-set of the customer at the checkout counter that determines if being undercharged presents a moral problem, and it is this mind-set that provides the frame of reference that is drawn upon when the decision to speak up or remain silent is made.

We should stop here to consider what this means, and what we typically do about it. If a person is a practising member of a religion, then they almost certainly possess an appropriate mental environment which they can consult when contemplating moral issues, and usually nothing stops the problem-solving process for them at this point. The most important function of any religion is to build such a mental environment, to teach followers what to believe and how to behave (that is, to provide solutions that resolve various kinds of moral problems). The "religious environment," the neural networks constituting memories that those following a religion have spent time building within their minds, is available for exactly these occasions. It is rare (although perhaps now becoming more common) to encounter a moral problem that has not been already solved by others within the doctrine, but, if ever this does occur, then the adherent is expected to think about what has been written in religious texts, taught by their religious teachers, or said by a religious leader. The devout likely solve most of the moral problems they encounter by referring to one or more of these sources. More complicated issues might involve talking to a theologian or other respected authority. But there exists, for people following a religion, a relevant environment to consult, in which can be found the criteria to judge which solutions are acceptable, as well as the valued purpose that provides reasons for making the "correct" choice.

(However, it may be that many moral problems are not actually solved this way today, even by the devout. Perhaps some, or even most, everyday "moral" problems are in fact solved by recourse to the individual's social or cultural environment.[10] In other words, perhaps when a person wants to know the "right thing to do," they [possibly quite subconsciously] might think along these lines; "now, what does society sanction?" Or, "what would my group expect of me?" They might even think, "what can I get away with?" Or, "how far can I go without being caught?" The last two examples might be a little extreme, but they serve to make a point: that in many situations today we may actually be obtaining our values, our standards, the criteria we use to judge which solutions are morally acceptable, from the social sub-set we inhabit, not from our religion.[11] I suspect that, to the extent that this may be true, it is mostly so because our religions are failing to keep up with the changing times.[12])

So be it for those who have a religion to follow, or those who can be satisfied by adopting their society's criteria of what a "good person" should do. People with these ideologies can make decisions (and feel or be certain that they have behaved morally) by consulting their knowledge of these constructed environments. But, what about those who have no mental religious environment to guide their decisions and disdain the vagaries of social standards? How can these people solve moral problems? Admittedly, there may be relatively few such people today, but there must have been many pondering such dilemmas before religions became common features of social life. Since we will shortly be investigating the emergence of religions, it is particularly important to explore what such people might do.

Presumably, some who have thought about such issues will have worked out their own value system, perhaps one based upon standards drawn piecemeal from one or more existing religions or societies they know about, but personalized in some manner. Others might just "play things by ear," letting their emotions and feelings tell them how to behave as each situation unfolds. But a few, surely, would not be satisfied by such methods, and would want to work out solutions in a careful and rational manner. Where are these individuals to obtain the criteria they need to make moral choices? The physical environment holds none. The social environment has been ruled insignificant. Every religious source has been deemed artificial or irrelevant. And, they lack an appropriate internal, or mental, environment. How can such individuals solve moral issues rationally, and make decisions they can live with?

We are not quite ready to answer such questions yet but will do so in Chapter Three, where we explore how decisions are made. Before then, there are a couple of other issues that should be addressed. The first has to do with what people consider to be moral problems; the second asks why such problems arise.

It is difficult to provide examples of moral problems because what may be a concern for some, may not be so for others. But I will propose a few that may illustrate the point to be noted.

Consider a woman who has learned that the fetus she is carrying has a life-threatening defect. Some may see this situation as a moral issue, others may see it as a practical one. However, the point is, for this discussion, a religious person might have fewer options regarding the fetus than others; for example, abortion may be out of the question for those of certain faiths, and the woman may have no choice at all regarding her situation. Those without such a religion may have a greater number of options, but may lack guidelines of any kind; they would likely find it very difficult to make a decision about the fetus.

Another example: consider someone whose spouse is terminally ill, in considerable pain, and who expresses a wish to die. May the healthy spouse act to fulfil such a desire? How does a non-religious person make this kind of decision, if they see it as a moral issue? How do they justify the choice they make? (And, is this justification likely to be acceptable in law, or to society?)

An example that shows the global nature of moral dilemmas today: what criteria should nations use to determine if intervening in another country's affairs is justified? Is committing genocide a moral problem? By what criteria is this decided? What "environment" defines the situation as a moral, rather than a practical, one? What "greater purpose" is there to be achieved that permits overriding the tradition of respecting another nation's autonomy?

One final example: many see acts of terrorism, when innocent bystanders, children and adults, are maimed or killed, as morally reprehensible. But an unknown number of others see such acts as a short-cut to paradise. One act—two diametrically opposite views, with seemingly no middle ground to enable reconciliation.

Clearly, by providing the otherwise non-existent but needed mental environment, religions fulfil a necessary role. Just as clearly, current religions are unable to provide a singular environment that could apply to and be adopted by all nations of the world. Consequently, humanity has no common moral authority to cite, and no collective conscience. The sudden collapse of energy giant Enron Corporation illustrates what can happen to organizations that lack moral environments. We might ask ourselves if such things as terrorism or the wealth disparity between nations (which affects maybe a billion or more people) illustrate that civilization lacks the same thing and if global collapse is a possible consequence.

The second question we should touch upon before moving on is: what prompts the appearance of "moral" problems? If individuals possess no inherent mental "religious" environment and have to be taught in order to construct one, then why would any "moral" problem have arisen in the first place? What would have prompted its appearance?

This question is easy to answer. Moral problems arise simply because the mind has the words and language that makes posing such problems possible. It is our mind's ability to manipulate words that causes it to ask, "is it right to do this?" Humans are so used to mentally seeking the best course of action to take when practical alternatives arise that it is done automatically whenever more than one choice is offered. To put it crudely, we simply daydream moralistic alternatives, and then become stuck when trying to decide, "what is the right thing to do now?"

Without the mental ability to pose and answer questions (i.e., to note and solve problems) we could not ask ourselves if anything were right or wrong. In short, we don't agonize over moral problems because we must, we do so simply because our mental ability with languages makes it possible, as the "moral" problems presented earlier in this section demonstrate. Our daily requirement to decide how to behave (together with the fact that religions have made the words "moral" and "ethical" part of most people's vocabulary) is all that is needed to prompt such inquiries.

We are now well equipped to investigate the nature of decision making. Doing so will provide answers to the questions asked earlier: how can individuals solve moral issues rationally, and make decisions they can live with, if they lack a relevant (possibly religious) mental environment?

Summary

The mind uses words, phrases and thinking patterns that have developed as a result of dealing with real world situations. Questions such as, "should I take this path?" are perfectly answerable when walking along wooded trails, for example, because we may have a map that describes the territory, and because, presumably, we know where we want to go or what we want to achieve. The very same words seem to be meaningful when asked metaphysically, but often they are not—the question can arrive without a map or a goal of any kind in mind.

Mathematicians and theoretical scientists, it must be emphasized, do have a map and a purpose in mind when they begin their explorations. They, therefore, can pose abstract questions, and are able to find meaningful answers. Every iota of their maps is connected, each to another, joined by the glue of rationality, and logical exploration of the territories they describe is practical and possible.

Theologians also have maps, but the glue holding the pieces of their maps together is faith, which, unfortunately, may bear no relationship to logic or fact. This may not have mattered in days of yore, when logical consistency was of little importance, but every aspect of modern society is driven by technology and its computers, and humans living in modern environments are beginning to demand that their religions become as rational as they themselves are being forced to become. A modern age is calling for a modern religion, a call that might be very dangerous to ignore.

Chapter Three

Making Decisions

Chapter Two observed that we solve problems by consulting their relevant environments, and that this is both to understand the problem and to find the criteria that an acceptable solution must satisfy. We glossed over the fact that there are frequently several solutions to each problem that will satisfy these criteria. This chapter discusses how the mind decides which solution to adopt. The answer in brief is: we make decisions in order to achieve a valued purpose.

1. Practical Decisions

Almost every problem can be solved in more ways than one. A simple example, that of going to work, for instance, illustrates this, and also the fact that we choose a solution to achieve a valued purpose. Thus, there may be several ways to travel from home to work: by bus, bike, car or by walking perhaps, and there may be a choice of several routes. The decision made is a successful one if we arrive at work, on time, and have also met any other valued purposes (such as obtaining some exercise, or buying a newspaper on the way).

Or, consider our previous dressing-for-work example. Our work environment may dictate that we dress somewhat formally, but we may be able to do so in a number of ways. Consequently, we might decide based upon what was worn yesterday, or we may let our feelings decide, simply satisfying our mood of the moment. We discussed these kinds of choices earlier, and we noted that the criteria we use to make our decision is found in an environment that is external to the mind itself.

However, situations are never as simple as those portrayed in the examples mentioned. Probing more deeply will show that every decision we make is affected by attempts to meet one or more psychological needs that exist entirely within the mind. For example, what we finally choose to wear may have been decided in an attempt to impress the boss, or to win our friends' admiration, or to heighten our self-concept. These goals or purposes are seldom known to others, and may be only partly known to ourselves.

We may think that some decisions can only be made objectively, and that private, subjective, or personal goals may play no part in them, but this is incorrect. As an example, imagine that we have to choose a bolt to anchor a structure we are building. We decide what size to use based upon what we know about the structure's mass and orientation, the strength of materials, type of foundation and so on. We are using our knowledge of the external physical environment, of course. But we also make this choice based on our personal desire for the structure to endure. Quite a different choice could be made if our private purpose was to sabotage the result. Whether or not our private purposes override the public purposes depends upon our psychological state of mind.

Thus, every time we make practical decisions we consult *two* environments. One is external to our mind and public; it contains all the facts and criteria required to select solutions that will satisfy its needs, and any suitably knowledgeable person could make an identical decision. The other environment is internal to the mind and private; it contains all the personal goals, self-chosen purposes, and maybe several (probably unrecognized) psychological needs that also influence each final decision.

However, only one environment is involved when making *moral* decisions—our own internal mental mind-set. It has to provide the environment, the criteria to be met, and the goals to value and seek. Thus, there may be no constraints upon what people may decide is moral or what are moral actions. Of course, religions provide environments and guidelines (i.e., criteria), but those without a religion, or who reject their society's norms, have nothing other than their own personal mental constructs[1] to consult when deciding how to act. Having only one's own mental environment to guide one's actions can have significant and terrible consequences (as the activities of numerous psychopaths throughout history have demonstrated).

2. Moral Decisions

Now we are ready to return to the situation introduced in section four of the last chapter. We were imagining a person who has no religion, yet who wants to live a moral life. Consider what such a person faces—where might he or she find the valued purpose needed to guide moral decision making? The physical environment holds no purpose in the moral arena. The transitory social environment is nugatory. Religious sources are considered unreliable or even false. No external environment holds a purpose worthy of being used to make a moral decision, and the mind, when lacking any belief system, holds none.

Search as they may, individuals in this position cannot solve moral problems, for there is nowhere else to look.[2]

Since the mind has to know and value the attainment of some purpose before it can make any decision rationally, minds lacking relevant purposes cannot make moral decisions rationally. For some, this mental state of affairs may churn for years. Such individuals may eventually give up the search, and simply choose to abide by social customs. Others in this condition may look at various religions and find a way out by adopting one, or bits and pieces of several. For a few, neither choice is feasible, and the dilemma escalates. Every decision to be made appears to be causally related to this missing purpose. The mind's primary function of directing the body's behaviour becomes incapacitated, and its owner may sink into depression, claiming, quite correctly, that they see no purpose to life, and that without purpose life has no meaning[3] and they have no reason to live. A mental breakdown can easily result.

In all of this behaviour, we must remember, the mind is being entirely rational. If a moral environment of some kind is not available, then, although everyday language allows moral problems to be posed, no satisfactory solutions can be found, because without a desired purpose decisions can't be made rationally.

Apart from insanity or death, there is only one way through this impasse. The mind has to accept a solution that it has been considering, possibly consciously, certainly subconsciously, but which has hitherto been rejected for one reason or another. Some formerly unacceptable metaphysical purpose must be reclassified as desirable. For this to happen such a purpose has to be accepted as representing the truth—it must be sanctioned by the mind itself. The mind's decision-making expertise will then be freed from its confining tangle of unacceptable choices, its state of constant stress will vanish, and it will at last find peace. This acceptance of a purpose almost always happens in a split second, occurring unexpectedly (and often appearing fully formed) to the affected individuals. They experience it as a "revelation" and may undergo a "conversion." (Chapter Five further discusses these phenomena.)

It does not matter what this purpose is.[4] Absolutely any criteria can be used to judge behaviour as "good" or "bad." (A "moral" person could even be considered an "evil monster" by another's standards.) What matters is that the mind's previous quandary has vanished, and it can once again resume its function of thinking rationally as it directs the body's functions.[5]

But let us return, for a moment, to the instant of reclassification—the mind's conversion from an absence, to an acceptance, of some mental environment containing both criteria and purpose. For the mind to take advantage of such a contrivance it must have already been stored in memory. Most of us have religious memories provided to us by our parents or teachers, and we all have some understanding of the beliefs in vogue in our society. This formerly discounted knowledge is often the environment grasped when the mind is under the kind of stress earlier discussed.

The newly converted typically accept unconditionally all that is contained within the religion (whether spiritual or secular) whose purpose they have suddenly adopted. Not infrequently, the intensity of emotion associated with this metamorphosis moves the converted to tell others what they have come to believe. That which, when they were non-believers, was simply "good" or "bad" behaviour, has suddenly become "right" or "wrong" behaviour to the new believer. This kind of distinction marks the transition—moral judgements have replaced value judgements for them.

Very occasionally, the straw grasped during conversion is not an existing religion but some abstraction, probably imaginatively pieced together by the mind's owner in earlier, restless, years. A new metaphysical purpose may be recognized to be valid, important and desirable. This new purpose may or may not centre around a belief in a god—but there are not many choices when it comes to inventing a purpose deemed important enough to guide moral decision making. (This is why people normally convert to existing religions; they have no alternative in mind. This book will be suggesting one later.)

A few, undergoing such a transformative mental revision, become convinced that they are another messiah, another prophet who has "seen the light." The conversion they experience is so real to them, so significant—the vision and clarity of the new truth so bright—that they cannot contain their emotions nor refrain from trying to convince others that they have found the most important manifestation in life (for, to them, it is the most important). They proselytize. And the vivacity and clarity of the words they speak attract the undecided. Cults and sects form, and eventually (as Chapter Four notes), if their followers continue to grow in number, the originators may be remembered as the founders of great religions. We will be exploring this phenomenon in Part Two.

Making Decisions 51

Summary

Before moving to Part Two, it may be helpful to summarize a few of the points that have been made in the past three chapters. The following are important.

- The universe's causal construction dictates that inhabitants who think and act rationally have a greater chance of surviving, procreating and succeeding, than those who do not. This, in turn, has favoured the genetic continuation of mutations which help minds to work in this manner.
- Practical problem solving and decision making entails consulting external environments to find the criteria that acceptable solutions must meet, then consulting the mind's internal environment to find what personal purpose is sought.
- Moral problem solving and decision making entails consulting the mind's own environment to find both the criteria for acceptable solutions, and the purpose being sought. Mental environments are always invented ones (composed, as we saw in Chapter One, from linked memories of perceived events, experiences and learnings, all tinged by the choice of words used when envisioning them consciously), and have no reality outside the minds of those who subscribe to them.
- Religious environments are made real to individuals through faith or belief. Belief provides a feeling of certainty; however this exacts a price. Belief can cause us to ignore, override, or transcend some of the more substantive reality that constitutes the rational universe we inhabit. In time, this may lead us into grey pastures.

(A postscript to this chapter titled "Purpose and Meaning" is to be found commencing page 218.)

Conclusion to Part One

What a wonderful manifestation is the mind. From its elemental beginnings when it simply helped the body to survive, the mind has become an instrument exquisite. It creates individuals of us all, and provides flights of fancy any time we care to climb aboard. Is there anything it might not do in the future?

But, does the mind do all this on its own, or does some Guiding Hand help it on its way? These flights and fancies; these revelations and beliefs—from whence have they come? Are they solely the product of a rational mind working in a rational universe, or might some of such thoughts have come from a god?

It is important to the theme of this book to determine how beliefs, in particular, come to mind, for they have greatly affected our past, are certainly affecting our present, and may well dictate our future. If we contend that certain beliefs are god-given, we might act in one manner; if we discover that all beliefs may have a more mundane origin, then we might be persuaded to think and act more circumspectly, for we would expect no saviour's help should anything go wrong. Thus, Part Two explores the origins of beliefs.

Part Two

Religions and Their Source

Introduction to Part Two

Many millennia ago, humans living in caves would have asked questions that could not have been answered with the knowledge they then possessed. Questions about events seen in the natural world, of course, but also questions about what might happen after death, for minds then (just as they do for us today) would have appeared to have an existence of their own, somehow separate and distinct from the body they inhabit. Shamans solved such abstract problems, and from the practices they suggested, followers likely built the early religions ancient humans once possessed.

As communal living tends to unify concepts and actions, enlarging clans and evolving tribes would have had to unify their beliefs about the unknown, if only to reduce internal conflict and standardize rituals and behavioural norms. Tribal trading and assimilations would periodically introduce new ideas, and undoubtedly these would have disturbed the status quo and created debate about the validity of existing practices, thoughts and even beliefs.

Now and again different kinds of leaders would appear and systematize practices. Military leaders would unify people and property. Philosophical leaders would unify facts and theories. Religious leaders would unify beliefs and dogmas. Successful leaders would attract followers, and these would help to consolidate and strengthen fiefdoms, as well as understandings and theologies, for such is the way societies are built.

Part Two examines the critical role that leaders play in originating and developing religions. It explains the source of the inspirations that illuminate and empower leaders' activities. Details about some of the world's major religions are then provided; these serve to illustrate our religions' diversity, to highlight some of the many benefits we derive from religions, and to provide a background to a list of failings that I think detract from their current utility, leading me to suggest that something better is needed.

Chapter Four

Religions' Origins

Beliefs, and their accompanying religious practices, have influenced the thoughts, decisions and behaviours of humans for thousands of years. Stonehenge, rock sculptures, pyramids, temples, stone altars, tombs, churches, cathedrals—all attest to religion's long history, but also demonstrate that our beliefs can and do change over time.

Religious beliefs and practices have influenced the development of all civilizations, all societies and all cultures; to varying degrees, they wend their way through and affect everyone's thoughts and deeds.[1] Yet, clearly, our religious mind-sets must have had a beginning, and there would have been a time when thoughts of a god did not exist. Presumably there would also have been a time when no one knew "right" from "wrong." This chapter discusses why and how early humans added such concepts to their thoughts and vocabulary. The central question being implicitly examined is, "are all of our many religions, beliefs and values, divine in origin—or could some, many, or even all, be man-made?"

1. Assumptions

No one knows just how religious beliefs and practices began, but a plausible explanation is that such ideas and customs grew from the assumptions that early men and women would have had to make. Let me elaborate.

Everyone makes thousands of minor assumptions every day, and normally these all transpire unnoticed. We get up, dress, eat, do chores, go to work, return home, prepare a meal, and so on, continuously making subconscious assumptions that determine the way we act. For example, we assume that other people will behave in much the same way as they always have—and they do. We assume that the bus will arrive, that stores and offices will open, that we still have a job to go to—and we are usually right. Any incorrect suppositions we might make are generally inconsequential, and corrections are easily, and mostly subconsciously, made.

We make assumptions because we can never know all there is to know about any facet of our lives, or about any object or event we encounter. Our true state of ignorance is seldom apparent to us, but our lack of knowledge makes itself known every time there is an important decision to be made, one whose consequences might seriously affect us, or the lives of those we love, for instance. On these occasions we quickly discover how little we really know. Anyone considering marriage or buying a house for the first time, for example, knows this feeling. At such times we may temporarily be unable to make a decision, for fear of the consequences were we to make a "wrong" choice. When such feeling arise, we spend much time gathering and evaluating information, trying all the time to replace assumptions with accurate knowledge. Thus, although we rarely notice that every decision we make has its fringe of assumptions, such is the case.[2]

Early humans would have faced exactly the same difficulty. They knew even less than we do about the true state of most affairs, and making assumptions would have been the only way they could have made decisions. And—just as happens to the assumptions we make—after a while many of the useful assumptions they made would have become indistinguishable from facts.

2. Ancient Assumptions

Traces of the assumptions made by early men and women still exist in tangible form today. Two in particular are important to the theme of this book and will be examined: our ancestors assumed that they would experience life after death, and they assumed that gods existed.

2.1. Life after Death

The earliest evidence yet discovered that our ancestors believed in some kind of life after death is to be found in graves of the Neandertals (who lived from about 200,000 to about 25,000 y.a.). Careful arrangement of the deceased, as well as accompanying flint implements together with broken animal bones (likely to have come from food buried with the body), suggest that these accoutrements were considered to be needed by the dead. (Neandertal cave artwork depicting burial rituals also supports the premise that they assumed a life after death.)

At least as early as 30,000 y.a., Cro-Magnon followed more complex rituals. They buried their dead in sewn clothing, covered them with ornaments and bead decorations, and surrounded them with tools, weapons and food.³ One grave, 28,000 years old, in Sungir, Russia, contains the body of a sixty year old man wearing bracelets and necklaces, and dressed in a tunic sewn with hundreds of mammoth-ivory beads; he was accompanied by rich grave goods.

For some as yet unknown reason, ornamenting the dead with red pigment has also been a long-lasting and wide-spread custom.⁴ The skeleton of a young man some 25,000 years old, discovered in a cave in South Wales, was covered with red ochre and accompanied by a shell necklace, ivory beads and bracelets. Ornamentation continued until at least 6,500 y.a., for the head of one of seventeen Stone Age bodies (dated to that age and found in a cemetery at Bøgebakken, Denmark) was surrounded by red ochre. Burial customs such as these and others provide strong evidence that early man believed in the existence of some kind of afterlife, for which the body needed to be prepared and provisioned.

Burial rituals increased in complexity during the Neolithic Age (9,000–5,000 y.a.), to the extent of including animal sacrifices, cremation, entombment in stone chambers roofed with huge boulders and body preservation. The Chinchorro culture of northern Chile conducted extremely elaborate burial rituals, as is readily evidenced by mummified bodies dating back 9,000 years. The head, hands and feet were removed, the body was skinned and soft tissue excavated, and the skull was packed with a mixture of grass, hair and ashes. The skin was then reapplied, the whole body plastered with an ash paste and then painted black and red. It is inferred from this elaborate practice that some intense religious assumption (one that sooner or later may well have metamorphosed into a belief) must have prompted such effort.

A different form of evidence suggesting early *Homo* had the intellectual ability to invent assumptions is to be found in several now-European countries where Cro-Magnon left rock drawings and engravings in caves. These sketches illustrate their prowess in hunting large herds of animals (and the skeletons of hundreds of early horses found in sites frequented by Cro-Magnon show how successful these pursuits were). Such hunting strategies require abstract thought, organization and planning, and from this it is deduced that they had a language complex enough to be able to conduct a discussion of options and to manage assumptions.

Another item occasionally shown in cave drawings, and of significance to this discussion, is a figure in clothing associated with shamans or medicine men. These figures appear to have a significant role in the behaviours being depicted in the drawings. Shamans are traditionally involved in caring for the dead, and their thoughts and practices would certainly influence ideas held by clan members.

The accepted conclusion from this kind of evidence is that our ancestors assumed that an afterlife existed—that they actualized the concept of an afterlife thousands of years before the same notion was incorporated into the religions of early Egyptians and, later, into many of ours. This suggests that when describing "heaven" today we are not simply repainting a vision first drawn by prophets or theologians—we are actually maintaining or embroidering a Neandertal assumption. Of course, we don't say that we are describing an assumption, but such is its origin. And our belief in an afterlife remains an assumption because there is no credible evidence that an afterlife actually exists, whether for the Neandertals, the Pharaohs, or for any modern-day human.[5]

2.2. The Existence of Gods

Man must have assumed thousands of years ago that the inexplicable behaviour of some or even many aspects of the world was due to the presence of powerful gods.[6]

We can understand why it was necessary to believe in gods. Prior centuries of rational thinking about practical matters (how best to take advantage of an animal's behaviour when hunting, for example) had led naturally (if only subconsciously) to the realization that everything that happens has a cause. It was therefore only logical to conclude that something must cause such events as thunder and lightning to occur, or the sun to rise always in the east.

It was entirely rational for our ancestors to ask what could possibly give rise to such phenomena. But the true explanations lay far beyond their ability to comprehend all those thousands of years ago.

Written records tell us how the Greeks later solved this problem. They assumed that such events were caused by some kind of invisible beings who lived behind the clouds, occasionally amusing themselves by teasing or playing jokes upon those who lived on Earth below. Today, we might think that this was an extraordinary fantasy to dream up, but what, in ancient times, other than some supernatural beings, could explain the occurrence of such impressive events?

The hidden existence of powerful entities was not an unreasonable assumption for even very early humans to make. Living in caves and huts, they were low in nature's hierarchy. There were many dangerous and more powerful animals lying in wait. Numerous awe-inspiring events took place daily that could not be explained. Mysterious illnesses and sudden inexplicable deaths occurred. Thunder filled the air for miles around, but lightning struck only certain spots seemingly randomly chosen. The sun, on the other hand, followed a routine—it moved across the sky in an orderly manner, regularly disappeared at night, only to rise again the next day. And eclipses—how could such rare incidences possibly be explained?

It was logical and sensible to assume that one or more mighty beings lived out of sight above, and that they contrived such events. This explanation so admirably solved many profound mysteries that, once put forward, it must have seemed the obvious answer and been immediately accepted. It seems certain that *H. sapiens* would have assumed gods existed almost as soon as they could form such a concept.

Moreover, in addition to being an explanation, this assumption had practical applications. It suggested ways men and women could act, if and when they needed to influence, praise or placate the behaviour of those who ruled from the skies above.

There is a great deal of evidence that magical rites with appeasement objectives were practised in many primitive societies. Early authorities, skilled in catering to capricious gods, devised and carried out often fanciful rituals. When the incantations and methods of these experts worked, when rain fell or eclipses ended, their reputation grew. When their best efforts were to no avail, someone or something else could easily be blamed.

The craft of such specialists continues today. Nearly all religions employ functionaries with similar roles, intermediaries who communicate the wishes of (and direct penitence to) a god. Their roles have remained roughly the same, but the communicants' rituals and ceremonial customs have changed because, over time, humans have modified their beliefs about what is the "correct," or "moral," way to behave (for example, we no longer hold that human sacrifices are necessary).

3. Beliefs

Assumptions can be indistinguishable from facts. A scientist might seek them out, but most of us would not. It would be impossible to sort one's general knowledge into facts and assumptions, and we treat them as if they were identical. Both are accepted as being correct until proven wrong, used as long as they are useful, then forgotten when their utility is spent.

This is what has happened to early man's assumptions that gods exist. Gods were taken for granted from at least as early as 5,000 BCE.[7] Their behaviours were discussed, subtle differences noted and character variations identified. Each deity became distinct, recognizable, understandable, named and worshiped by a few or by many; some because they created a fear that had to be calmed, others because they were loved. Assumptions had become indistinguishable from beliefs.

This early belief in many gods is still visible in Hindu communities. Colourful images of gods are displayed all over India, beckoning as clearly today as they did thousands of years ago. These deities are venerated and consulted in much the same manner as monotheists behave toward their one god. Some modern Hindus state that the images seen should be considered reminders that the one true god exists in many forms; others do not feel the situation is this simple, preferring to believe in the existence of many deities, each possessing different powers. However, the nature of Hindu belief is not the issue here; the point to note is that most of humankind once believed in the existence of many gods. Our shift to predominantly believe in a single creator is a relatively recent happening.

The belief in several gods (several dozens of gods, in some societies) gave rise to complex theologies, with many stories chronicling the interactions of multifaceted god-personalities to be memorized and taught to the next generation. It would have been fairly obvious to anyone, anytime, that monotheism is a much simpler belief. One supreme god could replace much confusion. Over centuries past there must have been many intelligent visionaries who argued in favour of a single supreme being.

We know a lot about one such idealist—Amaenhotep IV, a family-oriented Pharaoh who was married to a powerful wife (Queen Nefertiti) and who ruled Egypt for seventeen years, 1300 years before Christ was born. Amaenhotep changed his name to Akhenatom[8] in support of monotheism, and ordered all to worship the one sun-god, Atom. This practice didn't last long however; shortly after his death it was stopped by traditionalist priests who persuaded his successor (the boy-king Tutankhamen) to revert to polytheism.

Judaism was the first religion of modern significance to successfully institutionalize the belief that there is only one god. Christianity and Islam later adopted this concept, and have since conveyed their message to billions. Furthered by numerous persuasive practices (crusades, conquests, missionaries, inquisitions, torture, trials and burnings, to name a few), this lengthy battle for simplification (and influence over the minds of people) affected many over the centuries. Over time it remodelled nations, as they changed their laws to accommodate changes in beliefs.[9]

Today (as noted in Chapter Six) the majority of the world's population take for granted the existence of one god. Most prefer not to consider this just an assumption, first conceived to account for any number of seemingly mysterious events, then employed to explain how the universe and life began. The assumption remains in vogue because it is useful; it authenticates the purpose many refer to (see Chapter Three) when making decisions about how to live their lives.[10]

4. Leaders

A belief in a god or gods is not a religion. Religions add visions of purpose, ideals, behavioural criteria, rewards, punishments, and much more, to their core belief. (In other words, religions weave and maintain aspects of their followers' mental environments discussed in Chapter Two.) Many of the most critical of these ideas stem from the religion's founder. To understand how one person can conceive such notions then convince others that they are true, we must first discuss leadership.

Contrary to popular impression, leaders are plentiful in this world. Many lead for just a short time, but others retain their leadership quality for years.[11] Most guide only a family, a work group, or perhaps one friend, but some lead multitudes.

Social conditions elicit leaders—recall the French and Russian revolutions, India in the 1920's (and on), Germany in the 1930's, or South Africa more recently, for example. Individuals within, or emotionally close to, suffering communities feel driven to change conditions and metamorphose into leaders as they become captivated by powerful ideals.[12] Leadership skills strengthen as these ideals are expressed. Think of Jesus, Mohammed, Ghandi, and Mandela, or Churchill, Hitler and Stalin. Each held fast to an imagined ideal of some kind, their view of how society should be, a future to strive for, a dream of a better world.

All leaders have a vision of an enhanced future. A vision is critical because this is what leaders lead toward—their own mental image of a superior state of affairs. These visions can develop slowly, as perhaps for Genghis Khan; or in a blinding flash, as perhaps for Joan of Arc; or in intermittent surges, as perhaps for many parents.

Religious leaders differ from others in one important aspect: they credit a Supreme Being with providing the insights they convey. Moses, Jesus, Mohammed, Joan of Arc, and a multitude of saints and lesser religious leaders attributed the words they spoke to their God. Clearly they did so because they believed this to be true. But skeptics might be forgiven for thinking otherwise, reasoning that the vision expressed may have come from the visionary's "conversion" or "revelation" (terms introduced in Chapter Three and further discussed in Chapter Five), events that were possibly an outcome of their own desire to improve conditions.[13]

Please note that I'm not suggesting that religious leaders or founders do not believe in a God. Almost certainly all do, and many also believe that their God sometimes speaks to, or through, them. What I am stating, however, is that believing that their visions and words come from God does not necessarily make it so. They believe them to be authentic—that is what makes them convincing leaders. Their ideas can be entirely false, but as long as they believe them to be true, the strength of their convictions can convince and convert others.

This raises an important issue. What creates these beliefs? What happens in the minds of religious leaders to convince them that they are God's emissaries? The logical answers to these questions will be provided in the next chapter.

Summary

Experience has taught us that everything has a beginning, and this causes us to think that the universe, too, must once have begun.[14] The earliest origin-explanation was that it was created by a god, an interpretation based upon the assumption that such an entity exists.

This explanation has two great advantages over our modern understanding:[15] it is simple, and it is easily understood. However, it also has two great disadvantages: it tells us nothing about the universe and it does not help us to understand cosmological behaviour. If we want to understand reality, then we must work from what we know rather than from what we assume.[16]

Religious founders and leaders rarely state why a god created the universe. But they always attribute purpose to our existence, and they always teach us to live in a manner that demonstrates we value attainment of this purpose. Living to attain this purpose, we are told, presents problems; these, just like all of our everyday problems, can only be solved by understanding the environment that holds the conditions to be met (as we saw in Chapter Two). This is why each religion's environment is described and explained, and why their God's criteria or commandments, the existence of a judgement day, heaven and hell, and so on, are detailed. In explaining such things, these leaders all (except, perhaps, a few) confidently believe that they are carrying out the instructions of a higher Being.

A belief in any purpose creates a mind that can make decisions with the clarity of vision and the certainty of conviction. A strong belief in any leader's vision creates an ardent proselyte. However, belief only makes the believed-in concept real to the believer. It cannot make it true in the real world, for the real world is quite unaffected by what its inhabitants think. And it often cannot make it true to others, where many may simply adopt the views of the local majority to avoid arousing trouble for themselves.

Over the centuries we have significantly added to the belief we started with—that a god simply created the universe. Many of us now infer that this god has a purpose in mind, that humans are intimately linked to this purpose, and that God periodically intervenes in our lives. We have made these assumptions because we cannot solve moral problems or make moral decisions (i.e., obtain peace of mind) without first holding (or, for many, actually believing) that our existence has purpose. Directing our daily activities toward accomplishing valued purposes gives us the comfort of feeling that our lives are meaningful.

But some beliefs prevent us from thinking logically about what surely must be important in life—the way we act when living. Behaviour blinded by benighted belief can have terrible consequences, as acts of terrorism regularly demonstrate.

(A postscript to this chapter titled "Rationality in Science and Religion" is to be found commencing page 220.)

Chapter Five

Revelations and Conversions

The rationale for stating that humans need religions (given in Part One) can be summarized as follows. First, the universe has taught us that survival can depend upon thinking and behaving rationally. Second, to make a behavioural choice rationally it must be directed toward achieving some purpose. Third, real-world problems must satisfy criteria found in the real world to be successful. Fourth, moral problems are invented through mental word-play, and a metaphysical environment and valued purpose must be assembled before moral behavioural choices can be rationally made. And last, we invariably do our best to believe in the truth of our constructions, because belief that we are correct eliminates the stress that accompanies doubts about the validity of what we think, say, and do.

In the previous chapter we noted that religions grow from the visions of (mainly) one person, a person whose beliefs are particularly strong, clear-cut and convincing. This raises two questions that beg to be investigated. First, what makes these beliefs so convincing to such individuals (and, later, to their followers) that they may willingly endure torture, and even choose to die rather than change their minds? And, second, from where do such beliefs come—could there be a source other than a god?

Both of these questions can be answered by returning to the discussion of how the mind works. We begin with a short review of how memories become linked together.

1. Memory Linking

Memories[1] are synaptically linked to other memories, and these links can be made in several ways.

Transient links are made all the time. For instance, when preparing to take a holiday we typically think about where we are going, what the weather might be like, what clothes we should take, what money or documents we might need, etc. Our thoughts, in this example, might seem to be occurring more or less at random, jumping from weather to clothes to money, but they are not at all disconnected. If we really wanted, we could find the exact memory item that triggered the mental jump from weather to clothes, from clothes to money, and so on. There is always a path followed by our thoughts from one memory to the next; it creates what is often called a train of thought.

Sometimes, we make memory links in play. We build connections between memories in our thoughts and so make associations between events that may never have actually taken place. We do this, for example, when we daydream, or when we plan how we would spend the millions we might win in a lottery. Once chains of thought have been built in this way, they are often revisited.[2] Replaying any chain of thought strengthens it, which makes future recalls easier.[3]

A more definitive linkage, discussed in Chapter Two, occurs when we problem solve. Permanent links between previously unlinked memories are likely to form whenever significant relationships are found.

Memory chains can be short or lengthy. Many older folk, for example, can recall exactly where they were and what they were doing when they first learned of President Kennedy's assassination. This is likely to be a short sequence, robustly formed in association with strong emotions, but not often part of a longer sequence. On the other hand, a journey once taken, or detailed plans to build an elaborate addition to the house, for instance, might be stored as very lengthy chains of linked memories.

We all possess many useful, short and long, memory chains, assembled during daily living or taught to us by others. They form actual mental structures, just like the ones we have been calling the neural networks that store discrete memories, but longer and more complex. Whenever activated, they give rise to thoughts and actions that usually play out in succession.[4] As more-or-less permanent memory structures, they minimize the amount of thinking to be done (and therefore the amount of energy expended) when there is little novel to be considered in the triggering situation. Memory chains are important enough to deserve their own name: I term them constructs.

2. Constructs

Everyone's mind contains millions of constructs, most very small (such as the phrases we habitually use—our semi-automatic response ["Hello! How are you?"] to a neighbour's greeting, for instance), others much larger (such as those that auto-pilot the movements of our hands and feet as we drive to work thinking of other things). Every time a construct is used, additional synaptic knobs form along its pathways. These enlarge the construct's primary routes, which then offer less resistance to future biochemical transmissions. This, in turn, increases the probability that this route will be taken the next time one's locus of thought is in this region of the brain.

Constructs are supremely valuable for all animals because they facilitate rapid reaction to danger. Constructs automate some of the brain's activity, producing appropriate responses to stimuli for the least expenditure of energy and in the shortest possible time. Constructs in humans allow much mental activity to be carried out at the relatively fast, non-verbal, subconscious, second level of thinking. For instance, everyone (particularly athletes, musicians, and those executing rapid body movements) becomes more proficient through practice; an important part of practising involves the development of mental constructs.

However, acting solely in response to preformed mental constructs without at least some analysis of incoming stimuli to determine their implications can be dangerous for any animal. Constructs can undermine and limit the ability to perceive, analyze, understand, integrate and generally profit from observations. Furthermore, they diminish creativity and originality.[5]

Constructs cause each of us to become progressively more set in our ways, simply because biochemical flows take the path of least resistance through a neuronal maze. Thus thoughts tend to follow the same neural paths, constantly reinforcing them.[6] As we age, we encounter fewer situations where we need to think afresh about how to respond, for we have previously experienced many of a similar nature. Our thoughts simply follow patterns locked within earlier-formed constructs whenever more-or-less appropriate ones are found. Consequently, we begin acting in characteristic, typical, or even stereotypical, ways. Eventually, if we never try to break out of these neuronal ruts, we start to think that nothing is new, and we may slowly lose interest in external happenings.

Constructs may also monopolize thoughts. This is a particularly interesting feature from this book's point of view. If a significant amount of time or energy is spent thinking about any one subject, a construct-dominated mind can develop. Hobbies, careers, lovers, philosophies, food, business, probably anything we care to consider, can create this effect. We probably all know an individual with whom any conversation soon turns into an exposition of their particular interest. This happens because their mind has long pursued one particular theme and found relationships between it and many other memories. Ideas which might simply be interesting but unconnected bits and pieces of information to other persons can become linked to the central theme of interest in an obsessed person's mind. What once were dozens of discrete constructs can become one major Construct. This can change a fixated person's whole outlook on life.

3. Reformations, Conversions and Revelations

Understanding that the mind develops (and is, to varying degrees, dominated by) a wide variety of mental constructs prepares us to investigate the two questions posed in the introduction to this chapter: what makes conversions so convincing, and from where might they come?

Reformations, conversions and revelations all involve mental constructs; we will consider each in turn.

3.1 Reformations

Reformations might be divided into two types: minor ones (which change one's way of thinking but little else), and reformations which change behaviour. Neither kind is particularly significant to the current discussion, but will be examined because doing so helps us understand what happens when conversions and revelations occur.

We "reform" our way of thinking when we accept another's point of view. For instance, someone might point out that we have always maintained that such-and-such was true, whereas, in fact, it is not true. They might then provide justifications that we realize are valid and, after a moment's thought, we accept. In such cases, just a few, often secondary, neural constructs are disassociated. During this minor reformation, new links between a few memories will be formed, leaving the old associations to atrophy from neglect. This behaviour is usually the result of third-level conscious thinking, and typically happens during conversations or while reflecting upon something recently read, heard or seen. It is often permanent and will affect our thinking, but it may never affect our behaviour.

Behaviour-changing reformations are a somewhat more complex form of neuronal modification because more constructs are involved. However, the new neural patterns that form may not be permanent. For instance, recognizing that an excess of calories is going straight to the waistline and deciding to diet often produces a "reformation" that lasts no longer than a few weeks. More significant reformations, perhaps on the scale of forsaking habits such as alcohol, recreational drugs or gambling, may be more permanent. Reformations (of any kind) often fail without regular boosts such as those provided by support groups, because mental links to earlier constructs which present enticing goals (usually rich with associated emotions) remain.

More permanent reformations occur when some new mental purpose is held to be more attractive than a previous one, and decisions are then made in order to attain this new goal. As long as the latest purpose is sufficiently valued, the mind's decision-making process refers to this new purpose for guidance. This means, of course, that reformations last only as long as the new purpose is held in higher regard than the previous one. For any reformation to last, the prior purpose must be permanently replaced by the new one. For example, memories of eating favourite chocolates and of their pleasurable taste sensations, might be replaced by thoughts of looking slim and being fit. Using the terminology used in Chapter Three, we might say that the purpose guiding our activities must be switched from valuing a sensation of gustatory pleasure to valuing slimness or health.[7] For the reformation to be long lasting, a fresh construct must be deliberately built focused upon attaining the new end result. In short, it's not the diet that produces enduring results, it's the mind-set.

Reformations, then, are consciously made decisions to change one's behaviour in order to gain a newly desired goal. They fail as soon as the goal or purpose loses its attraction.[8]

3.2 Conversions

Conversions, on the other hand, create long-lasting effects. "Conversions" are the result of a change of belief, a belief that can be about anything. The following discussion relates only to religious conversions.

Religious conversions[9] come in two flavours; those induced by some external influence (a speaker at a mass meeting, or in a church, for instance) and those self-induced (the ones that seem to arrive "out-of-the-blue"). The first kind happen relatively often; the second, rarely. The prerequisite for either kind to occur is a prepared mind (one that is usually quite stressed—see the next section for more about this).

Externally-induced conversions cause the converted to accept the theology of an existing religion. The environment, beliefs and purpose-for-living, often remembered from past exposures to the religion and usually already present as minor memory constructs within the mind,[10] are accepted in their entirety. People undergoing induced conversions (whether from external or internal sources) are likely to explore and cement this happening by reading, talking to like-minded others, and thinking about what has happened. Mentally, they are realigning existing constructs, seeking and strengthening those that point toward the newly adopted purpose, and turning suddenly seen associations into connections, all the time reinforcing the new construct's position and significance within their revised mind-set. Eventually, if the conversion experience has been particularly powerful, many formerly small and unconnected constructs become realigned and joined to make one large Construct. And, as noted in the previous section, this new Construct may come to dominate much of such individual's thinking, and control much of their behaviour.

Externally induced conversions differ from reformations only in scale. Periodic refreshing is often needed if the adopted purpose is not to fade over time. This reinforcement is typically obtained by attending religious institutions or gatherings. Secular conversions occur, of course (to communism, for example) and these are commonly systematically reinforced by political boosts given in meetings. Terrorists, religious or otherwise, are often products of induced conversions; they, too, are given periodic indoctrination and training aimed at maintaining their level of commitment.

Self-induced religious conversions are also usually to an existing religion. Very rarely, they occur in the mind of individuals who do not convert to an existing religion but become the harbingers of a new one. It is this kind of event we must examine (although, as we will find, the causal mechanism in both situations is very similar).

Self-induced conversions are almost always the result of a "revelation."

3.3 Revelations

As mentioned in section four of the last chapter, leaders of any significance are invariably people who have thought long and hard about existing conditions and how matters might be improved. Some leaders only slowly realize they have a workable solution to offer and then act. They might write articles and books, as did Karl Marx. Others (in particular most everyday leaders) appear to decide and act without spending any appreciable time thinking about what to do. This is usually because they have already experienced (or have earlier spent time working through) alternative possibilities, and they come to the role armed with several appropriate solutions, primed and ready for different contingencies.

However, sometimes individuals recognize in one blinding flash that they actually have *the* solution. In such cases, they are often said to have had a "revelation." Such occurrences do not happen very often and only occur to those whose mind has been dwelling upon an apparently insurmountable problem for a considerable amount of time. For such individuals, there is an instant of recognition, when the truth is suddenly revealed. This has often been described (see next section for some documented examples) as being accompanied by misty patterns of light,[11] and the whole experience is marked by a plethora of intensely strong and pleasurable emotions: surprise, wonder, elation, euphoria, and sometimes a feeling of being united with the universe. These emotions erupt the instant it is realized, with unequivocal certainty, that the definitive, long-sought, solution-to-a-critically-important-problem has been found. Accompanying feelings of pure joy sometimes continue for weeks.

Revelations that produce this effect need not always follow a search for meaning, or be the result of a religious mental struggle. Many scientists and artists have reported identical feelings to those mentioned above. These experiences occur, for them, the instant they realize they have found the answer to a problem long worked upon. Their emotions, just as the emotions of those experiencing a religious conversion, gush forth the moment their mind replaces many of its old and disjointed constructs with one that is more appropriate and functional. The "eureka" solution transforms disorder into order, doubt into certainty, complexity into simplicity, and stress into delight.

Those who have experienced a revelation of any kind, are often forced by their new Construct to become leaders, devoted to communicating to others the truth that has been revealed to them.

4. The Source of Revelations

But what is the source of such revelations? Such perfectly fitting, almost complete, solutions to long-pondered problems could not have come from nowhere. Some, even many, might insist that revelations could only come from a divine being. While this supposition cannot be entirely ruled out,[12] it seems an unnecessarily complex explanation for the revelation experiences that have been reported by scientists and artists, and it simply obstructs further investigation when attempting to account for those of a religious nature. We should not accept the "divine origin" explanation too readily; there could be a more mundane source.

Once looked for, this source is not hard to find. The new-found solution, its organizing principle or purpose, and the accompanying Construct, all come from work done by subconscious second-level thinking.[13] In other words, from the individual's own mind. To fully appreciate just what happens to produce a revelation, we should first discuss a few non-religious (and therefore likely less controversial) examples of its more common occurrence.

We are all very familiar with third-level thinking, where we use words in our minds to think consciously about things. But, as noted earlier, this is not the full extent of our thought processes.

Second-level thinking (when associations between memories, or between memories and related incoming information, are found and when more or less permanent links between memories may be formed) occurs subconsciously all the time. While not discussed in depth previously, other stimuli besides incoming information can instigate subconscious neural link-formation or thinking. One cause, important to our investigations, is stress—in particular, stress caused by constantly ruminating about the same, apparently insoluble, problem.[14]

This kind of stress makes itself known in various ways—sometimes mentally, as with dreams or nightmares,[15] occasionally physically, with ailments such as headaches or upset stomachs.[16]

That dreaming is often related to stress is generally well-known. We have all probably experienced waking in the middle of the night, feeling anxious, and thinking that our problems are particularly serious. But, upon waking in the morning, following periods of REM ("rapid eye movement") or dream sleep, we may feel that our predicament is not so bad after all. (We even have a saying, "you'll feel much better in the morning," that acknowledges this.) Occasionally, something marvellous happens: we awake with the answer we have been looking for, and know that our problem has been solved. Such occurrences illustrate a little of what our subconscious mind is capable; they also help to substantiate the fact that the mind is continuously working, even though we are not aware of it doing so. Dreams are secondary manifestations of this work; remembered portions of dreams provide fleeting glimpses of what has been happening at the subconscious second level during sleep.

Many people have recorded how long-elusive solutions sometimes arrive suddenly, quite unexpectedly, out of the blue. Henri Poincaré, a great mathematician, in an insightful essay *Mathematical Creation*,[17] wrote that he discovered Fuchsian functions in a coffee-induced, semi-dreaming state, after spending fifteen days attempting to disprove their existence. In this essay, he explored how the subconscious must continue the search for a solution, then present the *"good combination"* to the conscious mind when found. He postulated that conscious thought liberated the elements of the problems, and that these might then fly about the subconscious mind like gnats or atoms of gas until a fortuitous encounter produced the sought-after "good combination."

Many similar examples of second-level subconscious thought breaking through into second- and third-level conscious awareness have been described in the literature. One probably known by all organic chemists is Kekulé von Stradonitz's 1865 realization that the benzene molecule is ring shaped. Kekulé reported thinking about possible structures while dozing in front of a fire, seeing long rows of carbon and hydrogen atoms dancing into different snake-like configurations in the flames, and eventually observing one snake seize hold of its own tail. He immediately awoke, recognizing instantly that this had to be the correct molecular arrangement.

Another example of this phenomenon was recently reported in the local press. The chairman of a company described how he was very surprised to find the answer to a problem he had been wrestling with for a week, written in his notebook when he opened it one morning at work. He remembered leaving the notebook downstairs when he went to bed the previous night, but nothing else. He then realized that he must have dreamed the answer, sleep-walked, written it down, and then gone back to bed, all without wakening. The answer in the notebook was perfect. It was immediately put into effect, and the company's efficiency doubled.[18]

Solutions so found are typically discovered upon wakening, but they can arrive, abruptly and unannounced, anytime.[19] A recent book relates how a daytime breakthrough suddenly occurred to Dr. Folkman, a dedicated cancer researcher, while sitting in Boston's Temple Israel.[20] In another publication, it is reported that Charles Darwin remembered exactly where he was when he suddenly realized why offspring differed from their parents.[21]

Returning to our main concern, it is now relatively clear what must be happening at the subconscious level before and during a revelation's occurrence.

When awake, our conscious mind seeks solutions to problems by searching for relationships between memories, or between memories and incoming stimuli (recall the "drill-bit search" example given in Chapter One). Using its knowledge of the properties of each element within the environment presenting the problem, the alert mind can determine when an appropriate solution has been found. Furthermore, both the conscious and subconscious are aware of ongoing searches and any resolutions. Similarly, when solutions cannot be found, this also is "known" both consciously and subconsciously.

However, unlike the conscious mind, the subconscious always addresses the same problem: stress. Any problem-related activity it undertakes is not aimed at finding a solution to a dilemma in mathematics, organic chemistry, cancer growth, or a reason to live, to use examples we have mentioned. The outcome sought by the subconscious is merely a path of lower bioelectrical resistance through the mental constructs continually being activated by the conscious mind. It seeks this because a path of lower resistance consumes less energy, and thus generates less stress.

The subconscious seeks routes of lower resistance when it can; that is, when its neural pathways are not occupied by incoming stimuli or pre-empted by demands from conscious-level activities. During this free time (obtained mostly when the body is sleeping), the subconscious seeks pathways of lower resistance (i.e., links that more directly join the involved memories) from within the mind's museum of memories and constructs. In finding networks that reduce its energy consumption, the subconscious solves problems that interfere with its primary task of directing a healthy body, not those related to the world outside its realm. But, the subconscious does solve such problems, indirectly, and must do so relatively frequently.

Thus, simply by seeking a network that produces lower resistance and lessened stress, the subconscious finds routes which position formerly overlooked memories within new constructs. It does all of this, it must be emphasized, with absolutely no knowledge that the solution it has uncovered has any possible meaning in the real world.[22]

Any time after a new neural network (construct) has been built in this manner, a revelation can occur. Revelations are simply sudden break-throughs, from the subconscious to the conscious mind, of the new understandings that a revised neural network denotes.

Revelations of any kind, scientific, artistic, managerial, or otherwise (including those that set the stage for, and result in, a self-induced religious conversion) occur abruptly and quite unexpectedly. And because the solution presented has been tailor-made by the subconscious to relieve stress caused by the conscious mind's incessant thinking about one particular problem, this solution solves that problem. It immediately feels right, there is a sudden release of tension, and a flood of emotion surges forth.[23] The solution's presentation, the instant it passes from subconscious to consciousness, may seem to be inexplicable, to artists, scientists and religionists. Some may see it as a divine act, and its nature may be such as to precipitate a self-induced religious conversion.[24]

What had taken so long to discover, comes, seemingly, from the unknown.[25] Most importantly, the solution appears flawless—all of the pieces fit perfectly and make a unified whole. While the solution may not yet contain answers to all the questions that will likely come later, the individual knows instinctively and emotionally, as well as rationally, that this new-found solution will be able to provide them. Every part of the experience is magnificent.[26]

Unfortunately, the found solution may be completely wrong. While the discovered solution is often accurate (for it is the result of much prior thought, both conscious and subconscious, by individuals well versed in their discipline), it can be erroneous, even for such individuals. The intense feelings and instant conviction experienced bear no relation to the truth of what is newly thought to be the answer. The solution always feels right, and it is right for the particular mind-set of constructs that conceived it. And it is also right in that it reduces energy consumption and stress. But the answer may be entirely false, and always will be, if the individual has had only incorrect knowledge or false assumptions to work with. Kepler's experiences can serve to illustrate the effect of working with unsound knowledge. Kepler (an extremely careful, sixteenth century mathematician and astronomer) deduced, via mathematical investigations into the properties of regular solid figures,[27] that there could only be six planets. (Of course, there are more than six planets, but no one knew this at that time.) Kepler was immediately filled with "great joy,"[28] because he believed that he had discovered one of God's mysteries.

The experiences related above demonstrate that hours of conscious, troublesome, problem-solving attempts usually preceded revelations. Since this kind of activity induces accompanying hours of stress-relieving, subconscious, mental activity, the most logical explanation for revelations (and the religious conversions that sometimes follow) is that they stem from this work amid the memories stored within the brain.[29]

Summary

This is an appropriate place to review a few of the major points discussed so far in Parts One and Two.

- The brain's chief function is to receive information detected by the body's sensors and to analyze and redirect this information so that the body acts in a manner that best enables it to survive and reproduce.
- Chunks of knowledge, experiences, thoughts, past emotions, etc., are stored in the brain as memories within neural networks, much like information is stored in computers as patterns in memory chips and on hard drives. The human mind accesses these memories both consciously and subconsciously.
- The mind evolved as the "problem-solving software" of a brain that had to manage an increasingly complex body. (The body's abilities became more complex over time as survival-enhancing mutations added structures upon existing structures. See Chapters Eight and Ten for an elaboration of this phenomenon.)
- The mind survives because it helps the body to survive. It does this by searching for and recognizing relationships between

memories and stimuli from body sensors, then creating an awareness of alternative courses of action.
- The universe's causality has led its inhabitants to think (to the extent that they possess this capability) and act rationally. This ability began, and will continue (evolving as it does so), because those behaving in this manner are more likely to survive and reproduce than those who ignore its importance.
- Solutions to everyday problems can only be found by consulting the environment presenting the problem situation. The criteria needed to draft and select rational solutions are always obtained from that environment. This environment can be the real universe, or it can be a social, cultural, artificial or other environment, including the private mental mind-set created by the blend of constructs each individual develops during his or her lifetime.
- A purpose, attainable in the environment presenting the problem, must be valued and sought before a solution can be rationally chosen (i.e., a decision made) and "meaningful" action taken.
- Language tremendously expedited the transfer of knowledge and understanding between generations. It has made humans the most adaptable species on this planet and it has accelerated the growth of their intelligence. However, language also allows us to expound metaphysical problems devoid of real world context. Such problems cannot be solved without first defining some appropriate metaphysical environment; furthermore, meaningful decisions cannot be made even within this environment without first defining and valuing a purpose.
- Religions declare purposes and describe accompanying environments. These conceptions exist entirely and only within the minds of believers, and differ widely throughout the world. In effect, religions provide an environment where otherwise-unanswerable metaphysical questions such as, "what is the point of living/what is the meaning of life?" may be answered. This environment contains solutions and criteria to be used by believers when making a decision or choice. The religion's goal (or purpose) is said to be attainable by anyone who chooses to live mentally within that environment. This purpose, once valued, is then used to assess options, make moral decisions or judgements, and regulate behaviour. (A similar effect is created when individuals adopt and conform to the behavioural standards defined by their social environment.)
- "Revelations" occur when the results of subconscious, second-level, stress-relieving thinking break through into conscious thought. This phenomenon is accompanied by emotions of

excitement, wonder and joy, chemically generated as the stress-induced tensions are released.
- "Conversions" of any kind, religious or secular, and whether externally or self-induced (by way of a revelation), occur when one all-encompassing Construct connects or re-connects, then supersedes, numerous formerly poorly integrated neural constructs. The new Construct profoundly affects the thinking, decision making, and behaviour of the affected individual.
- The intensity of self-induced revelations, the instant relief from stress they provide and the seemingly perfect answers they offer create conditions that convince recipient individuals that this is "the truth." Such individuals often become close-minded in their way of interpreting information and firmly believe[30] that their mind-set is the only correct way to think.

(Three postscripts to this chapter titled "Creativity," "Free Will" and "A Revelation" are to be found commencing page 223.)

Chapter Six

Present Day Religions

Humans have built, nurtured and developed religions of various kinds for millennia. Primitive people venerated animals, snakes, birds, plants and insects, as well as the more usual mystical gods. Forms of astrology and magic often accompanied and added complexity to their beliefs. The sun, moon and stars, human ancestors, imaginary demons and spirits, have all been thrown into the mix to flavour religious philosophies at one time or another.[1]

Over the past twenty five centuries or so, the number of major religions has contracted to nineteen.[2] However, each one of these includes many variations (Protestantism, for example, acknowledges over seventy), and each variation can be further subcategorized many times. In addition, an incredible number of minor cults lie half-hidden in the cities, towns, villages and backwoods of many nations. Society still has Satanism, voodoo, animism, warlocks and witches, all seeking (and finding, if occasional newspaper reports are to be believed) receptive audiences to extend their influence. In total, humans probably support a million or so different religions—and the number increases each year.[3]

This chapter presents a brief overview of five principal religions, summarizes some of their commonalities and ends with a list of issues that, in my opinion, devalue their utility. It is necessarily a very cursory glance at only a few of their most obvious features; doubtless many readers will be able to add much that has been left out.

1. Some Major Religions

Over half of the world's population claim to be either Christian (over 2 billion), Muslim (about 1.2 billion), or Hindu (nearly 0.8 billion).[4] Buddhists number over 0.3 billion. No other religion is supported by more than 200 million people, with most other doctrines claiming just a few million. Surprisingly, the founding monotheistic religion, Judaism, reports less than twenty million adherents. By way of comparison, over 0.9 billion people state that they do not follow a religion of any sort, and more than 0.2 billion call themselves atheists and deny the existence of any god.

1.1. Christianity

Christianity may be subdivided into four major divisions; Protestant, Roman Catholic, Orthodox, and Anglican. Each holds the Bible to be an important fount of knowledge.

Christians, in a doctrine known as the Trinity, believe that God exists in three forms. As God the Father, He created the heavens and Earth, He judges then rewards or punishes (but is always willing to forgive any sin in those who repent). As God the Holy Spirit, His presence can be directly experienced by anyone. And as Jesus, the Son of God, He came to Earth to teach us how to behave in order to join Him in Heaven after death.

Almost all of the information we have about Jesus and his life was written by proselytizing followers several decades after his death, and the veracity of the text is considered suspect.[5] Notwithstanding this dispute, the many stories about his life, the miracles he is reported to have performed, and the description of his resurrection after death are taken by the majority of Christians as proof-sufficient that he was, and is, the Son of God.

Jesus taught that humans are created in the image of God, and that they should be loved as God also should be loved. Christians emphasize the importance of private devotion and prayer, living in accordance with the will of God, participating in worship, communion and confession, baptizing adults or infants, and hoping for everlasting life. Prayer is deemed to open up a direct channel of communication with God. Christian rituals, practices, and precise beliefs vary greatly between the numerous factions, but Christmas (celebrating the birth of Christ), and Easter (commemorating His death and resurrection) are invariably important annual events.

All segments of Christianity state that one's purpose in life is to obey God's will, that sin exists, that there will be a day of judgement, and that there is life after death. God is taken to be merciful, and repentant sinners are assured that they will be forgiven.

Christianity is an evangelizing religion, with followers of some branches ever willing to relate their beliefs to others, and missionaries eager to convert any who show an interest. In this vein, some Christians see other religions (particularly extreme forms of Islam) as a danger to their well-being.

1.2. Islam

Founded in Arabia by Muhammad early in the seventh century, Islam spread rapidly following Muhammad's death in 632 CE. During the Dark Ages, Islamic scientists, philosophers and physicians formed the intellectual centre of the world. Islam's growth and dominance declined following the First Crusade (called by Pope Urban II), when a rabble of mostly Western European Christian armies took Jerusalem in 1099. (Jerusalem was regained for Islam in 1187 by the Muslim prince Saladin.)

Islam is practised today by approximately one-fifth of the world's population. Muslims state that Muhammad was the last and greatest of many thousands of prophets.[6] Muslims believe that all prophets were human and all were passing Allah's words to humankind, that all prophets are therefore Muslim, and that only Islam is acceptable to Allah.[7]

Muslims believe that the Koran (or Qur'an) contains Allah's revelations to Muhammad and is therefore infallible. Because the sections of the Koran were memorized and written down by many followers and recorded in full shortly after Muhammad's death it has retained its integrity over the years. The Koran teaches forgiveness, but allows punishment of wrongdoers. Martyrs who die in a jihad, or holy war, are assured a place in paradise.

A second significant source of Islamic doctrine is the Hadith literature, which describes what Muhammad did or said in particular circumstances. This text is not deemed to be infallible; it teaches that individuals should live to benefit humanity, and not live to seek immediate or future pleasure.

According to Islam, Allah created and sustains the universe and all within. Nature is subservient to, and may be exploited by, mankind. Mankind is in the service of Allah, must worship Him, and must construct a social order that is ethical and free from corruption. As in Christianity, Muslims believe that there will be a Day of Judgement, when all humanity will be judged, with some going to the Garden or heaven, and others going to hell. In the meantime, "virtuous" nations are granted license to judge and punish "corrupt" nations.

Muslims are forbidden to eat the flesh of swine or to drink alcohol, and must obey five duties. They must publicly profess their faith at least once in their life. They must pray five times each day, give alms or charity, fast from dawn to sunset during the month of Ramadan, and, if physically and economically able, make at least one pilgrimage to the Kaaba at Mecca. Men should cover their midsection and are forbidden to wear silk or gold jewellery. Women should cover their whole body, except for hands, feet and face. Men may have up to four wives but each must be treated equitably and justly. Women can initiate divorce. Possessions pass equally to all children. Racial equality is stressed, and the practice of different religions is allowed.

Islam is a way of life that covers all aspects of living. Its principles govern personal, social, political and economic thought and action with no aspect neglected. Consequently Islamic law contains and defines both legal and moral obligations, and several Islamic nations do not separate church from state. This practice has fostered the growth of Islamism (whose slogan is, "Islam is religion and State"). Islamists, a minority group of avid fundamentalists, particularly oppose "Western morality," and believe that modernization has resulted in the breakdown of traditional family, societal, and religious values. They strive for a global theocracy and are not above using terrorism to achieve their ends. Moderate Muslims seem powerless to counter this activity from within Islam and any attempt to do so from without is regarded as an attack upon the Islamic faith. Perhaps for this reason outsiders often see Islam as an aggressive and ruthless religion.

1.3. Hinduism

Hinduism, existing in India for some 5,000 years, has influenced many other religions, and has itself absorbed an enormous variety of beliefs and practices. These shape and colour every aspect of its very intricate metaphysics. Today, Hindus show more uniformity in their behaviour than in their beliefs; however, very few practices are universal to all.

The principal Hindu textual authorities are the three Vedas (the Rig-veda, whose content reaches back to the birth of Hinduism, the Yajur-veda, and the Sama-veda). These books are considered to be revelations about the Supreme Being (Brahman, who is said to be the source and ultimate reality of everything) and are not to be altered in any manner. A fourth veda, the Atharva-veda, is of lesser importance. There are many other Hindu sources of information, particularly the Brahmanas (rituals and myths) and the Upanishads (mystical meditations on the universe and meaning in life), however these authorities are too erudite for most Hindus to comprehend. Practical Hinduism is found in the Smriti (which is allowed to be modified, and which includes epics), many Puranas, and textbooks on sacred law.

Hindu beliefs include the notions that the universe contains many concentric heavens and hells (with India positioned at the centre), that time is both degenerative and cyclical, and that the universe is being intermittently destroyed and reborn. Many Hindus believe the soul leaves the body after death, to be reborn as another person, animal, vegetable, or other entity, with the "level" of rebirth being determined by past actions. Only continuously striving to improve both body and soul and the renunciation of all worldly desires can merit release from this endless recycling. Few Hindus actively seek this ideal. However, the pursuit of this goal has produced two distinct metaphysical and social systems.

"Worldly" Hindus live within an intricate, hierarchical, caste system that binds society and gives each person an identity and purpose. Born into a particular caste, each person is destined to perform certain appropriate duties—to marry within their caste, to raise a son, and to eat traditional food, for instance. Thus, for worldly Hindus, the key concepts of their philosophies are relationships, harmony and detachment or peace—not religion or a concern related to their god's requirements for them. "Non-worldly" Hindus (who renounce the world) attempt to unite their individual soul with that of Brahman, the universal soul. Many of their practices (such as vegetarianism) have been incorporated into worldly Hinduism.

Each Hindu community is responsible for erecting and supporting a temple which it then manages. Most Hindus worship one of the male gods, Shiva or Vishnu, or the goddess Devil. However, they may just as readily worship any of hundreds of minor gods, some of whom can be particular to just one village or family.

Social ceremonial occasions include birth, the first time rice is eaten, first male haircut, purification after first menstruation, marriage, pregnancy blessings, cremation, sprinkling funeral ashes in a holy river, and annual ancestral offerings. Less-public daily ceremonials include chanting a hymn to the sun at dawn, and making offerings to the household shrine, or to special garden or village objects. Temples vary from small stone boxes to complex temple cities. Priests offer prayers at sunrise, attend their god, give food remnants to those worshipping, and perform sunset rituals. Processions are normally held each year to carry the god image around the temple, and goats may be sacrificed on special occasions. Numerous colourful and vibrant festivals are held annually, with some allowing all castes to mingle freely. Periodically, individuals (usually male) and, less commonly, entire families make pilgrimages to holy places, often walking hundreds of kilometres en masse to fulfil vows, to seek blessings or give thanks for those received, and to collect water for the household shrine.

Despite its multiple gods, variety in religious expression, diversity and apparent contradictions, the Hindu society flourishes and continues to attract converts, perhaps, in part, because central to its teachings is the universal desire to satisfy the human striving for Shanti, or peace of mind.

1.4. Buddhism

Buddhism is based upon the teachings of Siddhartha Gautama,[8] known as Buddha, or Enlightened One. Born (circa 563 BCE) a Hindu and raised as a prince of a small kingdom in Kapilavastu in north-eastern India, Gautama abdicated at 29 to lead an ascetic life and to practice Yoga. After doing so for six years he adopted a middle path between indulgence and self-denial, meditated, and eventually attained enlightenment. He then preached in various places, and subsequently formed a community of disciples.

Buddha retained the Hindu idea of reincarnation and belief in the reality of many gods (although none are to be considered divine and all are subject to reincarnation and to Cosmic reality). However, he rejected many other Hindu beliefs, particularly the veracity of the Vedas. He welcomed all castes and taught the "Four Noble Truths": that life is suffering, caused by ignorance, to be overcome by wisdom and compassion, achievable by following the "Noble Eightfold Path." This conduct requires right views, intention, speech, action, livelihood, effort, right-mindedness, and contemplation. In turn, these are often grouped into three categories: wisdom, morality and concentration.

Records of Buddha's actual teachings were not written until around the first century BCE, several hundred years after his death. During the intervening years, the unity of Buddha's teachings was maintained by councils of monks who met (four times in five hundred years) to agree upon proper monastic discipline and what should be taught. Disagreements in early years led to eighteen schools of thought and caused many splits. Today two main forms survive, Theravada (which holds Buddha to be mortal), and Mahayana (which holds Buddha to exist in three forms, one immortal).

Generally speaking, Buddhists believe that individuals are composed of five, constantly changing "bundles," which are comprised of feelings, perceptions, predispositions, consciousness, and the material body. Since this constant bundle-changing precludes the possibility of a soul (atman), the causal reincarnation link is attributed to ignorance, thoughts and sensations. Buddhists also believe in karma, whereby each act has an ethical consequence that brings punishment or reward during life, and which can determine the outcome of reincarnation. Being charitable, non-materialistic and unselfishly kind, having compassion for all, supporting the monasteries, not killing or stealing, avoiding alcohol and harmful language and not sexually misbehaving are considered to be correct behaviours. Reincarnation can only be halted through attaining the enlightened state of Nirvana.

Theravada Buddhism is most widespread in Sri Lanka, Myanmar, Laos, Cambodia and Thailand, and is returning, via the Untouchable caste, to India. Mahayana Buddhism is dominant (in a variety of forms) in the rest of the Buddhist world, principally China, Korea, Japan, Tibet, Central Asia, Vietnam, and Taiwan.

Theravada claims to be perpetuating the true teachings and practices of Siddhartha Gautama, and traces its descent from the original monastic community. The Theravadin ideal is to become an arhat, i.e., in a disciplined manner, attempt to manipulate their dharmas (a complexity of transient aspects that comprise the human existence) in order to suspend karma and thereby achieve Nirvana. Only monks can attain Nirvana, but the laity may hope to be reborn as monks after many reincarnations. Women and laity enjoy only limited participation in the monastic life.

Mahayana doctrine (originating between the second century BCE and the first century CE) holds that Buddha has a triple body-form: essence, bliss and transformation. "Essence" represents the absolute, which manifests itself in heavenly form as communal "bliss," and which appears on Earth as "transformation." (Siddhartha Gautama is held to have been such a transformation.) Mahayana Buddhism teaches that the true nature of all things is emptiness, and that this concept can be used in meditation.

Mahayana Buddhists believe that any individual can attempt to reach the stage of perfect enlightenment (bodhisattva). Of those reaching this state, some then choose to delay their entry into Nirvana in order to transfer merit to others through acts of compassion and loving kindness. (Mahayanists therefore consider the bodhisattva state to be higher than that of the Theravadin's arhat—who have more care for themselves than they do for others. As a result Mahayanists can revere bodhisattvas as deities during their lifetime.)

Any sentient thing, animal, human or god, can become a Buddha, and countless Buddhas, each presiding over their own universe, are believed to exist.

1.5. Judaism

Judaism was the first ethnic and religious group to oppose the prevailing Greek and Roman beliefs in many gods and to permanently adopt monotheism. Many Jewish beliefs and values were later carried over into its two most powerful progeny, Christianity and Islam, and Judaism continues to exert an influence far beyond that which one might expect from a relatively small religion.

According to the Old Testament, in the thirteenth century BCE Moses was commanded by Jehovah to deliver the Hebrews from their Egyptian bondage.⁹ Aided by miracles, he eventually succeeded. On reaching the desert, Moses climbed Mount Sinai, returning after forty days with the Ten Commandments. These became fundamental Hebrew laws,¹⁰ and emphasize the importance of property, communal equality, individual rights, personal freedom and sexual morality.

Orthodox Jews believe that God gave the Torah to Moses on Mount Sinai. The written Torah is maintained on scrolls in every synagogue where each week portions are read aloud. This, and the oral Torah (recorded as the Mishnar and the Talmud by rabbis in the Middle Ages) are said to contain all of God's teachings for humankind.

The Hebrews, under Joshua, conquered Palestine, and later, under King David, established their capital in Jerusalem in 1003 BCE, unifying the tribes of Israel. There, King David's son Solomon built the first Jewish temple. Periods of prosperity as well as misfortune followed, and are recorded in the Old Testament. Assyrians, in 721 BCE, conquered northern Israel, then drove ten of the twelve Israelite tribes into exile. In 586 BCE, Nebuchadnezzar II destroyed Jerusalem and Solomon's Temple, and the Hebrews were later exiled from the southern kingdom of Judah. Eventually the Hebrew tribes were allowed to return to Jerusalem as subjects of the Persian Empire. After a brief independence, they became subjects of the Roman Empire. Jerusalem was destroyed by Roman legions in 70 CE during the Great Revolt, and again the Jews dispersed. Many centuries of persecution followed, and the Jewish people only regained a land of their own, Israel, in 1948.

Jews maintained their faith through the many intervening centuries because they demanded strict adherence (through study, prayer and observance) to Judaism and to the Jewish Law; because they utilized one common language that all are required to know; because they practised an integrated communal and spiritual life; and because they were guided by an irrepressible hope for, and faith in, the establishment of a messianic kingdom.

Jews believe that there is only one God, Yahweh, who created the universe, and who continues to govern it in an intelligible and purposeful manner. They also believe that they hold a covenant with their god, whereby they obey His laws in return for His acknowledgement that they are His chosen people, to be carefully cared for. In effect, Israel is to be the model for the human race.

The Jewish year includes five major and two minor festivals. Three of the major festivals were originally agricultural, and are thus tied to the seasons. (Passover celebrates their exodus from Egypt.) Practising Jews pray three times a day and recite benedictions (particularly before meals, which follow strict dietary laws). Male children, when eight days old, are publicly initiated into the covenant of Abraham through circumcision. Boys reach legal maturity at the age of 13, when they are considered adults and assume responsibility for observing all the Jewish commandments (bar mitzvah), and are called for the first time to read the Torah aloud in a synagogue. Girls reach maturity at 12 years of age.

Both men and women are expected to dress modestly, and are prohibited (by an extension of the requirement to separate the animal and vegetable spheres of life) from wearing any garment that combines both wool and linen. Men are required to wear a head covering called a kippah.

Orthodox Jews expect the Messiah to return, the dead to be resurrected, and there to be everlasting retribution.

1.6. Atheists and Non-Believers

Atheists (who deny the existence of any god), and non-believers (who lack any belief in a god), number about 1.2 billion. Agnostics (who state that there is insufficient evidence to prove or disprove the existence of God, and neither believe nor disbelieve that a god might exist), are likely to form part of this total. These individuals have been included in this brief survey because they constitute one-fifth of the world's population, and because their opinions are relevant to the subject matter of this book.[11]

Countless numbers of philosophers and writers, from Lucretius to the present, have expressed non-belief either in the existence of gods or in their power over humankind.[12] However, since no census, or its equivalent, sought atheistic or agnostic affiliations in past ages, we have no estimate of the number of followers such thinkers may have had.

Atheists typically consider the Bible, Koran, Vedas, Torah and other such texts to be simply records of myths or stories, and dismiss the idea that they could be revelations from a deity. They refute the existence of any god (as creator, or as a loving, caring overseer), and reject the concepts of divine creation, a soul, or an afterlife of any kind. On the other hand, non-believers simply do not believe in such things. They do not concern themselves with denying or affirming the possibility that a god or gods exist, and leave the whole matter for others to mull over.

Atheists may provide any of several reasons for their disbelief, the most common being the lack or inadequacy of evidence. In their opinion, all of the theological proofs that a god exists (particularly the Ontological, Cosmological, Teleological, and Moral arguments[13]) have been clearly refuted in one manner or another. Miracles, and such concepts as the existence or presence of a satan or a god, they argue, are so contrary to the behaviour of all everyday experience and knowledge of the real world, that incontrovertible evidence is needed for them to be credible—the ubiquitous hearsay evidence being particularly weak. They counter religious believers by asking how an "all-knowing" god can also be "all-good," how an "all-good" god can permit innocent children or animals to suffer, and how such a being could allow evil to exist.[14]

Atheism holds no particular philosophical position,[15] and preaches no particular code of behaviour in refuting all divinities, spiritual religions and their doctrines. Although atheists must therefore develop their own standards of behaviour, there is no evidence that shows them to be any more or any less moral than those who have adopted the moral codes of a religion.[16]

2. Common Features

Religions, in one form or another, have existed from prehistoric times and frequently include much of the old in their new formats. They share many characteristics, and some of these are listed (in no specific order) below.

- Most religions, if not all, seem to have developed from the ideas of one thoughtful person, frequently one who desired to change people's behaviour by educating them.[17]
- Religions and beliefs in a god or gods were once necessary to explain how the universe and life began, and why "mysterious" events such as eclipses and plagues occurred—roles now more skilfully performed by science (see chapters seven and eight of this book).
- Religions incorporate and adapt occurrences remembered from the distant past (such as the Flood), as well as myths taken from other religions (such as Creation, or the Garden of Eden), and give them some special significance.
- Religions differ from place to place,[18] with the majority of any population professing allegiance to the local creed. Periodically, differences of opinion arise that cause factions to split off and establish variants of the original belief.
- People generally adopt the religion of their forefathers.[19] However, individuals occasionally convert from their family religion to another, typically upon marriage to a person of another faith, or if pressing needs are not being met, if a compelling preacher attracts them, if converting brings financial or social benefits, or if practising their belief threatens their survival.

- Religious groups build or select special places (such as churches, shrines or rivers) that are held to be significant in the conduct of that religion.
- Religions develop formalized, hierarchically structured organizations that, whenever circumstances permit, grow larger, become more complex, and eventually build edifices of some magnificence.
- Religions formulate ways to communicate with their god (such as meditation, the Eucharist, or prayer).
- Religions develop rituals, life-cycle rites (such as baptisms, funerals and processions) and festivals to be conducted at particular times, on special days, or during certain seasons, when something of historical or seasonal significance is commemorated or celebrated.
- Religions frequently teach by relating stories or parables crafted to illustrate virtues or values deemed to be worthy of emulation.
- Religions prescribe how to behave (and, not infrequently, how to dress) and give reasons why this behaviour should be followed. They define procedures (such as confession, covering the head, or prostration) to be followed to achieve particular religious purposes, and they devise special behaviours (such as making the sign of a cross, undertaking pilgrimages, or genuflecting) that publicly demonstrate allegiance.
- Religions integrate with and influence the society they service,[20] affecting many of their laws, customs, traditions, institutions, and moral standards.[21]
- Religions hold faith and belief to be more important than facts or reason.
- Religions centre upon some kind of unity,[22] and state there is purpose to life. They give followers an identity and a morality, and provide solace and hope in times of trouble. Many religions hold that a heaven or paradise awaits all true believers after their death.
- Above all, religions attempt to simplify moral decision making. (Perhaps this is why portions of religious texts are often cited as sanctioning actions taken, particularly by fundamentalists seeking to justify reprehensible acts).

This summary is in no way exhaustive—for instance, while followers receive many benefits from religions, few are listed here. Being able to provide so much for so many is probably the second most important reason to support religions' continuance. (The primary function of any religion is to provide the purpose used in moral decision making.)

However, while we gain much comfort from the beliefs and practices religions foster, religions can also hinder our ability to think rationally and openly. This may never have been more evident than it is today, when we might arguably claim that religious differences are creating more discord in the world than any other single issue, yet this topic is seldom raised at international levels (such as the United Nations), presumably out of fear that the discussions would rapidly become unmanageable.

3. My Dissatisfaction with Existing Religions

Existing religions raise a number of concerns for me, and those that strike me as incongruous are listed below, not to disparage any religion but to illustrate why I think something better is needed. You may well be able to add additional aspects, both pro and con, particularly if you have a non-Christian background. Having been brought up in such a society, I find it easiest to write with its doctrines in mind, and what I have written applies to all branches of Christianity as I understand them to be. However, I suspect that many of the following issues hold aspects that apply to other religions.

- As doubtless you will have realized from the preceding chapters, I cannot even get to first base. I find that I am unable to believe in the existence of a god that intervenes in human affairs. The evidence that others seem to find sufficient just doesn't hold true for me. It is possible to think that a god was necessary to create the universe, but it is just as plausible to think that He, She, or It did so in a last, dying act. Furthermore, I do not see the point of replacing one inexplicable event (that which created the Big Bang, or the universe) with another inexplicable event (that which created God). If, as the counter argument goes, God always existed, then, just as logically, so could the universe, and one wouldn't need a god to have brought about its beginning. The Big Bang description, with its verified ability to explain subsequent events, is much preferable to me for this has a utility that is scientifically beneficial.
- I find that not one of the world's great religions is simple enough to be understood. In those most-rational of disciplines, science and mathematics, simplicity is often used as the compass that points to the truth.[23]
- I can't believe that Christianity's central figure, Jesus, performed miracles, nor that he was resurrected after death. Nor can I believe that the old bible's stories are anything other than embellished incidents, copied down, then repeatedly tailored, decades or centuries after whatever they purport to describe had

happened,[24] and subjected to all the vagaries of intervening (and likely biased) minds. I am much more inclined to accept the findings of the biblical scholars that have contributed to the Jesus Seminars.[25] How can the Bible be one hundred percent factual as some believe? And, if it is not, how does the average person distinguish truth from fiction?

- How can a young man or woman, not already indoctrinated into a religion and seeking something to guide their spiritual well-being, make a choice between competing religions? Rationally is not an option (since religions are based upon faith not fact). Emotionally seems to be the only way, but is this really the best method to make such an important choice—a choice intended to provide the rationale for moral decision making in the future?

  Consider a reputable representative of each religion, someone perhaps midway between a fundamentalist and a reformist, someone anyone is likely to encounter, anytime, anywhere. Each will have a certain way to pray, to dress, to behave, and, most particularly, will have an opinion about how society should be ordered and children raised to conform to their religion's teachings. Yet each representative will claim that these directions follow from the word of God or His prophet. How can such instructions differ, one from another, so radically?[26] Are we to infer from their many different beliefs that there indeed are many different gods? Or, should only one be taken to be correct? If so, which? When neither parents nor culture(s) dictate, how does one choose?

- It is clear to me that direction, particularly moral direction, is relative, not absolute.[27] Moral direction varies from person to person, society to society, era to era, even Pope to Pope.[28] Only in an artificial system, such as in the world of mathematics, can anything be absolute, and only then because it is defined to be so as a precondition to the existence and properties of such a (closed[29]) system. Thus, to me, if one states that God's word is absolute, i.e., true and unchanging, then one is stating that we are discussing an artificial system, a human-defined and invented one, one that may or may not conform to the reality that exists outside of that invented system.

  The reality, for me, is that direction of any kind, but moral direction in particular, is nothing more or less than what we choose to make it.[30]

- Most religions look to their history for guidance; thus members are continually reminded of past defeats and sufferings inflicted upon their ancestors, most often by other religions. Is this the reason so many inter-religious conflicts still occur? Surely the best way to lead, and to rise above the past, is to look forward,

not backward? Furthermore, texts written to guide behaviour in past times were penned with prevailing circumstances in mind. The authors never worried about an over-populated world, for instance, when censuring birth control.
- Western religions use fear as a tool to control their followers. Punishment following judgement; the Devil and Hell awaiting; these worries are as real to many as is their belief in God.[31] Is this really the mental environment we want our children to pass to our grandchildren—a state of apprehension? What does this say about the way we think of ourselves, when our belief systems use this kind of negative psychological conditioning to obtain conformity?
- Many religions only conditionally bestow inclusion and love. Apparently, gaining admission to heaven is not for everyone, only for believers within the faith. Are we to believe that love, stated to emanate from God, is actually so rationed and controlled?
- Many religions promote human selfishness; they centre upon and cater to humankind and what God can do for us. Our prayers focus largely upon our needs, requisitioning help to obtain what we want. Moreover, most religions pay very little attention to the fact that we are only one small segment of a whole living biosphere and global ecosystem. If religious people believe that all living things were created by God, why then is the average western religion silent about how we despoil the biosphere (for example, by spewing pollutants, clear-cutting forests, or over-fishing oceans), or the way we treat some of our fellow creatures (battery-raising hens, restricting-movement of calves, force-feeding ducks, and worse)?[32] Is it because we hold that animals are scarcely sentient, or because scriptures tell us we are to rule creatures of the Earth?[33] Ignoring the well-being of all that lives except *H. sapiens* has innumerable adverse consequences, a concern familiar to environmentalists everywhere, but one almost totally ignored by our religions.
- Religions ask believers to abandon rationality when it proves troublesome, to place faith above clear thinking, to deny what their senses tell them about the way things are, and to believe in things like miracles, the existence of an intervening omnipresent, omniscient god, and an afterlife. The world is as it is today precisely because religions (to the considerable extent that they have influenced the behaviour of people and societies in the past) teach such things. Surely, placing statements that cannot be substantiated above rationality is the very last thing we should do if we want to survive and grow in a universe that conducts itself entirely rationally.[34]

Present Day Religions

- Finally, and of crucial importance to my way of thinking, religions are no longer able to do the job we most need them to do. Developed many centuries and even millennia ago, they have nothing to say about numerous current moral and ethical problems. They offer no guidance (and may even issue conflicting instructions) as we wrestle with the moral "right"- or "wrong"-ness of, for example, controlling conception artificially, allowing therapeutic abortion or yearned-for release from terminal pain, altering the genetic makeup of unborn children, rejuvenating diseased organs by using embryonic stem cells, cloning a human, or using MRI to examine suspects knowledge of criminal events.[35]

    Certainly, I hear religious adherents stating with conviction their understanding of God's directives about these matters, but I do not value their declarations as much as others seem to. I believe that the words they attribute to God are those of various well-intentioned, long-dead, humans; words probably altered many times over the centuries, and I discount their importance. Indeed, the arguments of many vocal adherents seem to be based upon their own personal feelings (richly coloured by the emotions they generate) rather than upon facts and logic. Instead of telling me how to act in today's world, or how to prepare for life tomorrow, I hear them proposing a return to the behaviours of the past. I do not want to return to the past. And I do not think many of us would be willing to trade our current knowledge (and the many benefits of living in today's world of scientific, technological and medical marvels) for this kind of direction, once we understood that it also requires returning to yesterday's world of superstitions, intolerances and repressive practices.

    Instead of uniting and guiding us as we attempt to make necessary moral and ethical decisions (as all religions were originally developed to do) current religions and their texts seem more to divide and hinder us. Faulty religious guidance has caused some to abandon the Pope in favour of condoms, states within nations to pass laws that counter and contradict reality,[36] fanatics to kill doctors who perform abortions, terrorists to destroy buildings and kill thousands, and otherwise sensible men and women around the world to assault, maim and kill others who have simply chosen to follow a different faith. Would anyone dispute the thought that certain aspects of current religions' guidance are likely to promote the same practices, again and again, in the future?

In short, I find that our multifaceted understandings of God differ, our interpretations of what He wants differ, and our ideas of right and wrong differ. I lament the way many religions use fear and conditional love as forms of control, and how they ignore the damage we inflict on other life forms. (And—until I found the replacement that is discussed in later chapters—I missed the guidance that a religion's "purpose for life" once provided me.)

There is one central reason why none of today's religions satisfy me (or, likely others): religions promote fancies and deny facts. There is no valid evidence to show that there is an overseeing, intervening or compassionate god, none that shows a heaven to exist, and none that confirms there is an afterlife to value. All experiences purported to substantiate these assertions can be explained more mundanely. Such ideas were derived from assumptions made long ago when facts were scarce. They have been kept because they were made central features of religions that provide purpose, solace and hope.[37] Our mind's crucial need for a purpose has caused us to follow a series of myths.

If we continue to rely upon incorrect assumptions when making decisions that affect the whole of life's future, then we are imprudent and short-sighted. Furthermore, we will suffer the consequences, as biospheric degradations and humankind's many ugly acts are regularly demonstrating to those with the wit to recognize what they are seeing.

We must search for a better purpose to guide our moral decision making. It must be based upon facts, not fantasies. We must develop a morality that conforms to reality, thereby creating one that is less likely to lead us astray.

Summary

Religions have been developed by the efforts of prophets and their followers, men and women who refined ideas and beliefs about how human life might be improved, and then conveyed these ideas in a convincing manner to others. For this to happen, divine intervention has never been required—everything that such prophets and their followers experienced, witnessed, undertook, or relayed, everything that happened then, and everything that has happened since, can be more realistically explained as being the result of other causes. Nevertheless, approximately five billion (or about 80%) of the world's population state that they believe in a god, and most, presumably, try to obey what they have been told are their god's wishes.[38]

Today we have over a million religions, all vying for attention, with many of them, in one manner or another, decrying their competitors. Is there no way our moral thinking might be better ordered?

I, for one, am sure that there is. A way that does not deny or attempt to replace any of the existing religions—that would be an insult to some of humanity's greatest achievements and a nonsensical proposition. But it must be possible to unify beliefs under a banner that allows all to embrace both old and new. There must be at least one universal moral code that captures the essence of being human, that defines who we are, states what we stand for, and guides nations when there are difficult decisions to make. An integrated and forward-looking code that might one day constitute the backbone of a universal religion.

The second half of this book begins the search for such an ideal.

Conclusion to Part Two

Humans have learned much over the last two thousand years. In the past, we made incorrect guesses about the orbits of stars, today we build machinery that replicates their fusing atoms' behaviour; we used to speculate about the nature of blood, today we routinely replace failing organs; a thousand years ago men on horseback spread the news, today we employ the light-speed of electromagnetic waves.

All such progress depended, and will continue to depend, upon one thing—the ability to identify and root out faulty assumptions and replace them with facts. In other words, progress necessitates recognizing that the universe (and all that it contains and everything that happens) is rational. Once we do this, we realize that all situations can be analyzed and treated logically. Then, given enough time and effort, almost anything becomes possible—even by-passing emotionally-charged, long-standing, religious differences.

We have employed a rational approach in every field of human endeavour except religion. There, we fight new understandings, progress, and each other. No time has ever been more appropriate than the present to investigate alternative ways to meet our religious needs. Religions are not beyond betterment; they can incorporate new understandings, they can be redesigned. The rational approach can be used, even in the field of religious belief.

Science and religion have not always been strangers to one another. In Ancient Greece all speculative thought was considered to be philosophy; science and religion were (and often still are) speculative in nature. Both might profit from a tighter union for both address aspects of the same problem—our lack of knowledge. Most spiritual religions attempt to explain the creation of the universe and the planet's organisms; many scientists work on exactly the same questions. However, religion and science operate at different ends of the knowledge gap. Religion starts at the "big end" with all the answers, usually declaring at the outset that a supreme being created all; science works at the "small end" and begins by asking questions, slowly building an understanding of the whole from a thorough examination of its parts.

Religion and science have another feature in common: both are founded upon a belief. While the belief held by religions is invariably made clear for everyone, the belief held by scientists is usually overlooked—however, it is just as fundamental and important.

Scientists, without exception, believe that all of the universe's behaviour is rational, i.e., that effects follow causes which follow effects (the causality discussed in Chapter One). Religions, apparently sensing that some aspect of this belief counters theirs, invariably state (in one way or another) that some parts of the universe are not subject to rational inquiry.

Because science and religion are both based upon a belief, I suspect that unifying these beliefs would fully unify science and religion. Although not its intended purpose, the last half of this book seems to be showing how this might be brought about. Essentially, the belief that heads both disciplines is that which is used by each to make purposeful decisions. Religious beliefs regarding a judgement day and an afterlife influence behavioural decisions made by followers. Scientific beliefs that the universe is causal or rational determine the accuracy of solutions proposed by scientists. Both beliefs provide the "purpose" needed by the decision maker to make a choice about how to act—the religious in order to enter heaven, the scientist in order to have his or her findings accepted as valid.

To my mind, there is no reason for the purpose that heads scientific inquiry to be any different from the purpose that heads a religion. The problem is—how might such a joint purpose be stated? "To seek the truth," might be accurate, but this is too simple a statement to have any practical utility. (The purpose proposed toward the end of Chapter Nine may be a more useful one.) I leave this as a problem that some readers might like to take up. What a foundation for future civilizations to build upon would be created, should scientific and religious purposes become one!

Part Three

Purpose

Introduction to Part Three

What better way to commence our search for a universal religion than to examine what is currently known about the universe and its living contents? Using knowledge carefully compiled over many centuries and replacing assumptions with facts—this is, after all, why the majority of us no longer live in caves.

Communal decision-making (moral or practical) is facilitated by valuing the attainment of a communally valued purpose, one which is readily recognized as applicable to all—a universal purpose. Unfortunately, as the next two chapters relate, to the best of our current understanding nothing about either the universe or life necessitates that they be purpose-driven. Scientists can't prove that a purpose was necessary for the universe or life to form; neither can they prove that a purpose was not necessary. All they can state is that both the universe and life are present, both change over time, and nothing more than that described by a few laws, principles and theories of physics is needed to explain their existence and ensure their evolution. As Chapter Nine notes, our current physics is not powerful enough to determine whether or not a purpose existed before our universe began—the only place a predetermining purpose might be found.

However, there is a possible way around the dilemma created by our failure to find a universe-governing purpose. This is discussed in Chapter Ten which suggests that a possible consequence of life's behaviour could be used as a "surrogate" purpose. It turns out that this "consequence" has a number of valuable contributions to offer (it can readily be used to guide moral decision making, for instance—an exercise explored in Chapter Thirteen). Part Three concludes by constructing a reason to think that the "possible consequence" might even be a "probable consequence" (which would greatly increase its value, should it be adopted to be the "purpose" that heads a universal religion).

But first, we must update Genesis I.

Chapter Seven

The Universe

Most of our discoveries about the universe have come through collecting and studying electromagnetic radiations. For many centuries, visible light waves were the only kind of radiation we could detect, and we could not do much with them until Galileo constructed his telescopes. But the electromagnetic spectrum holds much more information than that contained in the light waves visible to our eyes. The full spectrum ranges from very long radio waves, microwaves and the infrared, through the rainbow's hues, to ultraviolet, X-rays, and highly energetic gamma rays. Our ability to understand what is happening throughout the universe depends upon our ability to invent, build and utilize instruments able to gather in these waves, remove spurious background noise, then to amplify, analyze and make sense of the minute differences so revealed. The past few decades have opened many electromagnetic inspection windows, and the next will undoubtedly open many more. Thus, what follows in this chapter will certainly need to be updated as we learn more, but the chapter's major premises will likely remain valid, for they are supported by many millions of solidly based observations.

Let us begin this explanation of what has been discovered about the universe by describing just a little of what everyone can readily see. We will then use the laws of physics and the "causality principle" to extrapolate backwards in time; this reveals how things must have been in the past to cause them to be as we see them today.

1. What we see in the Sky

Who has not looked at the sky on a starry, cloudless night and felt the wonder of living on a planet surrounded by so many mysterious shining points of light? Two thousand years ago, many thought that most of these were merely copies of each other, and that they were positioned on one of several "shells" which surrounded the Earth—a very uninspiring arrangement. We now know how incorrect that view was, and any reasonably good backyard telescope can provide hints about how our new perspective was obtained. It can be seen that these points of light are not all the same: many vary in brightness, some possess tinges of colour, and, while most hardly ever change their position relative to one another, a few move about from one night to the next, and the whole rotates with the time and season.

Even four hundred years ago it was not generally known that the Earth and planets are satellites of the sun. Although the Greek astronomer Aristarchus (around 250 BCE) had guessed as much, most preferred to believe otherwise. The Catholic Church had adopted Aristotle's cosmology, and it maintained that three concentric spheres or "shells" encompassed the Earth, with the sun and moon moving on the surface of the first sphere, the planets moving on the second, and all of the stars being at rest on the third.[1] This conformed to the notion that a perfect heaven awaited above (while volcanoes and hot springs were said to prove that hell and brimstone lay beneath). There is a well-known story of how Galileo,[2] after careful use of a telescope he had constructed, declared in 1616 that Copernicus was right and that the Earth and planets did revolve around the sun; this led to the Church placing Galileo under house arrest for the rest of his life.[3] However, the increasing use of telescopes gradually altered popular opinion, and by the middle of the seventeenth century most astronomers agreed that the sun-centred description was correct.

A six-inch telescope and some careful scrutiny will uncover numerous small, fuzzy patches of light in the night sky. Careful observation at higher magnifications shows that these are actually collections of stars, or galaxies. Galaxies, typically comprising thousands of millions of stars, mostly appear in one of three arrangements: elliptical, spiral[4] or irregular. Astronomers further find (through careful examination of photographs taken using giant telescopes) that galaxies themselves collect together in groups and clusters, and that these clumps form even bigger collections. The size of these massive groupings (called superclusters[5] and galaxy walls) can exceed many hundreds of millions of light-years.

Astronomers have also observed several pairs of galaxies colliding. This sounds catastrophic, but it produces nowhere near the (relative) damage caused, for example, when comets or asteroids crash into planets. This is because galaxies are vast (which is another way of saying that they are mostly empty space) and one galaxy can pass right through another with relatively few direct impacts (orbital disruptions would be much more likely to happen).[6]

The Universe

A number of dark patches are also noticeable in the night sky, areas which seem to be devoid of light-emitting stars. One well-known dark region can be seen in the Great Orion Nebula forming part of Orion's sword and lies some 1500 light-years away. (The reason such dark patches exist is explained in section four of this chapter.)

Stars, galaxies, superclusters, and other objects in the universe have been photographed, numbered, catalogued and intensively studied for decades. Their brilliance, variabilities, emissions, compositions, movements, ages, and much else, have been repeatedly measured by a wide range of very powerful instruments. Over years of study, it has been found that most objects and phenomena can be grouped into categories, and these have been given names (for example, white and brown dwarfs, red giants, neutron stars, gas giants, black holes, Cepheids, pulsars, quasars, novae, supernovae, and so on). Much has been learned in just a few decades about the nature and properties of members of each category, but a great deal more remains to be discovered.

By studying the variations in intensity of emitted radiation, astronomers have found how to measure the distance between Earth and a particular kind of varying star called a Cepheid variable. By associating these stars with galaxies, it has been determined that the light from the most distant galaxies has been travelling for more than thirteen billion years! This means that, when viewing those galaxies, we are looking at something that is about 12×10^{22} kilometres away (calculated by multiplying the distance light travels in one year by 13 billion), and, perhaps more significantly, it means we are seeing light that was emitted from them as they existed over thirteen billion years ago.[7] To see these galaxies as they exist today, we would have to wait another thirteen billion years for their current emissions to reach Earth (or we would have to instantaneously travel 12×10^{22} kilometres to where they are, an impossibility). Knowing how far an object is from Earth has allowed astronomers to "look into the past"—the farther away a celestial entity is, the older the light we are seeing. Thus, the properties of distant objects can be examined and compared to closer (i.e., younger) emitting bodies. Such analyses have led to many meaningful discoveries about the origins of our universe and its evolution over time.

Some eighty years ago astronomers discovered that the spectral emissions[8] from all distant objects are displaced, i.e., that their spectral dark bands[9] have been shifted from their normal position. All galactic radiation (except that coming from a few, nearby, galaxies) shows spectral lines that have been moved toward the red end of the spectrum; this has been termed the "red shift."[10] This phenomenon has been found to occur in every direction we look, and means that all distant objects are moving away from us. In fact, the farther away an object is, the faster it recedes.[11]

Unfortunately, for those who would have otherwise, this does not make us unique. Although it seems to place the Earth (and therefore humanity) at the centre of the universe, this is not the case. The true explanation is that everything is moving away from everything else, because the intervening space is expanding rather than the objects themselves moving. (They do move, of course, just as our planet moves around our sun. Our sun travels around the centre of our galaxy, and galaxies themselves move. But galactic recession is due to space expansion. Space expansion is perhaps most clearly visualized using the analogy of specks of dirt on the surface of a balloon. When the balloon is inflated, the distance between each speck increases, and those furthest apart separate at the greatest speed, but no speck is more centrally positioned than any other.)

Finding that billions of galaxies exist, each containing billions of stars, has been exciting. Finding that they are speeding away from each other was at first unbelievable, then astonishing, and it immediately claimed the attention of all cosmologists. This galactic recession (or expansion of the universe, which is another way of saying the same thing) was so fundamental and far-reaching an observation that few astronomers could concentrate upon any other issue—an explanation had to be found.

2. The Expanding Universe

Two competing theories quickly emerged to explain the expanding universe phenomenon: the Steady State theory and the Big Bang theory. The first postulated that the universe is self-sustaining, and claimed that what we see today is what will be seen in billions of years time; galaxies move apart, but the total picture remains the same. According to the Steady State theory, the stars that are moving outwards are being replaced by new ones that are perpetually being formed out of cosmic dust. This dust is being created from atoms, the theory went, that themselves are being continuously created from cosmic energy. (We cannot observe this creation, because the theory predicts that it need only occur at a rate of about one atom per 500 cubic meters, every 1000 years,[12] which is far too slow to be detected.)

In contrast, the Big Bang explanation stated that the universe began with an explosion, and that everything within has been moving apart since that moment, with the intervening space expanding and cooling[13] as it proceeds. In this theory, everything was created during, or shortly after, "the bang," rather than slowly and continuously, atom by atom.[14]

I remember reading some of the discussions reported in the press when these theories were announced, shortly after the second world war. They provided a stimulating intellectual alternative to the dreary task of becoming formally educated. At that time, I favoured the Steady State theory because I couldn't understand how everything could come from nothing in one big burst. Creation seemed slightly more feasible if it happened very slowly, and I thought that perhaps the atoms being created came from energy released as the matter in receding galaxies became stretched further and further apart.[15] The Steady State theory also seemed more appealing philosophically, because if the universe continued forever, one would never have a beginning to explain.

However, three observations eventually dismissed the Steady State theory. First, if the universe did start with a bang, then there should still be some trace evidence of this explosion to be found. And there is; it has been heard since radio astronomy first began. Everywhere one searches, in addition to the electromagnetic information received from stars and galaxies, there is a constant hiss of background radiation. This hiss comes from energy that remains (unconverted into matter) from the originating Big Bang.[16]

Second, the universe does not remain the same over time, as the Steady State theory requires; it changes as it becomes older. This was discovered when quasar locations were established upon a four-dimensional map of the universe. This showed them to exist only at great distances from our system, signifying that they were present billions of years ago but no longer exist today.[17] Astronomers also find (by searching far and near in distance, and so effectively far and near in time) that galaxies tend to change their shape as they age.

Third, scientists have calculated the variety and abundance of chemical elements that should have been formed following the Big Bang, and their calculations predict exactly the ratios that are found to exist in space. Furthermore, the particular mixture predicted by the Big Bang theory (and corroborated by observation) is quite different from the mixture that the Steady State theory predicts.

Various other kinds of evidence support the Big Bang theory, and it rules the roost today.[18] The creating Bang is calculated to have occurred about 13.7 billion years ago.

While no cosmologist doubts that our universe is expanding, there has been much debate about whether it will continue to expand forever. Should this be the case, our universe will end up as a diffuse, dark, frigid, dead junkyard, with no energy differences left to power change. If, however, the attractive gravitational forces are strong enough, the universe's current expansion will be slowed down, stopped, then reversed. This reversal would cause everything to be pulled tighter and tighter together, and it would all eventually be gathered into one gigantic black hole, presumably to continue shrinking until it reverted back to whence it came.

This uncertainty about the universe's future may have been resolved by measurements taken over the last five or so years. Measurements of the brightness and red shift of distant supernovae (see next section) yield the recession speed of the universe when it was young. Comparisons of that speed with the recession speed shown by nearby galaxies reveals that the universe's rate of expansion is increasing, not slowing down.[19] (It is currently thought that the slightly repulsive gravitational force of the "vacuum energy"[20] of empty space may be causing this acceleration.)

3. What Happened after the Big Bang

The Big Bang theory postulates that the universe came into being when what amounts to an infinitely large amount of energy suddenly appeared as an infinitesimally small speck (fittingly called a singularity). Where this energy came from—no one knows.[21] How so much energy could occupy next to zero volume—no one knows. One theory postulates the existence of another universe, vastly bigger than the one we inhabit and hidden in additional space/time dimensions, and suggests that it could have created and fed the singularity. This background universe could be periodically "blowing bubbles" that inflate into universes.[22] Our (relatively small, on this scale) universe could have originated within one of these bubbles.[23] Superstring Theory (see "The Conservation Laws," a postscript to Chapter Seven) supports the existence of many universes (of which ours is one), each being formed from, and eventually returned to, empty space.

Regardless of what actually occurred to "begin our universe," and what was needed before this event to cause it to happen, scientists can account for what is seen today simply by postulating that everything came from a single point in one Big Bang then applying some known laws of physics.

Rather than making guesses about what might have happened beyond and before our universe began (guesses that can never be substantiated—see section six of this chapter), let us start with what is generally accepted—a Big Bang/Inflationary origin to our universe. This theory is able to explain much that we observe, and it yields accurate predictions, hallmark properties of a good scientific theory. Assuming that the laws of physics as we know them today also applied almost immediately following the Bang,[24] we can reconstruct the history of the universe. This has been carried out by various people over the past fifty years, with modifications and revisions being made each time someone was able to improve the fit between astronomical observations and theory. Today, scientists think that something very like the following occurred.

Immediately upon the original insertion of energy, time in this continuum began, and space was created by separating energy components. This was followed by an extremely rapid expansion. Starting about 10^{-37} of a second after the Bang,[25] and lasting until about 10^{-34} of a second,[26] this minute bubble of pure energy that was to become our universe inflated to 10^{50} times its previous size.[27]

For the first one hundred seconds or so following the Bang, only energy (in various forms of radiation) could have existed.[28] Continued expansion and further cooling of this hot dense ball of energy continued until, after about 300,000 years,[29] the temperature was low enough (about 3,000°C) for atoms of hydrogen (and helium, the next lightest element) to remain intact. From this time onward the universe would contain matter.[30]

These atoms of hydrogen and helium[31] continued to move apart, and the temperature of the universe continued to drop. Gravitational forces pulled wisps of atoms closer together, forming tremendous, irregularly shaped clouds, and these eventually further condensed to form many giant gas balls. Condensation continued, with the gases at the centre of each ball forming first black holes, then supermassive black holes.[32] Electrically charged gases (spiralling ever faster and faster around these holes before being swallowed) emitted intense electromagnetic radiation fields that pushed the surrounding gases away. Clouds of these gases then themselves condensed to form additional smaller balls. As gravity pulled the gases in each of these balls tighter together they began to heat up. Eventually the temperature within each became so high that thermonuclear reactions occurred, and the gas balls began to emit light. These high-temperature, hydrogen-gas balls, are called stars.[33] The large collections of stars that rotate around supermassive black holes are called galaxies.

4. The Life of a Typical Star

Stars contain huge amounts of hydrogen, and the gravitational forces near their centre are extremely high. This creates a pressure which pushes the hydrogen nuclei closer and closer, eventually fusing pairs of them together, creating helium. Since one helium nucleus has slightly less mass than the two hydrogen nuclei that formed it, the surplus mass has to be released. This occurs, but the release is not in the form of a particle of matter; the mass difference is radiated away as energy,[34] and many such fusings quickly raise the sun's core temperature (which stabilizes at about twenty million degrees Celsius). Physicists replicate this process in hydrogen bombs,[35] and they are attempting to do the same thing in the laboratory. (Here the biggest problem is how to contain and control the high temperatures involved[36]—about 100 million degrees, or over five times the temperature of the sun's core, in some research reactors.)

The average star today[37] burns for about ten billion years. As a star's hydrogen continues to form helium, its core gradually shrinks. This causes it to become hotter, and its nuclear fusions become more complex. Through fusions, helium is converted into carbon and oxygen, then into other elements (those in approximately the first quarter of the periodic table). Further core shrinkage eventually creates enough radiation to induce a big expansion of the outer layers, and stars that are about the size of our sun become red giants, enveloping any orbiting planets in incandescent gases. Eventually, fusion can no longer be sustained in the core, and red giants shrink, lose their outer layers of gases, and become compact white dwarfs. This is likely to be the fate of our sun and its planets, some six billion years in the future.

A number of stars are large enough to avoid this kind of relatively slow death. Their extra mass creates higher core temperatures and heavier elements are formed. However, forming nuclei of elements beyond iron requires an input of energy (because extra energy is needed to hold together the many mutually repulsive protons such nuclei contain). This reduces the energy released during fusion to a point where it can no longer counterbalance gravitational attraction, and the star collapses. This sudden implosion releases tremendous amounts of energy and everything immediately heats up again. This, in turn, rapidly fuses many of the existing elements into the larger and more complex elements that exist beyond iron (over eighty of them; copper, silver, gold and mercury, for example). The core's raging furnace builds in intensity and soon explodes, scattering the star's chemical elements into space. Some massive stars undergo several cycles of explosions and collapses. (Astronomers occasionally witness these events; each explosion is termed a nova.) Other giant stars explode completely in one detonation; what is then seen is called a supernova.[38] Both appear abruptly as bright patches of light in the sky, often intense enough to be visible in daylight, occurring in the spot formerly occupied by a star.[39]

Observers find and study one or two new novae each year, and witness gigantic supernovae blossoming within our galaxy, the Milky Way, an average of twice a century. In the ten billion years of our galaxy's existence,[40] about two hundred million supernovae have spewed out the chemical elements we know from spectroscopic evidence to be present throughout its volume. The dark patches (mentioned earlier in this chapter), observed within interstellar and intergalactic space, are due to the presence of vast clouds of these minute dust particles. This dust (altogether amounting to hundreds of times more matter than is contained within the total of every galaxy's collection of stars and planets) is mostly composed of the elements formed and ejected during novae and supernovae explosions. These particles absorb and obscure light from the stars and galaxies that lie beyond, and it is the absence of this light that produces regions that appear to be dark.

The visible universe is estimated to contain some 100,000,000,000 (100 billion) galaxies, and an average galaxy (such as ours) accommodates a collection of some 2-300,000,000,000 (200-300 billion) stars. Thus, there are twenty to thirty thousand billion billion (i.e., 20-30,000,000,000,000,000,000,000, that is, 20-30 sextillion, or $2-3 \times 10^{22}$) stars all told in our universe.[41]

As mentioned, stars of all descriptions have been found.[42] Some, only about a half-million years old,[43] have been photographed via the infrared radiation they emit. These newly formed "baby" stars already show a spin (imparted by the kinetic energy of condensing gases as they are drawn into the star by gravitational attraction), which the star retains for its lifetime. Observations suggest that about half of all newly formed stars are also accompanied by a rotating disk of gases, particles, dust and debris. Matter that is not pulled into the star is gradually pushed away by the star's radiation and most eventually disperse into space. However, gravity also pulls some of the disk's matter and dust together to form aggregates; the largest of these we call planets.[44]

The brightness and remoteness of stars generally prevent us from directly observing any planets that might orbit them.[45] However, the presence of planets can be inferred by various techniques, and some nearby stars are now known to have orbiting bodies. One way to determine if a star has one or more planetary companions is to measure its wobble[46] (caused because the orbiting bodies together rotate about their common centre of mass, i.e., the star no longer rotates about its own centre and therefore looks as if it is "wobbling." A similar wobble can occur when a car tire is "unbalanced.") Another way to find planets is to look for lensing effects, when light from distant stars becomes bent due to gravitational pull as it passes close to large masses, such as those of giant (e.g., Jupiter-size or greater) planets.[47] Astronomers also look for emission intensity variations and dark spots transiting the face of stars (caused by planets crossing in front of a star and so preventing some of its light from reaching the observing telescopes).[48] The presence of rings of matter surrounding some stars gives observers yet another way to infer that planets have been (or are being) formed about a star, and circular gaps within such rings of dust almost certainly mean that planets are present. (Clumps of particles within a ring gravitationally sweep up additional dust as they travel around a star; this causes the orbiting bodies to gradually enlarge and leaves the gaps that are seen. These dust aggregates may ultimately become large enough to form asteroids and planets.[49] Most stars, including our own, lose much of their dust halo due to this process [as well as due to pressure from the star's radiation] in the first 400 million years following their birth.) Planets may also be sought and even studied by examining the doppler-shifted starlight scattered by their atmospheres.[50] Over one hundred exoplanets (as planets outside our solar system are called) have been found to date, a number that is being added to every few weeks. Undoubtedly, with time and as astronomers refine their planet-finding techniques, many more will be discovered.

5. The Earth

The Earth was formed (as were all of the planets in our solar system) from the aggregates that orbited our sun approximately 4.6 billion y.a.—less than half a billion years after the sun itself formed (and about 9 billion years after the Big Bang). As it was forming, the Earth's accumulating mass was constantly bombarded by matter-adding meteorites, comets and huge planetesimals (mini-planets), and this, together with the energy released by radioactive decay of the heavy elements that settled to its core,[51] kept our planet in a molten state for its first two or three hundred million years. The Earth's solid surface crust formed about four and a quarter billion y.a.[52]

Today, our planet consists chiefly of a liquid iron alloy core (at a temperature of approximately 5,000°C[53]), covered by a mantle of hardened oxides that float on the core's surface. The core is slowly cooling as convection currents and eddies in its upper layers transfer heat into the mantle. These currents also cause the Earth's continents to drift, almost imperceptibly, but constantly. In several places, subterranean tectonic plates bump into each other, inevitably pushing one under the other. The uppermost plate (usually the lightest one) lifts to form mountains, with rifts, or valleys, forming in between. The plate pushed underneath remelts to form magma, some of which may find its way to the surface again through volcanoes.

Most of the water that covers three-quarters of the Earth's surface arrived in the form of comets early in our planet's life, but another 500 tons or so is added daily as the Earth sweeps up space-dust (much of which is water[54]). Water is ubiquitous throughout the universe simply because its constituents (two atoms of hydrogen, and one atom of oxygen) are elemental and universal—hydrogen being the first element formed following the Big Bang, and oxygen being one of the elements produced as stars evolve, and later thrown into space as they nova.

As we doubtless remember from our school days, the sun's radiation evaporates water (that then condenses to form the clouds that produce rain, lightning and thunder). The sun's energy also heats the land and sea; temperature differences between these create winds and drive the water cycle that sustains life on land.

More than three billion years of continuously varying weather has eroded the Earth's ever-changing mountains, turning their rock into the sand, dust and silt that have become major constituents of our planet's soil and the bottoms of its lakes, rivers and oceans. Silt and material on the ocean floors, compressed by the weight of water and accumulated matter above, has formed layers of sedimentary rock that trap and hold evidence of the conditions and life forms that existed from the recent past to many hundreds of millions of years ago. Ice locked at depths within glaciers provides ancient liquids and gases that scientists have collected and analyzed, further adding to what is known about how our planet aged and changed. These sources have also told us much of what is known about how life evolved on our planet.

6. What Started it all?

Although we can conjecture, we are never likely to find out what caused the Big Bang; that is, what created our universe in the first place. The reason this is so is to be found in at least two places: Gödel's Incompleteness Theorem, and General Systems theory. These are not too hard to understand in outline, as the brief summary given in the next two paragraphs aims to show. (A little more information is provided in postscripts to this chapter.)

In his Incompleteness Theorem, Kurt Gödel proved that no system can contain all of the information needed to answer every question that can be posed from within that system. No matter how much we understand about the system we are examining from within, logical paradoxes will always exist. Asking what started our universe is posing just such a logical paradox

General Systems theory states that all systems are either open or closed. Open systems interact with (and obtain what they need to continue their existence from) their supersystem.[55] Closed systems are cut-off from the outside, and no energy of any form (e.g., radiation, matter, or information) can enter or leave such a system. All our current theories suggest that our universe is a closed system, and, if this is so, we will never be able to obtain information from outside.

Summary

The universe is not quite as mysterious as it once appeared to be. Cosmologists and astronomers now understand a great deal about its past, present and future, as well as what creates and controls its contents. Using computers and instruments to analyze photons collected by different types of telescopes, it is possible to infer what was likely to have been happening when these photons were created, and even what energies and matters were encountered in their journey through space and time. As we progress in this manner, we find that the science of cosmology depends upon—in fact, mostly is—the physics of energy and matter. In other words, the behaviour of the gigantic is controlled by the properties of the minuscule, the ultimate test of reality's rational conformity to causality.[56]

However, there appears to be no method of peeking through a singularity. If this is so, then no future beings, wherever they might live in the universe, will ever discover what caused the Big Bang, or what existed before time in this universe began.

This could be where a god once lived—or even lives now. If one exists anywhere at all, then this is the only place that modern science would position him—before the beginning, and beyond any possibility of interfering with the present.[57] Certainly, there is proving to be no physical need for a god's intervention within our universe. Once a universe possessing the properties we are discovering has been created, it will simply evolve in the manner our telescopes reveal, with stars, galaxies and planets (and life, as the next chapter explains) being formed along the way. A god's influence is seemingly not needed in the day-to-day operation of the physical universe. But isn't that to be expected of a creation if God Himself designed it?[58]

Well, so much for the universe. It started, and it evolves as time goes by. We don't know why it began or even if its existence requires a cause,[59] but we do know a lot about how and why it evolves, and the forces that regulate its development.

It is time to turn our attention to the phenomenon of life, and review what scientists can tell us about it. Two questions are most important to our discussions: how did life begin, and how has it given rise to the forms we see today? The next chapter will review the answers that have been found.

(Three postscripts to this chapter titled "Gödel's Theorem," "General Systems Theory" and "The Conservation Laws" are to be found commencing page 229.)

Chapter Eight

Life

Life's development has been much harder to definitively trace than that of the universe. This is because biology's countless combinations and permutations are exceedingly convoluted compared to the linearity of physics or the predictability of chemistry.

Experimental physics is often conducted by holding all variables constant, then determining the effects of changing just one. This procedure, together with the universe's constraints (which limit the number of particles [such as protons or electrons] there are to investigate and the number of ways they can behave) has simplified the discovery of many of the universe's secrets. Physicists now extrapolate with confidence from present to past, from past to future, and from here to the other side of the universe.

Chemistry is somewhat more complex than physics, because there are over a hundred chemical elements. This relatively large number means that millions of different combinations (as molecules and compounds) can exist. This complexity is being conquered, however, as demonstrated by the near-routine formulation of new and improved fabrics, explosives, alloys, drugs, plastics, and innumerable other products.

Progress in biology, on the other hand, has been considerably slower until just recently. Life's ability to mutate and change over successive generations has meant that investigators cannot simply extrapolate backwards to determine what previously existed, nor look forward and predict what might result.

Most of our knowledge about life's history has been obtained from fossils and preserved remnants of past life forms, but two factors greatly complicate the task. First, biotic matter provides food for other living things, so most of it never makes its way into the future to be studied. Second, the extensive (and ongoing) geophysical changes that the Earth has undergone during its more than four billion years of existence has left the story-telling remains of life's progress fragmented and incomplete. However, enough evidence exists and has been found for scientists to trace life's gross history on this planet. Moreover, each year new fossils and new facts (particularly genetic) about past and present inter- and intra-species relationships are discovered. These fill knowledge gaps and build confidence in the accuracy of what has already been deduced. What biologists now generally accept is related in the following pages.

1. Possible Origins of Life on Earth

One of the first theories to become widely known that described how life may have begun on this planet was proposed in the 1920's independently by Aleksandr Oparin, a Russian biochemist, and J. B. S. Haldane, a British biologist. They pointed out that some four billion years ago, conditions in the Earth's shallower seas and oceans would have resembled a chemical vat. This vat must have held a variety of ingredients that would have been warmed by sunlight, constantly stirred by tides and winds, bathed in ultraviolet radiation from the sun, and intermittently subjected to electrical discharges from thunder storms. This so-called called "primordial soup" would inevitably have become more complex over time, as interactions (mostly chemical) between the constituents occurred. Eventually, it would likely contain many of the molecules and compounds needed to create some elemental forms of life.

Stanley Miller, under Harold Urey at the University of Chicago in 1953, recreated many of these conditions in the laboratory. Together they subjected methane, ammonia and hydrogen (gases that very probably existed on this planet in its early years, and that are still present in abundance on Jupiter and Saturn) to electrical sparks in a sealed sterile flask. On later analyzing the flask's contents, they found many of the amino acids from which life's building blocks—proteins—are built.[1] Similar experiments have since yielded molecular components of proteins that regulate carbohydrate and fat formation. In other words, some of the major constituents of life have been fabricated from scratch in the laboratory.

However, it is equally possible that life on this planet began thousands of meters beneath the sea's surface, in total darkness. Clues to this conjecture have been found in north-western Australia, in sulphur-rich rocks that retain micro-fossils of single-celled organisms over three and a quarter billion years old. These rocks possess mineral structures that reveal they originated close to hot springs on the sea floor.

In 1977, a mid-ocean ridge of hot springs was discovered encircling the globe. The wealth of chemicals and nutrients it supplies nourishes a complex ecosystem of over 500 species, from bacteria to tube worms and crabs.

The energy source that sustains this web of life is the oxidization of hydrogen sulphide in a process called chemosynthesis (as opposed to photosynthesis, whereby sunlight powers life on the Earth's surface). Experiments at the Woods Hole Oceanographic Institution determined that when similar physical (high-pressure, turbulence, completely dark, etc.) and chemical conditions are constructed in the laboratory, large organic molecules containing over thirty carbon atoms form in less than a day. Thus, life on Earth may have first begun in the sunless depths of its oceans.[2]

Alternatively, life may have begun as some form of methanogen.[3] Methanogens are microbes that obtain energy by converting hydrogen and carbon dioxide into methane. Very few such organisms exist in any of Earth's typical, oxygen-abundant, environments (because methanogens are consumed by the more-efficient carbon life forms that now occupy these niches), but a complete food-chain community of them has been found in Idaho living in 58°C water two hundred meters underground. Presumably these have survived from very early times. Methanogen communities may have been common on this planet before oxygen in gaseous form became abundant (see section two of this chapter) and they may also exist where conditions are similar, such as upon some of the sun's other planets or moons, for instance.[4]

While several situations and mechanisms might have given rise to life on this planet, it may in fact owe its origins to extraterrestrial events that first happened in water, frozen in space, long ago and far away. Although space temperatures average just 3° above absolute zero, recent experiments have found that amorphous ice (the kind that forms when water vapour freezes in a vacuum) flows when subjected to ultraviolet radiation (as it would be in space). In the laboratory, when carbon monoxide, carbon dioxide, and methanol (gases all abundant in space) are dissolved in water before freezing to form amorphous ice, subsequent ultraviolet radiation produces hundreds of complex organic molecules. Moreover, if this frozen ice flows (or is melted or added to water), membranous vesicles (similar to those found in the 1969 Murchison meteorite[5]) are formed, together with even more complex compounds (some able to convert ultraviolet energy to visible light).

Laboratory findings such as these are reinforced through data collected by the European Space Agency's satellite Infrared Space Observatory (ISO). When scrutinizing selected objects, the ISO can detect the emission of infrared rays at particular wavelengths, revealing the presence of identifiable atoms, molecules and solids. These data show that complex, ring-structured, aromatic molecules form in the regions surrounding very old stars, over the relatively short period of a thousand years or so. Spectral analysis of interstellar dusts and gases have identified hundreds of different organic compounds, including amino acids of the type needed to build life's proteins.[6] Recently, sugar molecules (glycolaldehyde) have been spectroscopically detected in the dust clouds near the centre of our Milky Way galaxy. (What makes this finding particularly interesting is that such molecules can combine with other molecules to form ribose and glucose; ribose molecules are utilized in the construction of DNA and RNA.)

All these findings strongly suggest that life's precursors, including cell-like sacs containing organic compounds, could have been formed many billions of years ago[7] in space, and would therefore be part of all comets, asteroids and planets from their very beginnings.[8]

2. Development of Life on Earth

While we don't definitively know where life first developed, we do know approximately when it first appeared on Earth—it showed up less than a quarter of a billion years after the Earth's crust had formed. In other words, just about as soon as it could.[9]

For reasons noted in the introduction to this chapter, early evidence of life is hard to come by.[10] Nevertheless, indirect evidence suggests that it was present at least 3.7 billion years ago. This has been deduced from an analysis of rocks dating to that age, found on an island close to Greenland. These rocks contain a higher carbon-12 to carbon-13 isotopic ratio than chemical and physical processes alone would create. (Life processes prefer the lighter isotopes, and this concentrates carbon-12 where life exists.) More direct evidence, in the form of fossil micro-organisms, has been discovered in sedimentary rocks from Iceland that are between 3.7 and 3.8 billion years old. (Iceland is particularly suitable for finding early life forms because its rocks have not been greatly disturbed by geological processes during the intervening ages.)

Many of us were taught in school that there are three kingdoms of life on this planet.[11] The simplest and most ancient are called the Archaea (otherwise known as archaebacteria, the first cells).

Archaean kingdom representatives were first discovered in volcanic vents on the floor of the Pacific ocean,[12] three kilometres deep off the Galápagos Islands.[13] Archaea and very primitive bacteria are autotrophic (that is, they build their complex living molecules by chemosynthesis, a chemical process mentioned in the previous section).

The second kingdom, the Prokarya, are a later development; they consist of life forms whose cells lack internal membranes (and thus have no nuclei).

Prokaryotic life was flourishing within the Earth's shallow oceans as blue-green algae (a.k.a. cyanobacteria), over three and a half billion years ago. Once formed, the anaerobic[14] cyanobacteria began dumping its photosynthetic by-product, oxygen, into the Earth's oceans and atmosphere, and continued to do so without much competition for over two billion years. Eventually a new form of bacteria evolved that was able to use this oxygen through a process we call aerobic respiration; this opened the way for the more complex (and more energy-demanding), nucleated, eukaryotic cells to evolve. (Bacteria, of course, still exist in abundance everywhere conditions permit, and they still lack cell nuclei.[15])

The third kingdom, the Eukarya, first appeared about two billion years ago. The cells of eukaryotic life forms contain membrane-bound nuclei, and all plants and animals (including humans) belong to this kingdom.

While one billion years ago the continents were still barren (with the possible exception of primitive algae), the seas teemed with unicellular life. Many of these life forms reproduced asexually through division, although some used sexual means. About 700 m.y.a. (million years ago), multicellular sea plants appeared. They rapidly developed in form and prevalence as they made the most of their added capabilities. Multicellular sea plants stayed at the forefront of life's evolution until the beginning of the Cambrian era, about 540 m.y.a., when multiple forms of marine animals developed from simpler varieties of roundworms. This transition occurred because possession of body cavities and an alimentary canal allowed worm-like creatures to grow more than a few cells thick (as nutrients and waste materials could now be readily passed between internal cells and the external environment). Larger bodies meant that supporting structures would be valuable adaptations, and any that evolved would be retained. The first vertebrates developed soon thereafter (about 500 m.y.a.).

By 400 m.y.a., plants, fungi and primitive arthropods (invertebrates, similar to crabs or lobsters, having an external skeleton and jointed appendages) had colonized the ocean shores and moved inland. (The ongoing evolution of early arthropods eventually produced spiders, centipedes and insects.) Around this time, fish utilized their swim bladders and fins to spend temporary periods on land. These organs gradually evolved into lungs and legs, and the animal class known as amphibians arose. The fluid-filled amniotic sacs we call eggs allowed amphibians to reproduce and give birth on dry land, and some later evolved into reptiles, dinosaurs, lizards, snakes and turtles.

The earliest mammals appeared some 200 m.y.a., evolving from a group of reptiles called therapsids. These mammals were small (about five centimetres long) and possibly lived in trees during the dinosaur age. They remained rodent-like creatures[16] until the dinosaurs became extinct 65 m.y.a. One branch of these early mammals evolved (some 30 m.y.a.) to become Proconsul, our hominoid ape ancestor, and their descendants became the gibbons, orang-utans, gorillas and chimpanzees we know today. About six million years ago, the ape and hominid lineages separated; today our closest living relatives are Central African chimpanzees (demonstrated and verified by comparative DNA sequencing[17]).

The genus *Homo* appeared about two and a half m.y.a. (although stone tools have been found that date to earlier periods). Artifacts left by "technologically advanced" clans of early humans (who used stone tools to chip bones and antlers into refined shapes) have been found in Israel's Dead Sea Rift Valley and dated definitively[18] to 780,000 years ago.

Neandertals (who first appeared in Europe about 200,000 y.a. and whose ancestors were hominids who moved from Africa to Europe some 500,000 y.a.) holed up in valleys to survive the ice ages and so avoided the many challenges that constant moves would have brought. Perhaps as a result, their tools changed little during most of their existence, and this suggests that their intelligence also did not greatly change. However, fossilized bone structures show that Neandertals did have the means to utter words, and they probably developed and used simple languages.

The tools and ornaments of *Homo sapiens*, on the other hand, changed greatly over very short periods of time. Our species first appeared in Africa over 100,000 y.a. and moved into Europe (as Cro-Magnon) around 40,000 y.a., and they seemed to have confronted and surmounted the various challenges successive ice ages introduced.[19]

How do we know these things? Specimens of life and associated artifacts have been trapped in muddy sediments, chalk, glacial ice,[20] peat bogs, dry sandy deserts, tree resin[21] etc., for millions of years. These entombments often preserve complete specimens in date-stamped strata for scientists to examine.[22] Painstaking observations over many decades combined with more recent sophisticated analytical techniques (such as DNA analysis and various imaging techniques) consistently show that life's development demonstrates an overall progressive trend from simple to complex.[23]

3. Evolution

Millennia ago, humans realized that greatly different animals (deer, birds and fish, for example) possess body organs and systems very similar to their own, but could not explain why. Over the centuries various explanations were proposed, some theological, some scientific; two centuries ago most people accepted the theological interpretation—that life in its different forms was Created. Papers read to the Linnean Society in 1858 written by Charles Darwin and Alfred Russel Wallace (who had independently reached similar conclusions) did little to change this situation—attendees simply did not understand the importance of what they were hearing. However, when Darwin's book *On the Origin of Species by Means of Natural Selection*, was published a year later, evolution became a topic of discussion for every learned person and things changed forever.[24]

It is easy to understand what immediately happened. Darwin and his ideas were ridiculed by almost everyone; scientists said he could not prove what he was saying, and the religious said that mankind was created—as proven by texts in the Bible. Humans simply could not be "descended from an ape."

Darwin's work, and its attendant publicity, resulted in widespread use of the words "evolution" and "natural selection." These terms are sometimes treated as though they hold the same significance—they do not. One is a fact, the other is a theory, and we should take a moment to discuss the differences between the two.

There is plenty of evidence to show that evolution occurred—is still occurring—and that all life on this planet is interrelated, with a common ancestry. Palaeontologists study fossils of once-living organisms, and their work demonstrates that the bones and structures of ancient life forms gradually changed over time. Comparative studies of the physical and systemic structures of living plants and animals uncover the same kind of gradual change. Genetic mapping[25] adds to the information obtained, and shows beyond any possible doubt that links between living species, and between living and extinct species, exist.[26] Weiner, after discussing work done by Seymour Benzer and his wife in the 1980's, noted that flies, worms, seeds, yeasts and bacteria possess thousands of very similar genes or gene sequences.[27] This could only have occurred if they all had a common ancestor. (In fact, a pre-Cambrian common ancestor must have existed, well over 540 m.y.a., for such widely separated species to possess so many similar genes.) Moreover, as Weiner pointed out, the genomes of mice and men (and women, if it needs to be stated) are about the same size and contain corresponding genes.[28] (de Duve actually states[29] that the evidence showing all Earthly organisms to be descendants of one common ancestor is "overwhelming.")

That evolution occurs is something animal and plant breeders have known and profited from for centuries, and it is a fact that few educated people today dispute.[30]

However, we can never be certain that we know all of the factors that *cause* evolution to occur, so any explanation of why evolution occurs may someday be modified or even overturned. While we have what we think is a very good idea, there could be additional or different reasons why evolution happens, so scientists continue to call this very good idea a theory. Natural selection[31] is Darwin's very good idea, and it has withstood all manner of challenges to its ability to explain and to predict. But it can be thrown into doubt, and even discredited, any time a fact of evolution is found that it cannot explain. (All scientific explanations are like this; any or all of them may one day be shown to be inadequate or inaccurate, and we remind ourselves of this limitation by calling many of them theories. All will remain theories forever.[32])

Thus, that evolution occurs is a fact; however, the explanation why evolution occurs will always be called a theory. This, presumably, is why controversy continues. A few people, wilfully or mistakenly, capitalize upon the word "theory" to imply that the concept is untrue, and that evolution does not occur. What they might better state is that the natural selection explanation of why evolution occurs is a theory, good only until some better explanation is found.[33]

Returning to the theme of this section, it is estimated that some two billion species have evolved on Earth during the past six hundred million years (the period for which we have some of the best fossil records, and during which all of our land life developed). Today, about 99.9% of these are extinct.

The two million species that exist today exhibit a multiplicity of forms. Variations range from the large, most-obviously complex, multi-system animals, down to the minute, single-celled, relatively simple bacteria. As might be expected, it is the tiniest of these which demonstrate the greatest diversity and resilience.[34] The habitats of bacteria range from the plus 91°C boiling hot springs of Yellowstone Park, to the minus 50°C super-cooled brines found in the Antarctic. Bacteria also flourish under tremendous pressures on the ocean floor, spread prolifically throughout the soil we walk upon, waft through the air we breathe, and luxuriate in every kitchen.

When the papers written by Darwin and Wallace were first read,[35] no one had seen evolution occurring. Today, experiments demonstrating its thesis can be conducted using fruit flies in high school science laboratories. Evolution was thought to be too slow to be witnessed in nature, but the real challenge to demonstrating its ubiquitous occurrence comes from the need to detect and measure small changes over a number of generations while also recording every possible factor that might relate to (or be causing) such changes.

Some of the earliest decisive documentation of evolution occurring in the wild was obtained by Peter and Rosemary Grant through studies of "Darwin's" finches on the relatively isolated Galápagos island, Daphne Major. For more than two decades, the Grants, with the help of many colleagues, captured, numbered, precisely measured, banded, catalogued and released, almost every finch that lived on the island (sometimes only a few hundred, sometimes several thousand in a year). This period included years of drought, as well as wet and more normal years. In this manner, they recorded the features of close to 100,000 finches, together with many details about their varying habitats.[36]

These records were run through computer programs that sought correlations between the number and variety of finch, and changes in their environment such as rainfall, seed plant variety and abundance, and so on. Drought years drastically reduced the number of softer seeds, leaving the number of hard-shelled cactus seeds about the same. Finch species with large, strong beaks that were able to crack hard-shelled seeds, survived in stable numbers during those years, as might be expected. However, measurements of surviving members of the other finch species showed that only those whose beak was larger than average for their species were surviving and reproducing. The net result was that the beak size of each finch species drifted toward a larger and stronger shape during drought years. This drift continued in successive generations for as long as the drought continued. Wet years produced the opposite effect, and resulted in a drift within each species toward a finer beak structure (because the cactus plants began to die, and thinner beaks could better retrieve the smaller seeds of other plants that fell into the many tiny cracks in the island's volcanic rocks).

Others have conducted parallel work. John Endler, for instance, working with guppies in various South American countries, observed natural generational variations in colour which were brought about by changes in the environment. Dark water favoured brilliance (better to attract females); light water favoured camouflage (better for hiding from predators).

Any change in an environment may affect species living within that environment. An accumulation of adaptations within one species eventually produces what becomes described as a new species. Collections of plant, animal and insect fossils in museums and universities around the world show that time, environmental change, and geographical separation are all that are needed for species to evolve from old into new.

Changes over time cause descendants to either diverge (i.e. increase in difference, one from another), or converge (i.e., increase in similarity). The factors that promote species divergence are predominately food (which favours the development of tools—for instance, the beak—that better exploit the particular kind of environment which supplies that food) and sex (which favours the development of partner-attracting displays or like-attracting-like matings). The forces that promote species convergence include the presence of enemies (which favours the development of camouflage and herd behaviours, the latter because there is safety in numbers) and the physical features of the environment being exploited. Hybridization, whereby closely related species merge genes, can produce fairly rapid convergence or divergence. The prevailing environment determines which outcome predominantly survives.

Evolution, we now realize, is often not a slow and gradual process. It can occur in small or large bursts, and these may be followed by long ages of slow consolidation.[37] A common sequence is as follows: an environmental calamity occurs, followed by a rapid collapse in food supplies. The calamity can be localized and relatively insignificant (a fallen rock, for instance) or something very pervasive (the eruption of an immense volcano, the impact of a large comet, or the rapid development of an ice age, for example). Each environmental change causes the death of some or perhaps almost all of the existing, previously well-adapted species.[38] The decline in numbers of some species (or the environmental change itself) opens niches that were previously occupied, blocked, or non-existent, and this provides opportunities for suitably different members of surviving species to thrive.

The mutations that make life's evolution and continuance possible need not be large, as the work with Darwin's finches demonstrates. However, even drastically mutated offspring may survive and flourish under some kinds of environmental change. Evolutionary change following extinctions is rapid, because many of the previously well-adapted (and presumably competing species) completely die out. This may open niches accommodating to some of the more extreme variants (that might not otherwise have survived); without competition, they may now proliferate. Evolutionary change slows down again just as soon as successfully adapted species fill all available energy niches.[39]

Massive extinctions have not been uncommon in our planet's history. Two of the more infamous were probably caused by asteroids or comets hitting the Earth. The first of these occurred around 208 m.y.a., creating the environment that early dinosaurs exploited to become the Earth's dominant animals (this impact produced the changes that mark the junction between the Triassic and Jurassic periods). The second collision happened around 65 m.y.a., and ended the dinosaurs' supremacy. Other extinctions occurred around 438 m.y.a., 367 m.y.a., and 245 m.y.a. Each of these cataclysms resulted in the demise of more than fifty percent of the prevailing marine species, and an equal or greater percentage of the existing land species.[40]

Records of growth from tree rings as well as ice core samples show that large calamities, due to one cause or another, have also occurred relatively recently. The most prominent events happened around 3200, 2300, 1628, and 1159 BCE; the most recent took place in 535 CE.

Catastrophes rapidly and radically transform the planet's various environments, and life forms that do not adapt (i.e., evolve) do not survive. (And, as a corollary, it must be emphasized that if life does not continue to evolve it will not continue to survive, for it is certain that changes will occur to life's environment in the future just as often as they have in the past. Moreover, it is worth noting that the environment currently changing the most rapidly is not the Earth's biosphere, it is our human mental environment—a change brought about by the mix of facts, ideas, opinions, fantasies, beliefs, etc., that worms its way into our thoughts every day. To survive, we must discover how to adapt to the changes occurring there.)

Fossil records show gross evolutionary changes in *Homo*'s body structures that took thousands of years to develop. Detecting subtle changes necessitates making fine measurements, and we currently lack the detailed records covering several generations that would unequivocally demonstrate human evolution in action. Doubtless, as computer record-keeping increases in scope and depth (particularly if DNA profiles are to be stored), we will soon have plenty of evidence to show that, like all else that lives, humans evolve, and evolve continuously.

Humans have always acted to minimize the effects of events that may influence their evolution. We store food and survive most food shortages; if we did not do this, the average body mass and size of *H. sapiens* would drift downwards. We capitalize on niches and specialize in occupations; if we did not do this, our numbers would decrease because there would be too many competing within each energy niche (read money, thus food, for energy) and fewer would survive. We stress universal literacy and education; if we did not do this, the total number of energy niches would decline over time. Together, forces such as these select for particular skills: musical, mathematical, artistic, and so on. In effect, ever since we have had the ability, we have acted in a manner that influences the way we evolve. Genetic engineering is about to vastly extend this ability.

4. The Probability that Life exists Elsewhere

It is not difficult to estimate the probability that life has developed on other planets in the universe. All we need do is calculate the total number of stars, the number of these that may support habitable planets, and the likelihood that any of these planets would support life.[41]

First, the number of stars in our universe. It is estimated that our Milky Way galaxy contains between two and three hundred billion stars (2-3 x 10^{11}), and that there are about one hundred billion galaxies (10^{11}) in the visible universe. If the average number of stars in other galaxies is similar to ours, then there are 2-3 x 10^{22} stars all told. Using the smaller number we have 2 x 10^{22} stars to start with.

Second, there are many inhospitable zones within all galaxies (the planets of stars too close to the centre of a galaxy or to radiating black holes, for instance, are being sterilized by microwaves[42]) and stars in these regions are unlikely to support life-bearing planets, at least, not life as we think of it.[43] Let's guess that only one tenth of each galaxy's stars are clear of these areas, giving us 2 x 10^{21} stars in hospitable zones of the universe.

Third, using observations noted in section four of the previous chapter, we can guesstimate that some fifty percent of all stars possess planetary systems, so about 1 x 10^{21} (or 10^{21}) stars are predicted to have orbiting planets.

Fourth, many exoplanets likely do not possess the conditions we consider necessary to support life (water, appropriate temperature ranges, appropriate elements and minerals, energy sources such as sunlight or planetary heat, etc.). A reasonable guess might be that of those possessing planetary systems, only one star in ten will hold a planet that is habitable. This gives us 10^{20} stars or 10^{20} habitable planets.

Fifth, we do not know if life will always arise on habitable planets.[44] If, as is turning out to be likely, the molecules from which life originates can form in space-ice, then probably all of the universe's planets will have been inoculated by now. How much of this material then goes on to create life can only be a guess. Presumably, if the right conditions exist, eventually all will; but, to err on the conservative side, let us say that only one in a hundred habitable planets becomes a host to life.[45] Thus about 10^{18} (1,000,000,000,000,000,000 or one quintillion) life-bearing planets possibly exist in the visible universe. Of these, about 10^7, or ten million, could be in our own galaxy.

As we learn more about the nature of life and our universe, we will undoubtedly revise our estimates of the number of planets that could be home to living entities. The number may decrease or increase, even significantly, but it is very unlikely that the number will turn out to be one. Statistically, therefore, it is highly improbable that our planet is the only one to bear life; the universe contains an incredibly large number of stars, and the conditions and ingredients required to start and support life probably exist in many, many millions of places. Furthermore, these places may include intergalactic space, within gases where life's precursors may first have formed, then evolved, to create living entities that waft through the heavens in forms vastly different from ones we might recognize.

5. Intelligent Life

The contention that life exists elsewhere holds a mystery. If ten million planets in our galaxy alone are likely to support life, why have we not heard from any of it by now? It has been estimated that about a thousand of these planets would be supporting life that has evolved to the state of communicating by radio transmissions. Why has the SETI Institute (Search for Extraterrestrial Intelligence) not yet detected intelligence-bearing signals?

Moreover, why have we not found unquestionable evidence[46] that we have been visited by aliens, or by one of their devices? We have already sent probes far beyond our own solar system, and within a decade or two will likely send similar instruments to exoplanets orbiting neighbouring stars. Indeed, in less than a couple of generations we may be visiting these planets ourselves. (Current technology necessitates journeys limited to a dozen years or so, but ion-accelerated drives already in use promise an ability to travel great distances in that amount of time.) This being so, we will inevitably attempt to colonize any habitable exoplanets we find, and, from those bases, we will certainly move onwards and outwards. All intelligent life, needing to replenish the resources it consumes throughout its industrial development on its home planet, will want to do the same. A few plausible assumptions and a couple of calculations suggest that any such pioneering life form will have colonized the whole of its own galaxy within a period of five to fifty million years.

This may seem a long time relative to our life span, but it is minuscule in evolutionary terms (we have to go back farther than that to find living dinosaurs). And it is an almost infinitesimal period on the galactic time scale. Life on other planets could well have begun a billion or more years before it arose on ours. Why, then, have we not been colonized by any of the intelligent civilizations that should have been able to do so in the past hundreds of million years? Or, why have we not at least been visited by some form of von Neumann probe (see Chapter Seven, endnote 18, for a little more information about von Neumann probes) during that time?

Crawford[47] suggests that the answer to this puzzle (called the "Fermi Paradox") could be that, although the formation and evolution of life may indeed be universal, its subsequent development into intelligent life forms may be rare. An alternative explanation could be that von Neumann probes have already visited, or even now be present. If they were small enough—developed by aliens using nanotechnology, perhaps—we would not have noticed them.

However, the explanation may be even simpler. Perhaps life forms intelligent enough to use von Neumann probes, or to travel and colonize hospitable planets, avoid planets whose "intelligent" inhabitants are constantly at war among themselves. Landing would certainly lead to a transfer of technology, and would eventually equalize abilities of the two life forms. Far easier for them to wait to see if we mature to a stage where we no longer make war; seeking contact before then only invites trouble and is simply not what an intelligent being would do.

Summary

The major points in this chapter may be summarized as follows.

- We don't know where life started, but we do know how it developed once it took root on this planet.
- Evolution, meaning change over time, is a fact. Natural Selection is a theory, and it very satisfactorily explains why evolution occurs.[48]
- There is a high probability that life exists wherever conditions permit, in likely countless billions of habitats throughout the universe.
- Life's history parallels that of the universe in its change from simple to complex, because the same laws of physics govern the behaviour of both.[49]

(A postscript to this chapter titled "Origin Theory Modifications" is to be found on page 233.)

Chapter Nine

Looking for a Purpose

The previous two chapter's survey was conducted because, as emphasized in Chapter Three, a purpose is needed before one can make any decision rationally. Furthermore, to head a moral code or religion of universal significance we need a purpose of universal significance. We therefore seek a purpose that applies beyond our culture, our species and our planet—one that is ubiquitous, timeless, consequential and fundamental, immediately recognizable as worthy of unfettered support, one that is eternally compelling, able to attract and hold followers for many generations to come.

This chapter looks for such a purpose. If one can be found it should rectify two shortages: one, provide a basis for the rationale used when making moral decisions, and two, provide a solid foundation upon which a logical future universal religion might be built should this eventually be deemed desirable.

1. Can we adopt the Universe's Purpose?

Would the universe's purpose be such a candidate? The short answer is, no, because we know of no such purpose. The universe exists and functions and we can explain and predict much of what we observe. Nothing known to us requires its operation to be subject to the constraints of some purpose.

A number of writers have suggested that God, or some god equivalent, could have programmed the universe before it began, before the initiating singularity existed. This god could have bestowed the initial parameters and laws that would force it to ultimately achieve a precisely predetermined purpose.[1] This, these writers state, would explain why everything is "just right" for us to be here.[2]

Borrow and Tipler, two eminent scientists, have attempted to prove this proposition. In *The Anthropic Cosmological Principle*,[3] they provide their rationale for stating that this universe was designed to produce intelligent life. Further, they try to show that *Homo sapiens* is the only form of intelligent life that can exist within this universe, and that our descendants have a specific task to perform (to regulate all matter contained within the universe). Their book makes interesting (although complex) reading.

If we want we can choose to adopt the assumption that a god predetermined a purpose for our universe and the life that it spawned. However, when doing so we should remember that this is just what was done several thousands of years ago, and those assumptions led to today's religious beliefs. Implementing current knowledge to resurrect the same assumption ends up reintroducing the same god of old. This doesn't help us tackle current moral questions because these questions were never asked, and so never answered, in times when our current religious texts were written. We just don't know how prophets of old might have replied, so any statement made today is necessarily an extrapolation from what was reportedly said in the past—as such, it is simply an interpretation, and thus sure to be disputed by one religion or another.

If we are unable to know what a designing god wants, then there is little point in thinking about the possibility that a god existed (or exists) and had (or has) a purpose in its mind. This is primarily because, in our lack of knowledge, there are no bounds to what we could imagine. For example, the god could have been (or is) a spiteful monster (and a world-destroying comet could be right now on its way, because we are not turning out to be as malicious as he intended us to be . . .). Whatever we conjure up will be drawn by the pencil of our desires and fears, and limited only by the scope of our imaginations. We gain nothing by postulating the existence of a "designer" god as Borrow and Tipler have done. We allege several gods already, and different religions' interpretations of what each one wants seems to be adding to current confusions, not helping us rise above them.

If looking to the universe's past to find a purpose leaves us empty-handed, what about looking to its future? We know that the universe changes. It has evolved since its time and point of origin from the very simplest that such a thing could be, to what we see today—something vast and complex. Might this change be purpose-directed?

Again, no, it does not appear to be, or at least leading authorities find no reason to think so. As far as can be determined, the contents of the universe are simply obeying known laws of physics when they change from one form to another. These laws control matter-energy interchanges, and force certain physical properties to be conserved during interactions (see "The Conservation Laws," a postscript to Chapter Seven). As a result, the universe unfolds in a strictly rational manner, predictable effect following deducible cause every time. (Predictable, that is, in the sense that actuaries can accurately calculate insurance risks. For instance, we can predict that life will experience more catastrophes, such as the extinctions it has endured in the past, but we cannot say exactly what will happen, nor when it will occur. Predictions can become certainties if the number of variables are reduced—for instance, I can predict that my computer will show an "a" on its monitor when I depress the "A" key.[4])

The changes that do occur throughout the universe are not directed toward any purpose that can be discovered from within. From analyzing the universe's overall behaviour, we can expect only one of two outcomes. Either gravitational attraction between its contents will slow, stop, then reverse its current expansion, and everything will be pulled back again to ultimately disappear into one tiny, hot hole; or, as recent observations suggest, our universe will continue to expand forever, eventually fading into a vast, black, dead frigidity.

Thus, the answer remains no; there is no purpose to be found by examining the universe's past, or its future. And it doesn't help to imagine that the universe was designed before its beginning with a purpose in an external god's mind, because we have no way of finding out what this god had in mind at the time.

No; unfortunately, the physical universe, although meeting the conditions of being virtually infinite and everlasting, seems devoid of the kind of purpose we seek.

The next obvious arena to examine is the biological universe. Let's take a look at life itself, and ask if its presence or behaviour suggests the existence of any kind of purpose.

2. Can we use Life's Purpose?

Again, the short answer is no; life exists, and its various forms and capabilities change, as shifting environmental conditions favour first one, then another, chance mutation. And that's all that appears to be happening, as generation after generation meanders its way between birth and death. Biologists do not think that life is on a journey to anywhere. Evolution, they say, is natural selection and survival of the fittest, nothing more.

Some two centuries ago, Reverend William Paley wrote that life's complexity necessitated a creator (saying that, just as a found watch would require a watchmaker to explain its existence, so, too, do the complexities of life require a Maker). Although the concepts of mutations and natural selection readily explain how simple becomes complex over time, Paley's misconception still exists. This impelled Richard Dawkins to write a book to put an end to this mystification.[5]

Dawkins' text reminds us that although complex life might seem designed to non-biologists, it is simply the result of many mutational advantages being piled one upon another, generation after generation—the successful remnants of environment-surviving adaptations.

Most biologists maintain that life provides no evidence of being directed toward a purpose of any kind. However, they usually have no reason to look much beyond the collection and analysis of facts, and the formulation and testing of theories (this, after all, is their chosen mission in life). But we do have a reason to look further. It behooves us to take a second look at what is known about the origins and development of the biological universe, to see if a purpose might be hidden within the larger picture.

At least two factors that most biologists don't usually concern themselves with can be added to our considerations. First, as discussed earlier, we can be fairly certain that life exists in many forms, all over the universe. Second, if life is so prolific (and if scientists are likely to be able to construct it in the laboratory in the not-too-distant future[6]), then life itself may be nothing very special.

But, what might this be suggesting? If anything, it seems to be saying just the opposite of what we might like to hear. The probable abundance and possible triviality of life seems to imply the lack, rather than the presence, of a purpose.

If life's existence and behaviour seems purposeless, then let's see if life's beginning shows signs of being purpose-directed.

We earlier mentioned what is known about life's beginning. As far as we can tell, it is simply a matter of physical laws giving rise to chemical molecules that interact, with some of these interactions eventually creating molecules that develop into living entities.[7] There's no more purpose to be found in such a process than there is to be found in the mere physical presence of the molecules that assemble during that process. The presence and behaviour of all matter is just another result of the presence and behaviour of the universe, and can have no more built-in purpose than the universe itself has.

Well, if the past and present tells us nothing about life having a purpose, then there is only one other place to examine—the future. As we have just mentioned, biologists usually say that they can predict nothing about life's possible future. They know the mechanics of evolution; the fittest generally survive to parent fit offspring in greater abundance than those less fit. This behaviour doesn't have to go anywhere; it need have no future other than to favour life's continuation. In fact, the whole process of evolution, as it is usually described, appears to be a very laid-back process: evolve when conditions change, otherwise stay the same.

But, if we dig a little deeper, we do actually find that something more may be happening. Let me elaborate.

Evolution itself seems to be evolving. Evolution, we know, depends upon the occurrence of one or more chemical or physical happenstance's that reshape a few of life's molecules, which then occasionally give rise to descendants better fitted to survive environmental changes. But, this process seems to have become more than solely accidental in advanced animals. Evolution, once a passive occurrence, now occasionally seems to be an active one.

Active evolution involves two events. The first event is always passive: the occasional, random, unavoidable incident that produces a DNA nucleotide change in sperm, ovum, or zygote. A genetic mutation, which (together with its outcome—good, bad or inconsequential) will be carried into descendent generations, should they survive. These descendants may, or may not, be able to utilize this change.

Natural selection tells us that the environment provides the criteria that determines if the inherited change will be beneficial or harmful (dark stripes help to camouflage a zebra in dappled woods, for instance; they may make the animal visible to predators on sunlit plains. Thus, whether a gene mutation helps the animal to hide and survive to procreate depends upon where that animal lives.) However, there can be more going on than just passive use of an inherited feature.

Sometimes the modification to a body structure or system is passed on but lies dormant, unused, perhaps eventually to atrophy from neglect. However, occasionally, the evolutionary process is taken to a second level. Some circumstance (almost always an environmental change) causes the organism to discover how a latent ability might put to use. But, only organisms capable of learning can experience this second step, as will be illustrated.

This two-step evolutionary process seldom takes place in one generation. Mutations that are immediately beneficial are those that do not require learning anything new. Millions of these have occurred throughout life's evolution—for example, more appropriate body structure, more efficient energy conversion, more attractive plumage, more effective camouflage, etc. These and other such changes benefit with little or no learning curve to conquer. But some parental DNA mutations bring no immediate benefit (or penalty), and these may be passed on unused and un-noticed through many generations. Only when an environmental change offers a niche where these changes might be put to profitable use, may they benefit the bearer. Thus, for example, the uses to which an opposable thumb may be put, or the advantages vocal chords offer language users, must be learned before they can benefit the possessor. Steven

Pinker provides an example that illustrates how an ability most take for granted is actually the result of learning how to use an inherited capability.[8] He notes that we are able to see stereoscopically because we grow two, spatially separated eyes, but we each must first train our brain to use them efficiently, and then train our mind to interpret what has been seen. Bear in mind that eyes evolved from light-sensitive cells. When these first developed, no creature possessing them would "know" how they might best be put to use; each slight advantage would have to be discovered, then experimented with, to learn how to interpret the new perceptions. Evolved change by itself is insufficient in such cases.

"Learn" is an active verb, and learning occurs in animals, but not in plants. Animals use their brains and minds to direct their bodies to obtain food and mates, and to avoid predators. What an animal learns[9] and puts into practice can be copied by peers, and by offspring as they emulate their parent's behaviour. Learned beneficial changes in both mental outlook and physical ability are thus passed on to successive generations.[10]

Simple organisms like plants have not been able to evolve in this manner. Thus, the evolutionary process has itself evolved over time. In its original form, evolution benefits (or harms) future generations without their active participation. But in its later form, evolution can be a two-stage active process that operates only if animals learn how to take advantage of latent abilities.

Recently, evolution added a third capability and level to its repertoire: it can now plan its own future. Let me explain.

Two things happened after humans learned how to speak and write. First, we dramatically increased the speed at which we acquire knowledge, adapt, and change our behaviour. We learn how to extract metals, then build tools and weapons. We learn about genetics, then breed hardier crops and livestock. We learn about fats and cholesterol, then modify our diet. We learn how to survive in space, then go to the moon. What one discovers, others put into effect—increasingly within the same generation.

Second, we became able to plan our future. We have learned how to apply our knowledge to envision a desirable future, then chart a path toward that future. That is how we reached the moon; that is how we might one day reach other planets.

In essence, we now use our third-level thinking ability to consciously consider what the future holds possible. We then use it again to plan the actions necessary to obtain our desired goal.

This ability, I contend, is significant enough to be thought of as a third-stage in the evolutionary process. We have evolved to the stage of being able to take charge of—to be responsible for—our own future. Indeed, humans are verging upon the ability to take control of evolution itself. In short, we are no longer animals to whom change simply happens, or that must learn to take advantage of a latent ability before we can benefit. We have now become animals that can use words to select, far ahead of time, the kind of benefits we want evolutionary change to produce: we can then produce that change.

Is it not ironic that, just as we are learning how to plan and achieve our own future, this future can seem meaningless? If the universe and life exist with no discernible purpose, then everything subsumed within these two concepts also lacks purpose. No purpose, ergo, no meaning. What are we to do?

The answer is clear to me. If neither the universe nor life itself evince a purpose, if there is nothing anywhere that provides rational and universal direction and meaning, and if, as has been many times stated, we simply must have a purpose if we are to make decisions rationally, then we must invent one. To avoid stagnating in a moral quagmire, we must formulate a proxy purpose.[11] Our history of developing religions when searching for nonexistent answers demonstrates that we have done this many times in the past. We can do so again. Therefore, if, as concluded in Chapter Six, the invented purposes of past religions can no longer guide our contemporary moral decision making, then it is time to contrive a new purpose that will.

The question, nevertheless, remains: what purpose do we devise?

3. Learning and Purpose

To better understand the rationale behind the choice of purpose that I will be proposing, it is necessary to first say a little more about the nature and consequences of learning.

Learning brings understanding, and understanding opens doors toward modifying and controlling events and things. When humans first lit fires in caves to keep warm, they were using what they had learned. These days, just about every aspect of our environment can be modified using our knowledge. However, while we have become adept at modifying, our ability to control is still in its infancy.

Just think what we might be able to control in the future. Scientists may soon be able to use stem cells and a patient's DNA to grow body tissues and organs for "rejection-less" transplants, and physicians may be able to suppress the development of (perhaps even eradicate) most or all of the approximately 1,500 diseases thought to be genetically induced. Before long, we expect to be mining our neighbouring planets for rare minerals (NASA is already investigating the techniques needed), then manufacturing products on those planets. This increases the probability of eventually doing the same on exoplanets orbiting neighbouring stars. One day, perhaps not long now, physicists will learn how to build machines that will control nuclear fusion (the process that drives the stars) and so obtain virtually unlimited amounts of energy.[12] Some day we might even be able to scan and map the position of each atom within a living entity. All we will then need is a means of fashioning atoms to such a blueprint, to recreate the exact creature, with its entire memory intact, anywhere we position a receiver.[13]

Learning, then controlling, is limited by only two things: by our mind's capabilities and the constraints of the universe. There will always be facts we do not know and events we cannot control, but these will become fewer and fewer in number over the centuries and millennia ahead. Someday, perhaps a billion years into the future, perhaps sooner, life forms—possibly even remote descendants of humankind—may learn how to control the behaviour of the stars. Maybe even reposition galaxies! No law of physics prohibits such activities.

Learning how to progressively exploit our environment will not stop until life itself ceases. (We will see why this is so in the next chapter.) The extinction of one species does not prevent life from continuing. If, for example, all species upon an island are eradicated, the life continuing in the surrounding seas, the air above, on other lands, will soon encroach to colonize the empty niches. If we annihilate ourselves, other species will survive and fill the void we leave. The story of life would continue, and we would not even be missed, a few thousand years into the future. If some occurrence were to obliterate every living thing upon this planet, life would begin again once conditions permit. This is because all the while, everywhere throughout the universe, life explores and exploits its inherited options.

Inevitably, ultimately, life will learn enough to be able to control all that can be controlled from its position within the universe. Evolution will culminate in a life form that seemingly possesses god-like powers.[14] It won't be a god—it will still be just life. But what an entity!

It is easy to understand why this must be so: to those living just a few hundred years ago, people of this century would appear to have abilities approaching omnipotence. Any inexplicable controlling ability may confer such a title, and impart a mystical awe—ask any successful magician. If electronic, medical and technological progress continue at today's pace (to say nothing of the many other fields currently being exploited), then in no more than one or two hundred years time humans will certainly possess abilities that would be incomprehensible and astonishing if witnessed today. But think ahead another two thousand, or two million years. How would such powers not seem omnipotent, and where does this accumulation end?

Yet, we cannot say that it is life's purpose to develop such abilities. Evolution's consequences may produce a seemingly omnipotent[15] entity, but we cannot state that this endpoint must therefore be the inherent purpose that guides life's evolution. Immense competencies accrue simply because life compiles useful abilities, compounding one upon another as it evolves—progeny taking synergistic advantage of its inheritances. As previously stated, we cannot say that life is purpose-driven because we would first have to say that life's supersystem, the universe, was purpose-driven. And, since we can't position ourselves outside of our universe, this can never be determined.

This omnipotent consequence of evolution is just that—a consequence. It is not, and should not be considered, an ordained purpose.

4. What Purpose can we use?

So, life and our universe have no discernable purpose. Let us return to where we started this chapter and discuss what alternative purpose, if selected, might give us a vision that we can live with and, more importantly, live for.

Please do not misunderstand what I am about to propose. Life, as I have said, cannot be proven to be directed toward a purpose. Neither existing nor evolving is a purpose—these are simply states of affairs. Demonstrating a trend toward complexity does not demonstrate purpose—it demonstrates only what happens when something new is added to something old. Nor does the ability to learn then apply what has been learned prove that life has a purpose.

But we need a purpose to rationally make the many moral decisions thrust upon us by scientific and technological advances. And we need a universally accepted one if we are to achieve any degree of unanimity. So, one must be contrived.

What I am about to propose we adopt is based upon what we now know about the universe and about our abilities within that universe. Two millennia ago, we knew little and could control next to nothing. With ideas inherited from the Pharaohs and earlier civilizations, the only future we could imagine preparing for was our personal entry into an assumed afterlife. Times are much different now. Today, we think about the future of others, including other species, as much as we think about our own. And we are beginning to realize that, collectively, we have the potential to achieve and control almost anything we care to dream about.

A word of caution before we proceed. In selecting a purpose to guide us, we must be careful not to separate ourselves from life. Past religions did this—humans held themselves different from, and superior to, all other forms of life. We know better than this, nowadays. Life itself is our parent. Other living entities are our siblings. We have no more, and no less, purpose for living than life itself has. Thus, whatever we select to be a purpose for humans, must be a purpose that applies to all other living entities, including those beyond our planet.

What, then, do we choose to be our universal purpose?

Given that there is no detectable purpose pre-designed into life or the universe, then, if we must have one, *we must adopt a surrogate.*

To my mind, the only viable option is to support life's continual evolution and focus upon helping it to achieve an omnipotent ability. Such a purpose is universal and rational; it is a purpose that will last as long as life itself lasts. It accommodates the whole of life, and shows that we care about more than just our own well-being. It declares that we value life for its own sake and think little about the death that must follow, taking it simply as the price to be paid for living.

Such a choice, if made, would be so all-encompassing it would warrant being called a "meta-purpose."[16] If we indeed determine that all evidence points to life's evolution ultimately possessing omnipotent abilities, if selecting such an outcome could clear the way to making decisions that are both moral and beneficial to all forms of life (and this claim has yet to be substantiated, but we will examine both ideas later), then how can this not be the most logical "surrogate purpose" to choose?

(Indeed, we don't really have any other choice if the review conducted in Part Four has any merit, for, as we will see, no other purpose is as likely to ensure our future survival.)

What this might mean, and how we might obtain benefit by adopting it, must wait to be explored until Part Four. One other matter should be presented first; a speculation about what could be causing life to evolve toward such an end.

Summary

This has been a chapter of denials, where we finally acknowledge that the universe evolves only in obedience to laws that have been in existence since the moment of its birth—the purpose of which, if pre-programmed by some external deity, can never be discovered. We acknowledged also that life can arise and progress with no purpose apparent. The first life (wherever and whenever it arose) formed from atoms and molecules because conditions were conducive, and it has since evolved to become what exists today for exactly the same reason. When our star dies, so will our home, and all life that remains at home.

Some readers may find this Part of the book distressing. Such bold statements about the triviality of life and our species are not enjoyable to read. The real state of affairs is that there is no candy coating. There is no Father-in-Heaven looking down and caring for or about us—our prayers serve only to console ourselves. It is sobering to confront such truths, but are they really that much of a surprise? Haven't we all previously, at least briefly, suspected as much, deep down inside, at one time or another?

Much as we might like it to be otherwise, we are truly alone and adrift. Alone, but accompanied by all the other life forms that this universe contains. Adrift, but slowly finding our way from ignorance to wisdom. Constantly moving from the past, when life knew nothing, to the future, when life will know almost everything. God, if He ever existed, cut us all free when He released the universe. That was when free will began, and this is exactly what free will entails: facing up to the facts, recognizing that we make the bed we lie upon, and taking the responsibility to make decisions rationally as we travel along the evolutionary pathway.[17]

But, what a journey it is! Especially now, when we are at the cusp of understanding and controlling so much. So many possibilities, so many choices; the future can seem overwhelming—indeed frightening—at times. But life can become glorious and wonderful again, bright from a new guiding light—once we build the beacon.

I think that there is much to gain by adopting life's evolutionary consequence as a surrogate purpose, and using that to guide our decision making. Part Four examines some reasons for thinking so, and suggests what might be done with the visions such a choice generates.

But, before we rush ahead; what if these conjectures about life's outcome are fantasies? No one wants to be misled by yet another set of assumptions, inventions and falsehoods. Although life may well have learned how to control some things, is there any plausible reason to think that it will continue to do so? From where does this ability to learn and to apply such learning come, and is this source a permanent feature of life?

When I was able to step back from my "revelation" (see "A Revelation," a postscript to Chapter Five) a decade or so after it happened, I began wondering what could possibly cause evolution itself to evolve. Why should it change from being just a passive "reaction-to-events" process, to becoming an active "determinator-of-its-own-future" process? I knew of none; however, such a transformation has happened, so there must be a cause to be discovered. Chapter Ten explores one possibility.

Chapter Ten

Life and Exploiting

Leaving until later a discussion of the many advantages that might be gained by doing so, Chapter Nine concluded by suggesting we adopt as a "meta-purpose" the idea of supporting life's journey to its consequence of becoming an omnipotent entity. But, as it did so, it emphasized that this whole notion might only be a possibility, and cautioned against building edifices upon faulty assumptions.

However, there may well be a reason why life, very probably not a direct descendant of life on this planet, but life, somewhere, will eventually come to possess omnipotent abilities. What we may now think to be simply a fantasy may actually occur—eventually. This chapter looks for and attempts to provide a possible reason why this might be so by reviewing what we know about life's behaviour, then speculating about how it came to be this way.

Speculations usually have little merit beyond suggesting lines of further inquiry, but this one, to the extent that it has any validity, provides something more. It warns us to be wary of human nature, particularly as we accumulate knowledge. Thus Chapter Ten serves two purposes—it offers a theory that might explain why life seems to become ever more complex and proficient, and it reminds us that increasing powers bring increasing opportunities for "bad" as well as for "good" behaviour.

1. The Behaviour of Living Things

We begin by noting a few facts about life's general behaviour, starting with plants. Outwardly, plant life might appear to be passive and uneventful; endless cycles of germination, development, replication and death, with random mutations—possibly of significance to future species—happening in between. A cursory look at the life of animals might suggest the same pattern. However, as we will soon be reminded, the full story is much more complex. Each one of life's many species is competitive,[1] assertive, territorial, and occasionally very aggressive. Each does its utmost to expand into neighbouring territory, wherever it exists and whenever the opportunity arises.[2]

Plants fit this description, once we look at what happens over several generations. Most gardeners know that any plant will expand its domain unless curbed. Creeping Charlie is a good example; it will sow seeds and extend runners ad nauseam, and is very difficult to eradicate. Mushroom fairy rings graphically and accurately portray this expansionist behaviour, as underground mycelia spread, then fruit. In fact, the history of any plant species may be viewed as one long quest to gain territory, and an outside intercession of some kind or another is always needed to halt the process. Plants invariably enlarge their domain until prevented by an inhospitable climate or by soil that lacks nutrients or is toxic in some way, or until they are overcome by some disease agent or eaten by insects or animals.

Insects exhibit exactly the same behaviour. We have all likely read about calculations showing that the offspring from one pair of flies, unless checked in some way, would number enough to blanket the world after a few weeks. Only impediments such as lack of food, its own excrement, poisons of some kind, parasites, attacks from aggressors seeking to control the same environment—some kind of external force—will stop the population from exploding. Locusts dramatically demonstrate this phenomenon. Every few years, huge swarms of these grasshoppers arise and decimate vast areas. Insects, like plants, multiply, strengthen their control of local food sources, increase again in number, move outward, and repeat the sequence if not halted by an opposing force. In fact, it has been said that if a catastrophe killed most of the life on Earth, insects would survive and evolve to dominate what remained.

Animals, too, behave in this manner, as demonstrated by many animal population-cycle studies. Plant food supplies increase, so the number of rabbits increases; the fox population then builds, and a bunny take-over is prevented. The number of rabbits then decreases, so the fox population declines, and before we know it, we have rabbits galore again. (It is a seven-year cycle, roughly, in this example; eight years for the lemming/stoat cycle.)

No species self-limits its own population. Microbes and mice, birds and bees, fish and flowers, horses and humans; all multiply profusely unless prevented.[3] An external agent is always required to stop the expansion. Not infrequently, this external factor is itself living; it stops the growth of another by using this other as a source of food. The net effect of this has been to produce a precarious balance, maintained as our biosphere. The balance is preserved by each species defending what it possesses, and attacking to take what it needs.

Life and Exploiting 147

Now, let's consider what all this might imply. If every form of life behaves this assertively, then the assertive trait must have been present very early in the evolutionary chain. And, indeed, it was, because exploiting surrounding territory turns out to be the main characteristic that distinguishes living material from non-living material. To understand this more completely, we must again start at the beginning of the story.

2. Energy and Life

Biological life would not be possible without chemical interactions.[4] In turn, chemical interactions would not be possible without physical interactions, and no physical interaction occurs that does not involve an energy exchange; consequently, all biological processes depend upon energy exchanges. Clearly it is important to understand a little about this phenomenon if we are to understand how life began and how it proceeds.

We learned in school that almost all life on our planet depends, either directly or indirectly, upon the sun's energy, converted to useable form through photosynthesis.[5] During photosynthesis, chlorophyll converts simple molecules of water and carbon dioxide into more complex molecules (particularly sugars). Photons of sunlight provide the energy required to join the simple molecules together. This energy doesn't disappear, it becomes locked within the larger molecules (held within the electromagnetic forces that bind the chemical elements together). Plants utilize these larger molecules as nutrients fuelling other biochemical processes (breaking the molecules apart releases the binding energy). When consumed, these plants in turn fuel micro-organisms, other plants, insects and animals. In this way, the sun provides most of the energy needed by life on this planet.

Before delving a little deeper into what happens during energy exchanges within living entities, it is helpful to review a few features of non-living energy exchanges. The latter have been occurring since the universe began, and they hold the key to understanding life's creation—that instant when energy-processing chemical molecules first became energy-processing living molecules.

All chemical processes, living or non-living, involve energy transfers. Energy is either added to (or taken from) the involved atoms and molecules (by rearranging their electronic configurations). This energy is either taken from (or added to) the external environment. For instance, the energy required to form an iron compound when iron dissolves in an acid solution, is obtained from the energy released as the relatively complex configurations of electron orbitals in the acid are rearranged to form somewhat simpler ones. Forming iron sulphate in this manner needs no additional energy from outside the interacting molecules. (Quite the opposite; this process is exothermic—it releases energy in the form of heat as it proceeds.) Burning wood is another exothermic reaction; once started, the process sustains itself. When ignited, complex organic wood molecules break apart and release energy, only some of which is needed to join carbon from the wood and oxygen from the atmosphere to form carbon dioxide and other molecules. The rest of the energy is radiated away as heat and warms the universe.

Many chemical interactions do not release energy. These processes, termed endothermic, will not proceed, even after being started, without the continuous addition of energy. Producing plastics from oil, or forming sugar molecules by photosynthesis, are examples of endothermic reactions. In such cases, the final molecular compounds contain more energy than was originally held within the atomic structures of the forming components. This energy must be added before the bonds that hold the more highly structured molecules together will form.

Although every chemical process involves energy transfers, there is a significant difference between non-living (abiotic) chemical processes and living or biological (biotic) chemical processes. Abiotic chemical processes destroy or permanently rearrange the molecular structure of the constituents taking part in the process—the end products are different from those present at the start. However, healthy living cells do not permanently destroy, rearrange (other than when growing, learning or reproducing), nor deplete their own internal molecular configurations to obtain energy. They take what energy they need from their environment, eventually giving all of it back (in degraded form). While molecular configurations change continuously during life's many and varied processes, they are re-established before these processes end. A living entity, at the end of a long day of processing food, is much the same as it was when it started. (Indeed, unless growing, learning or reproducing, any difference between start and end configurations would be due to disease or damage.)

This energy transformation process, whereby molecules gather energy from their environment, utilize it in various ways, yet retain their unique identity unchanged after the energy utilization, distinguishes biotic from abiotic matter. Thus, the first molecular complex able to sustain an energy-transfer process unchanged, using energy extracted exclusively from the external environment, became the first living entity.

3. Life's Beginning

The transformation from non-living to living requires two steps. First, environmental sources must provide the energy needed to add an atom or two (also taken from the environment) to a molecular complex. This changes the molecule, as it now has one or more additional atoms and a little bit more energy (the amount needed to attach the extra atoms). In the second step, this process is reversed; the added atoms and energy have to be returned to the environment—otherwise nothing more than a chemical activity is occurring (or the entity is growing, see below). Movements within the fluid environment surrounding the molecule would bring new nutrients, and the process would repeat. (Fluid environments, liquid or gas, are vital to life's beginnings because life needs a continuous supply of energy and raw materials to survive.[6] A point of interest: the complex would be slowly propelled and could stumble upon its own supplies, if its configuration ejected surplus atoms repeatedly in one direction.)

(Where supplies exist to form one kind of molecular complex [see Chapter Eight concerning life's beginning], other kinds of biotic complexes might also arise. Once this happens, the most efficient process would sweep up available resources. Environmental variations would favour the formation of different complexes, however. Thus, right at life's beginning, natural selection seems inevitable.)

Occasionally, different atoms may have become permanently attached to the original molecular complex. Adding extra atoms to any molecule changes its properties; most changes would presumably prevent the complex from continuing its energy processing, and it would "die." However, some additions would not cause "death" and would thereby enlarge the complex, which might eventually grow big enough to split apart or replicate. However, it is not growing, nor even reproducing, that hallmarks life; it is the particular kind of energy transformations that extract from "without" to utilize "within," while the totality within retains its overall identity. Homeostasis first arose at life's beginning, and remains a fundamental property of life, equal in stature to life's ability to process energy.

Only one such molecule needed to form for life to begin. However, it is likely that conditions permitting the formation of the first self-sustaining molecular complex occurred in many places. If so, then many such molecules, identical or differing slightly one from another, could have formed more or less simultaneously.[7]

The first bounded, self-sustaining, molecular complexes might not have been able to grow and split. Many might have formed only to be broken apart by external forces after existing for a period of time. Nevertheless, this situation would provide opportunities for molecular alterations to occur, and thus a variety of molecular structures to have arisen. Eons probably passed before such complexes became capable of self-replication.[8]

Replication requires a means whereby each internal physical/chemical process is duplicated in the replicated entity. A bacterium reproduces by binary fission, whereby its single chromosome replicates and the bacterium splits into two. Some one-celled animals and plants also simply duplicate each internal component then split apart (amoebae, for example, replicate this way). At some time, one or more of the prototype living molecular complexes must have developed the ability to replicate (and probably did so by growing, then fissioning).

We can now expand upon the point made in section one of this chapter: life assertively reaches for and grabs hold of new territory because it needs the energy this territory contains to continue living. Life began as an energy-exploiting process and continued in that manner. It later developed the ability to replicate and hence to evolve in the sense we use that word. Subsequent beneficial mutations conferred an increasing ability to exploit different environmental energy niches, leading, slowly but inexorably, to the complexities of the many different life forms we see all around us today.

The phenomenon of life turns out to be just the behaviour of a bunch of complex molecules, co-operating within one body in order to exploit the many various environments inside and outside that body, to obtain the energy they need to sustain and replicate themselves. The whole body is said to be "living," but it is so only because each one of its constituent processing molecular complexes is living. In essence, biology is chemistry-in-action, and chemistry is physics-in-action. Feynman knew, decades ago, that life's basis had to be this simple.[9]

4. Exploiting

Now to return to where this discussion began. Living entities, like automobiles, need constant refuelling to run. Competition for resources, pitting one life form against another, is the inevitable result. The most able become parents to offspring that genetically inherit their parents' capabilities. In this way, the "exploiting" trait was strengthened as it self-selected down through the ages. The urge to exploit must by now be genetically encoded.[10] The natural world of plants and animals is not a paradise where every living thing exists in peaceful harmony with every other living thing. It is a battleground of constant aggression, each species against all others,[11] and within a species, one member against another. (In fact, it is precisely because species members compete against each other that species evolve into different species, as the Grant's work with the Galápagos finches showed.) Nature only appears peaceful because we rarely notice the underlying conflict. Expansion and conquest take place slowly, as with plants; or unnoticed, as is usually the case with insects; or hidden in the underbrush, as happens mostly with birds and animals. When we eulogize the peacefulness and serenity of nature we do not recognize the irony we mouth. All species compete for territory to obtain resources. As these resources become depleted it is inevitable that this competition will become more and more intense, most particularly between members of the same or closely related species, for they eat the same types of food and prefer the same kind of habitat.[12]

It may not be pleasant to think that life aggressively exploits its surroundings,[13] battling with any life form that gets in its way, but that is the nature of the beast. (In fact, as Dawkins stated, animal speed, eyesight, hearing, and so on, increases precisely because they are taking part in "arms races."[14])

The notion of a non-evolving, non-varying, non-exploiting, life form is non-sense. Non-exploiting life forms are dead life forms—living and exploiting are one and the same process. Further, much as we might dislike the idea that we humans exploit, we can find plenty of evidence that even the best of us live via exploiting and protecting what we have.[15] Who does not eat? Who would not buy stock if a genuine opportunity to gain presented itself? Actions such as these ably demonstrate that we all exploit when given the opportunity. Humans may not exploit every time, and we are usually selective in what, and who, we exploit. But some people are less circumspect than others, and some of their exploiting activities cause extensive grief and trouble to many.[16] (This is a topic to be discussed further, in Part Four, when we explore how excessive exploitation might rightly be identified and constrained.)

5. Complexity, Intelligence and Evolution

Once begun, life continued—exploiting, growing, replicating and diversifying, extracting energy from disorder, being occasionally knocked back many stages as environmental catastrophes occurred, eventually to arrive as we find it today. This continuous pattern is all that has been needed for life to become first, ever more complex, and second, ever more intelligent, as we will see.

The majority of life forms that populate this planet today are incredibly more complex than those that existed a billion years ago.[17] Of course, ever since Darwin proposed his theory of evolution we have known why organisms become more complex. Since most changes are merely modifications to an existing structure, their incorporation adds another layer to that structure. Complexity results, simply because amendments are necessarily added to what has existed before.[18] Many of the old abilities remain, most still active underneath—the new ones simply extend the entity's capabilities.[19]

But before they can serve any useful purpose, many changes in body structure and functioning have first to be controlled and directed. A slight increase in finger length or joint flexibility, for instance, offers no survival benefit at all unless the animal can manipulate the modification to gain an advantage over its competitors. This almost always calls for an increase in physical or body-activating skills, which in turn call for an increase in the mental skills needed to manipulate body parts, or to utilize improvements in sensory perceptions.[20]

Motor ability does not come out of the blue; in the modified finger example above, the change requires controlling by finger, wrist, and/or arm muscles, which in turn have to be exerted in new ways. As an example, random poking into crevices to extract bugs or maggots would flex and train these muscles, and this activity feeds information to the brain. Over time, the brain learns which incoming stimuli have been produced by which finger movements. Sooner or later, the brain reverses this process, sending impulses to a specific finger to produce the desired results. Thus, a genetic mutation that caused a body change has led to a new skill being learned, a result noted in the previous chapter in the suggestion that the evolutionary process itself has evolved due to an animal's ability to learn.

Yet the increased mental capacity is not inheritable. The animal's offspring learn, through observation, repetitive play and practice, how to use their body's abilities. Other times, as often with humans, they are deliberately taught. What is learned is stored via synapse development between the brain's neurons, and becomes part of one or more of the animal's mental constructs. Infants' brains explore the body's capabilities and limitations; they learn what can be controlled by attempting many movements and activities. Additional, mutation-created, physical capabilities require additional, learned, mental capabilities, to obtain this control. As noted in Chapter One, learning (linking the information held within neural networks) and intelligence are different aspects of the same phenomenon. Thus, evolution trends toward intelligence simply because a greater intelligence is needed to control a more complex body.

Intelligence is the ability to solve problems, i.e., in earlier terms, the ability to recognize new relationships amid the memories and stimuli present within the mind, to make new neural connections, then to apply this new understanding in some useful way.[21] It is not the mere possession of a large storehouse of facts, theories, or knowledge. These are just the material, the nuts and bolts, with which intelligence works to build theories and constructs, to solve problems and make decisions. Knowledge can be lost in one generation; intelligence cannot.

Two points must be emphasized. First, evolution trends toward complexity and intelligence, not toward humans. There is nothing inevitable or sacrosanct about our current dominance on this planet. Any language-using species will develop a similar intelligence, given time, although that species' morphology and history would likely nudge its intelligence to develop in different directions from ours. Second, the fact that intelligence develops is not evidence that life has been directed toward it. Life evolves the way it does solely as a consequence of the physical parameters present at the universe's birth, those that have structured every item and every event since that time. This accounts for all that exists and all that occurs. Intelligence is no different from other phenomena and needs no other kind of explanation.

Summary

Once again we have attempted to ascertain where we are directed by an analysis of the facts, and once again we are brought to the same conclusion. Nothing other than the universe's inaugural physics has been needed to bring into existence everything that lies about us. It has taken more than a dozen billion years to produce us. We cannot predict what billions of years more will bring, but we can predict that life's evolution will continue for as long as the universe has energy sources to exploit. And we can predict that life will continue its trend toward greater intelligence,[22] because we can foresee that the energy it needs to survive will become progressively harder to procure. Thus, the universe's initiating conditions alone seem to demand the eventual formation of an entity possessing what we would today call omnipotent abilities.

Barrow and Tipler reach the same conclusion. In *The Anthropic Cosmological Principle* they do their best to prove that life must continue to expand until it can regulate everything within every universe that exists.[23] I do not think that we can categorically state that such a life form must evolve, but I do think that its eventual appearance is highly likely. This is why I suggest making this consequence the "purpose" we are seeking. An artifice, certainly, but a necessary one, in the absence of any more-irrefutable purpose. A "surrogate purpose" if you like, but one that is more than adequate for, as we will see, it offers a profound morality-guiding potential.

Feinberg, in *The Prometheus Project*,[24] suggests that we deliberately choose the goal of creating a universal consciousness, then work toward its realization. It is preferable and more realistic, I think, to let life develop its own way to its ultimate "goal." All we need do, to survive and grow, is to support, rather than hinder, life's progress. Life's "goal" may not be to possess god-like abilities. But it seems likely that evolution's trend toward intelligence will bring such a being (or, at least, such a capability) into existence. I'm simply proposing that we consider this eventuality, think about adopting it as a surrogate "meta-purpose," and—if we think it useful to do so—use it to guide certain aspects of our global decision making. For just as long as it suits our needs. If it turns out later, when we know more, that life's evolution is trending toward some other outcome, then that will be the time to re-evaluate our choice of guiding "purpose."

Similar recommendations have been made by others, but perhaps none are as appropriate to the theme of this book as one made by Ursula Goodenough. She saw the need to have and be guided by a planetary ethic and proposed "The Epic of Evolution."[25] Yes, indeed. This is exactly what we need.

How we might go about developing such an ethic and what it might entail are topics that will be discussed in Part Four.

Conclusion to Part Three

That life evolves, and increases in complexity and in intelligence, is a fact. Why it does so is a theory, and natural selection is a very good one indeed. Life's exploitation of nature is a fact. The way it may have begun doing so, sketched in Chapter Ten, is little more than speculation. While we can ignore theories and speculations (all we lose is a degree of understanding), if we ignore facts we may lose our species' survival.

All life needs energy, and all life, wherever it exists throughout the universe, will be following the same steps; surviving if able to exploit an energy niche, dying if not, with survivors who possess the ability eventually moving out to exploit resources of neighbouring environments.

Life learns what it can about its environment in order to better exploit what is available. Increases in knowledge are accompanied by increases in the ability to control, a necessary feat if life is to extract all that is available from a declining resource.[1] This results in what has occurred on this planet—life becomes more complex, and its problem-solving ability or "intelligence" develops. In retrospect, humans of past cultures appear primitive. So will we, when looked back upon by life in the distant future.

A million years, even a hundred million years, is nothing to life. It has already existed on this planet for more than three billion years; our sun will still be providing life-giving energy another four billion years from now. Life here and further out in the universe, appears to have all the time it needs to reach its full potential.

To reiterate; the possibility that life will eventually evolve into an omnipotent being is not life's purpose (unless we return to imagining a god pre-designing the universe toward this end). Life needs no purpose to evolve; all it needs is the ability and freedom to exploit environmental resources. Nonetheless, possession of god-like or omnipotent abilities seems very likely to be life's eventual outcome.

(I will be referring to the idea of life evolving to become an omnipotent Being several times. This entity needs some kind of name. [As noted in endnote 14 to Chapter Nine, de Chardin called a similar culmination to life's evolution the Omega Point.] As an irreverent convenience, I'll call it oB, short for omnipotent Being.)

It might be simpler to believe that a god existed before the universe began, that it started the universe and that its laws created all that we find within. By believing so, all our unknowns are rolled into one, and we feel less driven to find the evidence required to support such an assumption. It would also be especially comforting to believe that this god plays some ongoing part in humankind's existence. However, miracles are rare and highly suspect to anyone with a logical mind. No rational person sits down and waits for a miracle to get them out of a predicament.

Furthermore, it is irrational to believe that solely one's own religion, and no other, holds the truth. Humans have thought this way for long enough, and, after centuries of disagreement, culture clashes, fighting and wars, have ended up where we are today—amid much religious bitterness, baggage, and confusion.

We can make a fresh start. We can learn from and apply, rather than deny or distort, the scientific facts we have uncovered. We can start by being rational, just as people tried to be hundreds or thousands of years ago when founding the religions we have inherited. We can consider what evidence there is to support the proposed meta-purpose, the conjecture that life itself will evolve to possess omnipotent abilities. Those for whom the evidence is strong enough may, if they also think the suggestion has merit, adopt it as the purpose they use to guide collective decision making (possibly in the manner suggested in Chapter Thirteen).

That many, even most, of the world will continue to follow the dictates issued by their current religion is inevitable. It also matters little, and is not unwelcome. Rather, it is desirable, for individual freedom (in all actions that do not harm others) is essential to life's vitality. The universal religion (whose development is touched upon in the last chapter of this book) does not replace existing religions. It is best regarded as an "umbrella" doctrine whose principle use is to provide moral guidance relevant to the collective action of communities and nations when guidance is otherwise confused or non-existent. With careful development, the old and the new tenets need not compete; they can reinforce each other, with one lending a hand when the other calls for aid.

Part Four

Developing a Universal Religion

Introduction to Part Four

Before we begin we should clarify the distinction between a "meta-purpose" and the "universal purpose" we have been seeking to guide our collective morality.

Part Three sought evidence that the behaviour of the universe or life might be directed toward achieving some kind of purpose. It found none. It then suggested that (and proposed a reason why) life might continue evolving until it became an omnipotent being (but emphasized that there is no proof that this must occur).

Since the universe behaves rationally, life's survival depends upon behaving rationally also. Sentient beings, able to plan ahead before acting, behave rationally when they pre-determine a purpose and make decisions that, when acted upon, help to achieve the chosen purpose. We might decide that "supporting life's journey to become omnipotent" is a worthy goal, and we could make it our "meta-purpose" to guide moral decision making. However, this is too loose a statement for many practical purposes. While it might convey some emotional desires or feelings, it is not precise enough.

A statement intended to guide the moral (and therefore physical) behaviour of an entire civilization must be able to withstand all manner of challenges—legalistic, moralistic, religious, economic, and many more. "Helping life to become oB" will never survive a rational attack; a more robust definition of humanity's goal is required. A clearly defined "universal purpose," possibly based upon the desire to help life evolve to become oB, could turn wishful conjecture into practical precision. Moreover, if a "universal purpose" were to be derived from the concept of assisting life to become oB, then a potentially dry legal document might come to life—the vision empowering the definition.

How a universal purpose might be defined is touched upon in the Postscript to Chapter Fourteen; it is difficult task but not one we need dwell upon. The question, "why bother to do anything?" is a much more important topic and must be addressed. Why should anyone go to the trouble of contemplating the precise wording of a universal purpose?

Chapter Eleven suggests some philosophical reasons why the effort should be made while Chapter Twelve offers some practical ones. I hope that one or more of the thoughts expressed in those chapters convince at least a few readers that the undertaking would be well worth while.

Chapter Thirteen delves into the nitty gritty of a possible new morality. Assuming a universal purpose based upon the premise of oB was crafted, just what behaviours would it support, and what might it forbid? And what is the rationale for the answers provided? My thoughts, hopelessly biased by my constructs, are provided only to initiate the discussion. Superior minds will hopefully someday undertake the task of developing a rational morality, one that might better guide us in solving the extraordinarily complex issues we face today and will surely encounter tomorrow.

In eras past, religions took generations to develop, with emotions playing a large part. Nowadays a sound religion might be rationally grown in a decade or two, via electronic communications. As shown in the subtitle of this book, my emphasis is upon the *need* to develop a universal religion, and where one might look, not upon actually doing so. Nevertheless, it seems appropriate to outline how such a fantasy might someday become a reality; Chapter Fourteen offers my musings.

Chapter Eleven

Why Bother?

This chapter attempts to answer some of the questions skeptics may raise. It suggests a few philosophical reasons why we should develop a universal purpose, why we should base it upon supporting the achievement of life's possible endpoint, and why we should make this effort. Other, more practical, reasons for developing a universal purpose are presented in Chapter Twelve.

1. Why Develop a Universal Purpose?

Purpose directs decision making. Even so, most of us start our careers and live our lives having no specific goal in mind. Perhaps as a consequence, many of us seem to actually like being told where we should be going and what we should be doing. We see this during election campaigns, and in the organizations we work for. We look for leaders with vision, people who can imagine possible futures, describe desirable ideals, then tell us how they might be achieved. We see it again in our religions: the current split between revision and tradition is all about direction. It is also pervasive in the advertisements that surround us; these wouldn't be effective if we weren't receptive to instruction and influence. Our willingness to accept direction in almost all walks of life suggests that many, if not most, may actually prefer to be told what to think, how to behave, and what to buy. Being told, I suppose, simplifies life.

If this is so, then perhaps the first reason why we should develop an overarching purpose is that the world today is arguably without united moral direction, and being in this position is disquieting. Religious dogmatists sense this void and are responding with an oft-surprising militancy. In that fundamentalism seeks to return us to the ways and notions of many centuries past, the possibility that a fundamentalist Protestant, Catholic, Islamist, or other extremist might generate enough support to globalize his or her religious views is rather alarming. Such an outcome would exclude the last thousand years' of progress in all fields of knowledge, and spawn an oppressive future. The world is not what it used to be—it no longer naturally overflows with abundant resources, and a population of six billion can only be sustained using the products of modern technology.

There are additional good reasons to seek and select a guiding universal purpose. For instance, heads of governments and large multinational corporations make decisions that cross many boundaries, affect the lives of multitudes, and determine how vast resources are spent. In our current society, these decisions are usually made as though each was entirely unrelated to any kind of a broader picture. (Moreover, and this would be worse, the organization's "bigger picture" could be completely at odds with the one that the majority of us would like to see.) If humanity's goal for life is to be more than just wandering and squandering, exhausting the world's resources toward trivial ends, perhaps even harming rather than helping our collective future,[1] then we must find a way to speak with a united voice.

Another, quite different, reason for individuals to adopt a universal purpose is that following one can provide an extra degree of personal meaning, something above and beyond that which we may already possess.

Fully one-fifth of the population (and, very probably, many more, once acknowledging ones adherence to atheism or agnosticism becomes acceptable in general society) openly states that they do not believe in the existence of a god who involves himself in the affairs of humankind. These individuals, and I am one of them, make moral decisions without referring to the guiding purpose a religion provides. Rather, we support a variety of purposes (commonly those that would be called moral or ethical) instead of just one: helping people or animals, working to improve communities or the environment, contributing to charities, and so on. Following such purposes and personally behaving in a manner consistent with these goals provides meaning. But none of these purposes, individually, can bring as much meaning as would following a single, all-encompassing, universal purpose—particularly one accepted and supported by the majority.

However, perhaps the most compelling reason to develop a universal purpose is that, for the first time in history, we now have the knowledge and power to direct our future by genetically manipulating life. This must not be allowed to happen haphazardly, driven this way or that by commercial or quasi-religious immoderates and their organizations, as such interventions represent the desires of only small portions of humankind. All must be heard in matters of such importance, for we are about to recreate ourselves in our own image.

This new-found ability was mentioned earlier, when we noted that survival has meant adapting to changes in the environment. In effect, life's future used to be (and much still is) externally determined. But our human future is about to become whatever we decide to make it, and we must proceed with great care. One mistake, and we may produce a virus a thousand-fold worse than smallpox or HIV. We may introduce factors that migrate between species,[2] or that mutate, then decimate entire biomes, and return life's whole matrix to an ancestral form comprising little more than bacteria.[3]

Our present and future actions in gene manipulation are fraught with danger, but they are also magnificently full of opportunities. We cannot ignore these technological and medical advances. We must learn fully the science of genetics, but we must also carefully control the use of what we learn. Only by everyone, at all levels of these endeavours, adopting, developing and maintaining a conscientious awareness of an appropriate humanity-guiding universal purpose, might this degree of control be achievable (a premise to be expanded upon in the next chapter).

The concerned rational among us must be the ones to take the initiative. We should adopt or define a judicious guiding purpose while we may, or in its absence someone will certainly come along and sell us theirs and it may become too late to make a rational choice. History provides us with many examples of this. Whenever we have found ourselves greatly dissatisfied, as a group or as a nation, someone offers leadership, then takes command. This is how Stalin, Hitler, Yeltsin, Milošević, and bin Laden gained or consolidated their power, to name just a few examples from recent history.

Humanity needs, I think, a collective purpose. This would be *in addition* to our many individual and religious purposes. Under such a unified objective, individual moral behaviour not harmful to the collective good would properly remain individual choice, accruing concomitant rewards as believed to come before or after that individual's death. However, the world's collective guidance is a different matter. It should be obtained from a purpose positioned far beyond any one individual's reach. This purpose should shine as a beacon to nations, guiding many generations. And its rewards should accrue to the living, not the dead, enriching the lives of all.

While no one should be expected to abandon their inherited or chosen religion, none should be prevented from adopting an additional universal purpose to guide their moral behaviour. No one should be asked to change what they have come to believe about themselves and their ultimate individual destiny, or to deny the god they worship. But an overarching universal purpose, used to guide humanity's collective behaviour should also exist—something that clearly helps ensure our species' and life's well-being and continuance.

2. Why choose Life's possible Endpoint?

Although life's imagined omnipotent climax is nothing more than a possible, perhaps probable, conclusion to evolution, it does seem to be our best choice of meta-purpose, the one that would then be used to guide the written definition of a universal purpose. Nothing else so focuses our attention upon ensuring that life (which includes us) has a future. When we select and use this meta-purpose we are forced to pay attention to the health of our planet, and our survival chances increase (to say nothing of the quality of life we live). No other purpose so aptly points out the criteria we need to use when making moral decisions (see Chapter Thirteen for illustrative examples) both today and in the future.

However, there is another, and, at first sight, strong, meta-purpose contender that has not yet been mentioned. In recent years, the idea of zero growth or sustainable development has been much debated. It would be quite possible to select this as our meta-purpose, and make moral decisions guided by the need to maintain the planetary status quo. It would be quite possible, but it would be an appalling choice.

In a zero-growth state, production levels just balance requirement levels. All life would exist in peaceful equilibrium, as some seem to believe was once the case. However, such a state never existed. Life has always exploited its environment for resources, and life forms that do not continuously attempt to take all possible advantages will be overtaken by others that do. Stagnant life does not survive.

A two-way disruptive process featuring life and its environment operates continuously. Environmental changes precipitate evolutionary changes, and life's evolution disrupts its environment, particularly the number and kind of other life forms that live in the vicinity. In the past, life-effected disruptions were minor and local in scale; today, due principally to population and technology, they are not. We notice environmental degradation now due to its extent and magnitude. It is pervasive and escalating, because we have just about shut down or eliminated many of life's formerly capacious buffering biomes, but also because we are running out of planet to exploit. This last factor, were we to adopt a zero growth rate, would soon create serious psychological consequences.

Mankind has not yet absorbed the fact that there is almost nowhere else on Earth to go. This planet has always provided new and interesting territory for humans to discover, explore and exploit. The open space and natural wealth found as our reach expanded provided avenues of escape for the oppressed and a challenge for the restless. This, in turn, helped to maintain the political and social stability of the countries left behind, and enabled the population explosion that has been our constant companion for the past three centuries. But we have reached our territorial limit. Today, only the oceans and space itself remain unexplored.

Psychologically we have not fully realized what this means. Subconsciously (particularly in the West), we still expect that limitless expansion—moving on, growing, and building a place of our own—will always be the intrinsic state of affairs. Life has been able to expand upon this planet, in one manner or another, for the past four billion years. Room to roam and exploit has always been at hand for all who so desired. It was always thus—but is so no longer. And, when we eventually have no place to walk that has not been trod before, have only food that has been artificially modified in some manner, have instant but sanitized and censored news and ideas, and have only vacations that are virtual, or made of fibreglass and plastic, how then will we feel?

I think that I would feel I was approaching the end of all that was good in life. I would begin to think about the end of the world and about death, for, in an entirely controlled world that was going nowhere, I would see no future and no hope. Indeed, this is just how things do begin to appear for many of us, in our final years. When there seems to be nothing new to put your hand or mind to, one becomes suddenly very old. And this is likely to be how the population of a zero-growth world would feel, once it is realized that the planet has been ravished and the opportune time to expand into space was missed.

Expansion is necessary for life's continued development— even expansion into space, throughout our galaxy and into others beyond. Yet life on this planet may have only the needed resources and psychological energy for one shot. It would dishonour all that life has accomplished to throw this opportunity away.

There is another aspect to this discussion about the viability of a zero-growth future. Evolutionary change occurs only when possible and advantageous: when niches open up, when food supplies vary, or when a mutation confers a bonus. If niches never alter, change brings penalty, not reward. If we choose zero growth, if we immobilize our niche, we will cease evolving. Without challenge, we do not advance. *H. sapiens* will regress and degenerate into obscurity.

There is only one direction to go, and that is forward. Returning to past views returns us to wars about beliefs, and ignores or debases scientific truth. Standing still amounts to slow death. We must go forward. Forward, eventually into space, amassing knowledge, understanding, and gaining an ever greater ability to control as we go.

As I have written earlier, there seems only one logical consequence to going forward forever. Life eventually, surely, must become an entity possessing omnipotent capabilities—oB. If this is so, or indeed, even if this is just a possibility, then why not adopt this endpoint as a surrogate "meta-purpose," use it to define a robust "universal purpose," then make collective moral decisions aimed at achieving that purpose? What better choice could we possibly make?

3. Why do Anything?

Why bother to do anything, when life will continue no matter what we do, and when, anyway, life may be ultimately purposeless and meaningless? These, indeed, are compelling questions.

If we take the short-term view, say for the next one hundred years or so, then, exactly, why bother? Why not just enjoy ourselves? Who cares what happens to life after we and our immediate descendants have gone? Does it matter that the world's quality of life will deteriorate as resources run out and pollutants pile up—people will get used to it and will know no better. If all that really matters is we who are living right here and now, then, certainly, why bother?

I suppose that narcissists, despotic and repressive dictators, psychopaths, and perhaps a few others may think this way. But I'm certain that you do not, for you would not have read what I have written so far were this the case. We must bother, because we care, and the majority of the world's population also cares about others and the future they will have. Proof exists everywhere: thousands of schools, libraries, parks, museums, art galleries, speciality hospitals, and institutions throughout the world, owe their origin to individuals who cared, and their continuance to others who still care. Millions of individuals dedicate their time, energy and resources to help others less fortunate. Caring about and for others is part of the human condition.

The choice of meta-purpose and definition of a universal purpose must not be left to our various levels of government. Those who govern are seldom inclined to look more than five or ten years ahead—we need to think in terms of five or ten *hundred* years and more. Surely it is aggregated actions of individuals, not governments, that instigate enduring change.

However, it is important that the choice of meta-purpose not be left to any single individual—it must be a collective judgment. Consider inaction once more, but from this perspective. Let's say that we do nothing, that we ignore the eventual need for a universal, integrating, fact-based religion. Almost certainly, some visionary will see the need and will come forth to lead us into a new (or back into an old) world-correcting religion. Many scenarios are possible, of course, but, to me, none seem attractive, for in all of them we would be lead by a single mind, and relinquish our freedom to choose. No matter how pleasant our existence might become, no matter how benign or how benevolent such a person might be, it would be their personal bias, their mental construct, we would be following. Effectively, life would just be putting in time until that person's conception was overtaken by events or facts and required rewriting, just as may now be happening with our old religions. We would merely be swapping existing imaginings for a new set, repeating history (possibly even locked into a never-ending cycle), with humanity slowly decaying under its load of competing faiths and goals.

It is for this precise reason that the impartial facts must show us the way, not one individual's emotional constructs. Let a multitude work together to interpret the known universal facts, then collectively design a morality that fits both reality and human needs—one that can be up-dated as new knowledge dictates. (But more about how this might be done later.)

Again, we could do nothing, and just aim to enjoy ourselves. And, why not? Isn't this, more or less, the way many of us already live? Does it even matter—for in the long run the human species will certainly be replaced by another, just as has happened with other species so many times in the past.

Yes, certainly, humans will eventually be overtaken by, or evolve into, other species. So, in the longer run of things, why should it matter what we do today? Is there significance to anything we do? If not, why should we exert ourselves?

We must make this effort because, within the past quarter-million years or so, life has attained the ability to build upon the *intellectual* gains of the past. This development is extremely valuable, and to simply throw it away would be an enormous setback to life. Previously, life's evolutionary masterpieces left little more than decaying matter and a minuscule amount of knowledge for future species to utilize. This is no longer the case. Humans now leave records of their errors and achievements that others can use and benefit from. Our knowledge and understanding, often almost in its entirety, is passed on to the future. We must care about what purpose we select to guide our moral and practical decision making, because the lives of our descendants will be affected by how we behave as we follow our choices. We must not sit back and let unreasonable fundamentalists or irrational fanatics set our path, for they often destroy records of the past in trying to ensure the future of their fantasies.[4] We cannot risk having our hard-won knowledge destroyed, as we now have so much to contribute.

Let me describe what I think we present-day humans have to contribute to the future. I might best do so by discussing three time periods: the near term, the middle term, and the ultimate.

As we begin this new century we bring with us more than two millennia of religious conflict. This discord exists at the personal level, where, in many minds, fears of afterlife "penalties" battle with hopes of an everlasting reward. And it exists at the community level, wherever the Catholic vs. Protestant, Christian vs. Muslim vs. Hindu, and all the other religion-based conflicts, occur, in so many places around the world. If we do not attempt to unite differences under a collective universal purpose, this situation is bound to continue. But if we choose a new purpose that looks forwards instead of continually backwards, there is a chance that these conflicts may eventually die out. What is preferable to pass to our successors: fears, bitterness and outdated notions from the past; or consideration, vision and reality-based hope for the future? The best short-term contribution we could possibly make would be to revise our view of what is important in life. We bequeath a disturbing legacy to our children if their only choices to satisfy their need for a religion are those that rule by fear and ferment discord. We must offer an alternative—one that might be developed if a suitable collective meta-purpose were first adopted. In my view, this would be the best short-term contribution we could make to humanity's path forward.

To appreciate the possible value of the middle-term contribution I will be suggesting, we must project into the future. Eventually, although perhaps not for several hundred years, we will encounter intelligent life elsewhere. This may be via electromagnetic radiation of some frequency, such as radio waves, light waves or the like. Perhaps this will occur by way of interacting space probes, or through quantum space tunnelling. Or, maybe we will develop something like telepathy, if ever such a transmission mode is uncovered.[5] However it occurs, when we do interact with an intelligent alien species what will matter most in what we communicate will be our identity, not our knowledge, because they will more than likely possess at least our level of understanding about the universe. As part of assessing our merits, what will likely be of most interest to exospecies will be who we are, what we think about ourselves, and what is important to us. To convey that we periodically take up arms and kill each other, that we routinely destroy our own habitats, that we have not supported the continuance of other species—these attributes should disgrace us, not to mention alarm those we communicate with. But to also reveal that the majority of us fear death while nevertheless believing that after death we assume a loving relationship with the "Creator" after destroying what He has created—what kind of fallacious thinking is this? (I am glad that I will not be here to witness us tell aliens this, for I would be so ashamed of our human condition.) I would not blame any sentient being for immediately terminating contact with entities advocating such beliefs and actions.

But to convey that we think, or even believe, that life, everywhere, is embarked on a journey of discovery; that it will learn and grow in ability as it voyages; that it will unite in learning with other sentient beings along the way and eventually coalesce into one entity that possesses "god-like" abilities—would be wonderful. Were I in their shoes, I would want to learn from a civilization with such concepts, for their convictions accept and embrace me, as well as all of life. Indeed, a universal belief such as this could well be our most valuable medium-term contribution to life's future.

Our possible long-term gift may be to contribute to the way this universe ends. Let me elaborate.

I fantasize about life's potential behaviour as it approaches an omnipotent state. This may take place in several locations throughout the universe at more or less the same time, or it may happen only once, in some well-favoured locale. I ask myself what such an entity would do next. All its history has been spent acquiring knowledge and learning how to control matter and events, but this magnificent endeavour would be reaching an end. Presumably, it would have long since sought and found other pockets of advanced life, then merged and consolidated knowledge and abilities. Presumably too, if there were other such beings, all would unite to form one "oB" for the same reason. Eventually, there would be nothing new to learn, nothing which hadn't been experienced at least once, or couldn't be experienced if considered worth the effort.

And ultimately, this being would be all alone. After maybe thousands or millions of millennia spent learning from, being with, and perhaps uniting with a multitude of other complex life forms, there will be none of equal capabilities remaining in the universe. In effect, oB will have consolidated all knowledge and experience into its own being. It will have no mental companions and few challenges left to surmount. What might such an entity do?

Moreover, time within the universe may be coming to an end for life. There may be very few energy differences remaining to exploit, as expansion and entropy take their toll on all that is physical, or as the universe collapses into a terminating singularity. And this entity's abilities will be retained only as long as there remain energy differences that can be exploited and put to use, for even it must obey the laws of physics and the demands of its supersystem, the universe.

Surely, as the sole and complete repository of all that is to be learned from within the universe, oB wouldn't just wither and expire. I find that very hard to imagine. But, there might be one last endeavour that it might undertake, some deed that would represent a fitting end for a being of such capability. Conceivably, oB could perhaps arrange matters so that the universe would rebound and restart, creating a new one from the old. Such a scenario might just be possible. Knowing all there is to know might point to a way that this could be done. A complete fantasy to us, yes, but to it? We do not know enough to judge.

The additional challenge for oB then, would be to see if it could somehow improve upon the past universe, perhaps slightly modifying one or more parameters, so making it possible for life in the subsequent universe to develop in new ways.

This, to me, is a very attractive thought. It opens the possibility of life being truly without end. In this fantasy, life effectively hibernates at the end of each universe, its existence to be reconstructed in the next. Each successive universe is given its initiating parameters in the final act of the oB of the universe past. In this way, we might have an endless, continually varying succession of life-bearing universes. Reincarnations without end.

Indeed, if this is what might come to be in the far, far distant future of this universe, then it follows that it could also have happened in the past, before time in this universe began. What can happen endlessly in the future can also have happened countless times in the past; an infinity of times in one direction necessitates an infinity of times in the other. And (but, I think, only in a context such as this), we could then even say that a god did create this universe. A god of the universe past, formed from the life that evolved in that earlier universe, itself created by the succession of gods of prior universes, without beginning or end. Who knows; perhaps this past god did implant the conditions necessary and sufficient for life to form, when it structured the laws of physics that we are beginning to understand and utilize today.[6]

In this scenario, if we need to give praise to anything, it would have to be to the life within universes past that created the universe present. And future life, in future universes, would be indebted to the final life form that evolves within this universe.[7] Formed, perhaps, with a contribution from us—if we survive to contribute—for this is where we might provide our long-term contribution.

In the very long run, millions or even billions of years ahead, what we have to contribute, I think, is our emotional perceptions of life's significance. We don't have to contribute our rationality, or our knowledge and understanding, because life forms everywhere will evolve toward intelligence, and will uncover exactly the same facts about life and the universe as we are discovering. The universe is everywhere governed by the same physical laws, and any conscious life, anywhere in the universe, should eventually be able to discover its properties and underlying controlling forces. However, humankind's emotional outlook is unique to our species, and much of it is fleeting.

What might perhaps become our long term contribution is sometimes called our "spirituality" or our humanity. We feel it when we look at the stars, when we are alone by the sea, or in a quiet forest clearing. A wonder, an awe, a sense of beauty or mystery, a feeling of immense peace and oneness. We sense it, but it is very difficult to convey to others because words are defined by personal memories—individual mental constructs and their meanings reside only in individual minds. However, these very emotions may be what is important to contribute to life's evolution in the long run.

We can't precisely contribute these feelings by words, paintings or sculptures; such items are culture-bound and contain nuances that could never be fully comprehended many, many, millennia into the future. But we may be able to contribute our emotions through our music. The music of Mozart, Beethoven, Brahms, Sibelius, and of so very many more wonderful composers come to mind. Their symphonies, concertos, requiems, sonatas, masses, love-songs, blues and jazz—all convey something of the essence of what it is to be human. Just possibly, morsels of music might survive passage through the ages, a million or more millennia, and contribute a little of what it has meant to be human toward the final shaping of that which life will become and may do.

But exactly what difference would any of this make, in the very long run?

One last dream. Maybe, just maybe, perhaps through music, perhaps by some other means, the essence of our humanity, what we feel about life, now, in these still early stages of life's intellectual journey, will be conveyed through time and make its way into the thoughts of oB, the god-like entity that life may become. Maybe our contribution will demonstrate how we feel about this marvellous life we live. Maybe our emotions today will affect oB's outlook at time's end.

And, maybe, just maybe, this is where we have most to offer. Maybe our feelings of happiness in simply being alive will influence the way oB designs the parameters that control life's evolution in the next universe, if it were to take that last, final, step. For instance, oB might make a change that could allow all future life to know more frequently the joy in living that today most of us only intermittently feel. To enrich the design of that which follows—what a contribution to make! To participate in creating a new beginning! That act alone adds purpose and meaning to each speck of life that has ever lived.

But, to make such a contribution, we must survive. And, we must make efforts to sustain our feelings of joy and spirituality, by living in expectant anticipation of the future. We must cease living in fear, mired in ideas from the past, as many of us seem to be today.

Summary

So, why bother? Because the media and globalization—if nothing else[8]—is forcing us to improve the way we think and act. Because we cannot continue indefinitely arguing and fighting among ourselves. What better time to stop and think about all we have endured, experienced and learned during these past millennia than now—now, at the beginning of a new millennium, and before we travel too far in the wrong direction. Now, now that we realize just how completely our minds shape all of our thoughts and actions.

Consider our new-found abilities—what might not be possible in just a few years? Our future can be wonderful, exciting and long, or it could be frightening, aimless and uncertain. The difference is simply a matter of taking the time to think, choosing a sensible direction to follow, and planning a path forward. We have gained the ability to think rationally. We have cultivated the intellect to discover the properties of matter and energy that open so many opportunities to us. And we are developing the technology that will allow us to colonize the planets, one that may later take us to the stars. The power and ability to control being unleashed by our increasing understanding appears to be unlimited. The choice of future is ours, and we are being asked to make it now. We can do nothing, and humanity may wither and die. Or we can unite in purpose and action, and humanity may flourish in ways it never has before.

Chapter Twelve

Possible Applications

This chapter turns from conceptions to reality, and looks at some current global situations which might be improved were humanity to focus upon its collective future much more often than is the case today.

There are three factors related to purpose which are critical to the success of any organization's endeavour—whether it is a corner store or an international conglomerate, and whether its aims are to make money, obtain power or preserve peace. These factors are vision, clarity and commitment.

Vision is important because visions, not purposes, excite efforts to succeed. It is the vision the preacher paints that holds our attention, not the bare statement that heaven, or hell, awaits. It is the vision of living in luxury and leisure that attracts many, not the target of amassing a million dollars. Visions are vastly more compelling than statements of purpose, but both are required when deciding how to act to solve problems.

Clarity of purpose is important because clarity determines how well subordinate goals can be defined and prioritized, and how well actions can be planned, resourced, carried out and evaluated.

But commitment is most important of all, for no effort succeeds if those involved lack the desire for success.

These three factors are also collectively important, because together they help to foster unity of mind, thought and effort. Not a carbon-copy identical-ness or single-mindedness, but a common desire to attain a common goal, where individuals each play their part in their own way.

The possible applications discussed in this chapter thus call for these three components. The "vision" stems from adopting the idea of supporting Life's journey to become oB as our meta-purpose; this provides the visionary power to surmount any distracting lesser purposes. "Clarity" stems from translating the meaning of this concept into a robust statement of "universal purpose," a definition that allows practical actions to be planned and undertaken. And "commitment" will likely stem from involving many throughout the world in defining both of these concepts. (This third step is a fairly straight-forward [although lengthy and complex] procedure, and need not be discussed until later in the book.)

The possible applications of a universal purpose are many, but only a few will be raised here. The first issue below discusses how world problems are currently managed, and attempts to show in general terms why "purpose" is key to success. Subsequent examples are provided to illustrate the range and scope of our vision's unifying possibility.

It is by no means certain that adopting a universal purpose, in an attempt to develop unity of desire and action, would change much in any of the situations presented below. Many of the issues are so large, and involve so many people, that any kind of change (particularly one of the magnitude and pervasiveness being suggested here) will require multiple years to take effect. But please do not dismiss the idea as naïve, simplistic or Pollyanna-ish before asking yourself whether what is being suggested offers any possibility for improvement over our present state of affairs.

If we grant that commitment to a clear purpose has critical organizing value and much to do with organizational success, then we are ready to examine some possible applications.

1. World Problems

Large scale problems exist throughout the world. A few words can readily bring some to mind: famine, diseases, polluted water and air, drought, climate change, deforestation, resource depletion, species extinctions, soil loss, wars, genocide, corruption, social and economic disparities—once begun the list may run for pages. Lumped all together they are immensely depressing. Many seem irresolvable—how can we even hope to improve such situations?

It's not that efforts haven't been made. We have addressed these issues as nations by setting up international organizations. The United Nations, the World Bank, the International Monetary Fund, World Trade Organization, G8, UNESCO, NATO, OECD, and numerous other international bodies, are all intended to support, improve and preserve what the concerned influential regard as important.

Consider just one institution, the United Nations. Its web-site (www.un.org) illustrates the scope of its activities. At the time of writing, the UN site linked to the following sub-sites: Peace and Security (which stated that there were over 750,000 military and civilian personnel participating in some seventeen peace-keeping operations); Economic and Social Development (which linked to Environment, Population, Trade and Sustainable Development); Human Rights; and Humanitarian Affairs. From just one of these sub-sites (Environment) there were links to Climate Change, Ozone Depletion, Acid Rain, Hazardous Wastes and Chemicals, Biological Diversity, Fish and Marine Resources, Marine Pollution, Desertification, Forests, and Fresh Water. Within another (Population), data were presented that traces the world's population from 300 million two millennia ago, doubling to 600 million three centuries ago, increasing ten-fold to six billion today, and predicting a fifty percent increase—to hit nine billion—within the next two generations.[1]

We have also tackled these matters on a somewhat less formal scale. There are hundreds of Not-For-Profit and Non Governmental Organizations (NGOs), staffed by paid and voluntary workers. The World Health Organization alone, for instance, lists close to two hundred NGOs whose activities are related to health. There are countless others to be located via the web. Their sites typically outline their concerns, what has been accomplished, and what remains to be achieved.[2]

And we have also sought solutions as concerned communities. There must be thousands of small groups:[3] churches, schools, colleges, clubs, associations and modest organizations, all striving to address issues of importance to them. Yet, even with all of this work being carried out, the overall number and magnitude of major world problems never seems to diminish.

Some problems are quickly solved, of course. Small groups, particularly, often make an immediate difference. Eyeglasses are delivered and fitted, a school is built, a well dug, water pipes laid, land irrigated, wind generators erected, hospitals staffed and supplied. Many beneficial results have been achieved.

Mid-sized organizations may not be able to act as promptly as smaller ones; however, money, tents, equipment, medical aid and food supplies usually do reach those in need, once the frequent obstacles (of a political, financial, religious and, all-too-often, military nature) are overcome.

It is the large scale institutions and interventions that seem so often to be ineffectual—neutered during conception, continually delayed, and acting too late. (The United Nations actually apologized not long ago, acknowledging that its lack of swift action had permitted the slaughter of over half a million people in Rwanda.)

There is something to be learned from a comparison of these results.

Large international governmental organizations become unable to carry out their mandate whenever national interests are allowed to overrule collective good. Representatives of different nations all too often seek results that favour national, rather than global, interests, and this then obstructs unreserved agreement upon a common objective. Speeches are used to obfuscate, delay or prevent, rather than as means to consolidate, collaborate and obtain action. When something is achieved, it is, too frequently, too little and too late.[4] This is irresponsible behaviour on the part of the organization's members.[5] Loyalty to their own national interests causes them to act irresponsibly with respect to the aims of the global organization, and to their own purported reason for participating in that organization.

Smaller organizations, associations and groups generally succeed perhaps because they are able to work more effectively than more expansive ones. More compact groups are not too large to consult local authorities, to collaborate and jointly build a vision of some desirable outcome, and to use the know-how and skills of both giving and receiving groups to solve problems and so obtain success. They use, perhaps unwittingly, techniques that every successful enterprise, small or large, uses. They try to involve as many stakeholders as possible in their attempts to improve the situation, and they collectively find ways to overcome or neutralize subsidiary purposes that might distract or confuse by focusing upon achieving their mutual, overriding, purpose. This is responsible behaviour: responsible to those who support and fund their efforts, to the jointly built ideal, and to those who will ultimately benefit from their actions. Collectively building, holding and valuing a clear vision of the desired result, in my opinion, accounts for much of the success achieved by participants in small-scale endeavours.

Of course, visions of an improved future can also be effective on broader scales, and have been used to unite international interests in the past. When England and her allies were battling the Nazis and Fascism in World War II, indecision and bickering between and among the various leaders likely occurred on numerous occasions and at many levels, but these distractions must have been surmounted. The Allies' conviction that they were fighting to maintain a civilized society provided a common vision, which would have given all involved the same purpose. It was the common goal that united, providing an integrative reason to ignore parochial differences.[6]

One last point on the topic of obtaining success in large and small organizations. There are many instances of leaders turning dying organizations into successes. A common factor in all such turnarounds is that the leaders were attempting to achieve some sort of vision—their vision of how the organization might be improved. The vision, of course, was used to define one or more practical statements of purpose, which were then used to determine intermediate goals, plan activities, motivate, measure successes, etc. Accomplishments such as these suggest that organizations (of any size, international as well as local) benefit from being guided by a consolidating vision.

2. Exploitive Excesses

Chapter Ten pointed out that living entails (and is inseparable from) exploiting the environment for resources. Exploiting therefore, at its roots, is constructive. Indeed, the exploitive ability of the creative[7] has improved the quality of life for billions.[8] We should never fear our exploitive nature, but we must manage its excesses.

Over the centuries, we have developed different techniques to curtail humanity's exploitive excesses, each practice yielding an increased measure of civilization as it took effect. For example, in religious doctrine we command ourselves to love one another and covet not. Progressive nations separate the Church's power over the mind from the State's power over the body, to limit the damage that both acting together might do. In the Magna Carta,[9] we placed limits on what a king might bring about. In democratically run countries we expect opposition parties to uncover and expose dishonesty and exorbitance in those we elect to govern. We value freedom of the press for a similar reason. We try to ensure that competition exists in free markets,[10] because monopolies act to satisfy themselves before satisfying their clientele. We develop and enact laws that constrain the ability of individuals or organizations to excessively exploit others or the world's resources. We set up courts, build prisons, and enforce contracts. Stockholders and legislators hold meetings and hear from auditors. Most definitely, we have learned that humanity's ever-present inclination to over-exploit must be controlled, and we have developed specific means by which to do so.

Unfortunately, the world has grown into the idea that the most expedient way for one nation to behave toward another is to "live and let live." Collectively, nations have come to regard other nations as families regard other families who live in separate houses: we avoid meddling in their internal affairs. Even in extreme situations, when excessive exploitation is not being contained and one country, for example, declares war on another, those outside the war zone usually sit on the sidelines and observe, hoping the conflict will be settled without their involvement.[11]

This "hands off" outlook primarily developed because, in the past, the world was large, and distant wars were often little more than topics of detached discussions. However, this is not the case today. Globalization is making the world's conflicts everyone's conflicts.

This view that nations should not intervene in the affairs of other nations is slowly changing. We are coming to hold that ethical atrocities (particularly genocide) must be opposed, even when they occur within the boundaries of another nation. We act (although usually not soon enough) if world opinion seems to support an intervention. Presumably this is because such immoral activity, if unopposed, would affect how we view ourselves, and devalue our concept of who we are and what we believe in. We feel a kind of moral obligation to do something, but can't clearly state why this is so, or what is right for us to do. The universal rationale needed to justify intervention is missing, weak, or unclear.

Section one of this chapter referred to some of the world's major problems, and to the impression that so many seem to be beyond humanity's power to prevent. International organizations like the UN are frequently rendered powerless because membership nations lack the moral authority and supporting wherewithal to require other nations to behave responsibly, as various recent (or current) issues relating to countries such as Rwanda, Iraq and North Korea demonstrate.

It is not impossible to influence the internal behaviour of organizations or individuals within any one nation from outside that nation. The clearest evidence of this is the European Union, where Common Market Standards have been developed that constrain a wide variety of activities in member nations. But other examples abound—Interpol and the International Criminal Court being obvious ones. The key to success for any such endeavour is a willingness to participate, brought about by the recognition that participation offers benefits that outweigh the costs.[12]

The means of curbing exploitive excesses within the boundaries of any one nation noted in the second paragraph of this section were originally developed, directly or indirectly, from that society's collective beliefs in what was "right" and "wrong" behaviour. Frequently, this authority stemmed from ideals espoused by the nation's major religion. But, globally, humanity holds no common religious ideal. A first step in this direction might be the formation of an organization to explore the possible benefits of developing a meta-purpose and defining its specific meaning. Widening the support for such a purpose might become a second step, and using it to unite dissenting nations might follow.

3. Globalization

Globalization's expansion is rampant, and its consequences are being felt everywhere. Money sloshes from shore to shore. Crime syndicates become multinationals. Trade patterns gyrate and jobs spring in and out of existence. Immigration and the media blur cultural boundaries. Terrorists infiltrate and create havoc. The world wide web provides instant gratification. And the future no longer resembles the past.

Globalization disrupts traditional ideas, challenges cultural identity, exposes acts of degenerate human behaviour that few knew about a generation ago, and clouds our self-images. Our national identities are waning. Once, we looked to the past to define what is important; this is becoming harder and harder to achieve and justify. Old information becomes obsolete, old ways become inefficient or ineffective, and old religions seem unable to cope. Conflicts between ideas, cultures and faiths erupt everywhere.

However globalization is not all doom and gloom. To me, it is little more than the industrial revolution being applied world wide. As it was occurring, the industrial revolution was thought by many to be a detrimental development—introducing new ideas, instituting different methods and means, and forcing people to change their traditional manner of earning a living. Nonetheless, few today would deny that it bought great benefits to humankind. In industrial societies, since the 1870's the average life expectancy has nearly doubled, working hours about halved, years of schooling tripled, and the range of consumer goods immeasurably increased.[13]

However, the industrial revolutions that occurred in various countries were simple compared to globalization because each took place within the confines of a nation's traditions and laws. No such regularizing principles govern the globe's activities. So we cope. Each nation does its best to patch up and modify existing structures. Organizations, municipalities and schools educate their employees, citizens and students, showing how different cultures can live together in harmony. Minority opinions are given full weight in crafting legislation. Institutions of global scope such as the International Criminal Court, the World Trade Organization, the World Bank, the European Union, and others of their ilk, are established, adjusted and strengthened. Nations meet to draft international standards, revise trading practices,[14] debate subsidy elimination, enact pollution-limiting laws, constrain land and ocean harvesting, and so on. Immigration policies are developed, money-laundering controls formulated, child labour laws sanctioned, statements of people's rights prepared, and more.

Behind the bustle of activity associated with the machinery of globalization one senses an ideal—the unformulated, perhaps unrecognized, notion of what is best for humankind. This notion should be made clear to all, so that it might properly influence what is occurring. For instance, a global legal system is emerging and, certainly, one global legal system will eventually have to be created—but ad hoc, in disconnected units, as is now being done? Sub-committees of various international organizations are hacking out multiple statements of right and wrong, seemingly unconcerned about the need for consistency and unification. This is producing a series of disjointed compromises (few of which will fit seamlessly together) and creating a tangled playground that high-priced lawyers of the future will have to unravel.

Much the same is happening with respect to trading practices and human rights, to name just two examples. This multiple approach toward global standardization may be expeditious, but it clearly cannot be the best way to proceed. Far better would be to first develop a centralizing universal purpose, one that encapsulates a grand vision of what human life is aiming toward. Working backward from a single desired goal is how supporting sub-goals and "right" actions are properly developed; it is the only way international laws and controls can be linked rationally together.

To grow as living organizations (whether as individuals, companies or as nations) we must provide the condition that life demands—the freedom to exploit available resources. And this condition must be fostered world-wide. Encouraging growth within one's own country while neglecting or suppressing it in others will inevitably generate significant disparities and problems associated with inequality.[15] Global media networks, which show the world what some, but not all, possess, turn this prediction into a certainty.

A world view of "correct" behaviour and a global legal system are important pieces of the solution, but they cannot be forced upon all nations. Perhaps a world federation with appropriate admission standards might be developed, much like the European Union where countries desirous of participating must first arrange their affairs to conform to certain principles. These admission standards, for reasons that were developed in Chapter Ten, must centre upon the provision of freedom for individuals and organizations to exploit, but they must also include democratic measures to control exploitive excesses of any kind, wherever they occur, in any of the member countries.

Concomitantly, if we recognize that every individual is a potential contributor to life's well-being, we must provide as many equalizing social programs as we can afford without jeopardizing the operation of the other (means- and money-generating) conditions. These three ideals—freedom to exploit, democratic control of excesses, and social progress—can be imagined to be corners forming the base of a triangular pyramid. The pyramid's apex represents the vision that guides our decision making—the vision that tells all where we intend to go, and why these three ideals form the base as our foundation. Hopefully, a federation built in this way, and that begins as a relatively small group of nations, might end up becoming a global amalgamation of civilized countries.

History tells us how we have solved problems of excessive exploitation in the past. There is no reason to think that similar solutions can't also be utilized in the future, once we learn how to apply them on a larger scale. Legislation enacted by an elected parliament has typically been our method of control, and is likely to remain so. Thus, global law, seeking to regulate nations, their institutions, and their citizens, enacted by elected representatives, must become a reality before a working global civilization can be fully realized.

But how realistic is it to expect any nation to subordinate itself to an international body of law as matters stand today? The United States, Russia, China, or, for that matter, any nation, would never let troops of an international agency, even one seeking to uphold "global law," intrude upon their institutions without retaliating. In our conventional view of the world, national interests are paramount, and such interference is unthinkable. But it need not always be so.

Willingness to abide by international regulations by all people, at all levels, and in all walks of life, depends upon these individuals believing such precepts to be more important than other desires or demands. A belief that life's continuation—our children's children's future—is more important than our country's shorter-term goals (or those of any of its organizations), may give rise to such a willingness, were it made the bedrock of global law.

Stable societies eventually enact laws which parallel those taught by their nation's significant religion. Globalization can only succeed if the same principle is applied globally. Loyal Rue recognizes this in the concluding chapter of his book, *By the Grace of Guile*. He writes that a "robust moral order" which embodies a "core of (shared) moral values" is needed to attain and sustain social "coherence and stability."[16] Exactly so.

One overall vision, generated by a belief in the importance of some meta-purpose, together with an accompanying definition of what this rationally means (the "universal purpose"), must guide global law-making. Only this kind of focusing foundation can integrate, then ensure wide spread recognition and acceptance of the validity of such legislation.

4. Terrorism

The western world was facing an emerging, potentially devastating, crisis when I first wrote this. Islamist terrorists had hijacked aircraft, destroyed monumental buildings, and killed several thousand innocent people. It was feared that, if not prevented, others of like mind might use chemical, biological or nuclear devices to kill millions. This is still a commonly held concern today in many parts of the world. If, as seems likely, such terrorists are motivated by some insidious, mind-controlling, vision or purpose, then those on the receiving end can expect terrifying times ahead.

Fanatics of any kind are driven to act according to the dictates of their central mental construct.[17] Their construct centres upon a purpose, and that purpose is made real to them by way of a vision of some kind—a vision of an Islamic world, perhaps, or a vision of a paradise that is soon to be theirs. To my mind, we cannot win a war against any well-organized, single-minded, terrorist organization, whose cells lie hidden within different nations of the world, unless we become equally single-minded. To win the fight against any ill-intentioned extremist organization, we must first develop a mental construct that is more powerful than theirs.

The construct used to hold the anti-Taliban coalition together following the September 11th, 2001, tragedy, was the ideal of a civilized world and freedom from terror. To the extent it worked, it did so because the calamity was fresh in everyone's mind, and because the United States is currently powerful enough to enforce its demands. But unfortunately, it was a weak construct and has little power left today, some years after the event. Not all agreed upon what this objective meant, what it required us to do, nor where it would take the coalition nations after the fighting, both overt and covert, had ceased. The world will need a construct more substantial and enduring if it is to maintain its vigilance. A globally respected universal purpose may well provide the guiding beacon civilization so badly needs.

5. Genetics

What will research into human genetics uncover next? Curbing the growth of (or even curing) many kinds of cancer; correcting conditions that may contribute to heart or lung disease; regenerating organs, tissues and bones on demand; pre-screening ova and sperm to remove genes causing hereditary diseases; all, and much more, may be achievable over the next few decades. Even an extra fifty or one hundred years of life expectancy may be on our grandchildren's agenda. These advances promise a wonderfully healthy future.

New possibilities resulting from genetic manipulation unfold every week or two. We routinely manufacture plants, adding disease resistance and increasing vitamin content, changing size, shape, colour, scent, texture, height, growth rate—whatever wished for—to suit any market.[18] We do the same with animals, creating living factories that duplicate top-rate fish, meat, milk, and egg-producers at will.[19] Parents select the sex of their next child. Before long, they will likely be able to pre-determine its size, shape and colour; choose its probable intelligence, artistic aptitude and physical dexterity; and replace genes likely to precipitate diseases or cancers. And, as each gene's role is deciphered by researchers, humanity treads closer to learning how to control the future of life itself.

New knowledge always brings both opportunities and challenges, and some of our past bio-engineering activities have already caused problems. Plants bred to resist herbicides have crossed with others to produce weeds that cannot be eradicated by conventional methods, and fish engineered to double in size have escaped captivity to breed predators that have decimated wild species, to give only two examples. Once produced, life evolves, and a future spent seeking and eradicating escaped and possibly dangerous genetic misfits can be horrifying to imagine.

There are many questions related to genetic manipulation that should be answered before rushing to apply research's findings. Perhaps the most important include: What practices should be permitted? How can the applications of each discovery be controlled? and, Who should benefit?

(The question of who should benefit is not a trivial one. Gene treatments that alleviate or cure diseases are turning out to be very expensive, at least currently. If only the wealthy—individuals or nations—are to benefit, then we will have created yet another worldwide inequity that will likely provoke retaliation.)

Part One noted that rational decisions are made by referring to the purpose to be achieved. In making decisions about gene modification, what are we seeking? Do we declare that all knowledge is important, and thereby allow any manner of research, or do we state that some knowledge can be dangerous and try to regulate certain lines of genetic inquiry? Do we decide that only those who can afford it deserve to benefit from research because it is they who have paid, or do we desire the best for all humanity? Is it morally right to allow prospective parents to make any kind of genetic choice they desire concerning their future children, or should there be some universal standards drafted to protect the interests of the unborn?[20]

And, whatever is decided, how will we ever be able to enforce our decisions?

A whole industry is rapidly developing to take advantage of our ability to control life by manipulating genes. Biomedical companies are springing up everywhere, run by entrepreneurs, staffed by well-trained scientists, and funded by venture capitalists, all eager for recognition or gain. Again, this is natural, not wrong; it is an expression of life exploiting a potential opportunity that may bring success to those that exploit. The problem, as usual, is one of control. How does society control an industry whose products need long-term screening, yet whose markets will clamour and pay for immediate gratification? Nations can legislate, but what good might that be when organizations can move offshore anytime they wish? One nation can act responsibly toward its people, however nothing requires all nations to act responsibly toward all people of the world. And the problems that may arise in this arena could be world-threatening.

Developing new life forms, beneficial or otherwise, is becoming a simple task. But it is next to impossible for an outside agency to detect the covert pursuits of another country until too late, as Russia, Afghanistan, North Korea and other nations, have taught us. There may be several ways to counter such activity, but one stands above others in effectiveness—that derived from individuals within an organization whose moral sensitivity is affronted by suspect endeavours. Disaffected individuals are prime sources of intelligence and counter-activity.[21] Unfortunately, individuals have different concepts of moral correctness.

As noted in Chapter Five, most ideas about morality stem from religions, and most religions have as their focus individual benefit, not that of the community. Consequently, how human activity in one location is affecting distant communities and different life forms is seldom considered until the damage has been done if it is considered at all. A global religion would generate a global awareness and conscience. While developing a global religion is a tall order, as a first and more practical step, developing a universal purpose is possibly the best countermeasure we may currently be able to adopt.

6. Summary

The world is plagued with problems. That a universal purpose may help us to more effectively address some of them may seem a far-fetched idea, but those who lead organizations and nations already know that people will strive to attain a purpose they have come to believe in and consider important. Perhaps the benefits to be obtained from a universal purpose (as sketched in this and the previous chapter) are overstated, but we won't know the true extent of its possibilities until we have tried. As the saying goes, "nothing ventured, nothing gained." Can we really continue the way we have been, letting the winds of chance blow us hither and thither? Should each nation continue acting independently and as they wish? Or are we ready to think collectively as we shape the future our grandchildren will inherit?

If the idea of developing a universal purpose seems implausible, the idea of eventually developing a universal religion based upon this purpose must seem preposterous. How could anyone think that adding a new religion to the existing mix might simplify the situation when religions themselves often contribute to—and may even create—some of the very problems we are trying to solve?

The idea of deliberately trying to develop a new religion might have seemed nonsense when first opening this book. But, if it did so, perhaps this was because so little has been generally understood about how the founders of our various religions obtained their ideas, and why those who followed these leaders created religions. Religions are commonly thought to be based upon ideas that came from a god, but one of this book's purposes has been to show that this may not have been what actually happened.

Religions are social tools, designed and fostered quite deliberately by human beings to ameliorate social ills. What was done with success in the past can be done again with success in the future. Please re-assess my contention that humanity needs a universal religion. Is it not actually quite a plausible suggestion? And would developing a religion that is consistent with our current understanding of reality actually be so difficult to do? I do not think so.

How we might begin to undertake such a task is discussed in the next two chapters.

Chapter Thirteen

Determining Moral Behaviours

Currently our "universal religion-to-be" is an undefined figment; it needs substance to give it shape. Just what is entailed in supporting life's journey to possess omnipotent abilities? What moral injunctions might be imposed by adoption of such a doctrine? This chapter begins a discussion of questions such as these.

Because moral decisions made within a religious framework are intended to further the attainment of a religion's purpose, then moral codes must be logically linked to, and derivable from, this purpose. When this connection is not readily evidenced or traceable, behavioural codes appear to be adrift and may fall open to different interpretations. Moreover, various codes may well be at odds with one another, for without sound links connecting them to the desired purpose any injunction may be embodied. In short, causal relationships are as important in religion as they are in science and for exactly the same reason: the universe is causal, and correct explanations will bear witness to this causality. Similarly, correct behaviour will also be causal—the event sought determines the causal action required (i.e., "correct behaviour" is purpose directed behaviour). Further, our rational minds need the ability to cross-check their analyses, because they have evolved to operate this way through being successful in a rational universe. Causal links provide this ability.

But until the precisely worded universal purpose is defined, we must work with our proposed meta-purpose concept.[1] This renders the process more complex; moral behaviours derived from a meta-purpose rather than a universal purpose will almost always be imprecise, and some may be completely off the mark. This chapter simply serves to illustrate how a "moral" direction might be deduced—a feat that will be more judiciously accomplished once a universal purpose has been defined. Thus, in that they serve only as examples, my derivations in this chapter are of limited practical application other than as a spring board for further discussion.

We again set out from the beginning by restating the facts that form the basis of our current understanding of reality.

1. The Facts of Life

The facts of life presented in earlier chapters can be summarized as follows.

- Life is a process whereby chemical complexes exploit their environments to obtain energy and resources. Living and exploiting are inseparable activities, present at the base level in all life forms. Replication is a secondary function that (if sexual, rather than simply division) facilitates diversity. Diversity helps life to survive in a changing environment.
- The elemental nature of life's underlying process (chemical processes exploiting their environment) implies that it can, and will, arise anywhere, whenever suitable conditions exist. Once begun, life continues until all useable energy differences are exhausted; ceasing prior to this point would simply leave niches where new life could arise and evolve.
- Sporadic mutations that improve or have no negative effect on life's ability to successfully exploit environmental resources are carried through into subsequent generations.
- Living organisms add new structures and cell processes to those they already possess, making entities more complex as time goes by. This creates an evolutionary trend toward intelligence because, to become beneficial, compounded body augmentations require more elaborate controlling abilities. Furthermore, since energy-exploitation becomes more difficult as energy resources are consumed, the very act of living creates conditions that necessitate enhanced problem-solving ability. That is, declining resources (and challenges of any kind) beget increased mental ability or intelligence.
- Life learns how to exploit and control its environment by perceiving, investigating, understanding, then utilizing the relationships that exist between objects and events. This is possible because the universe is causally constructed.
- Causality's chain seems to break, from an insider's point-of-view, at the physical and temporal boundaries of our universe. Internal causality cannot be connected to anything external to this universe because the properties of that which lies beyond (if anything does exist outside) cannot be understood from a position within.

There are many other important aspects to the nature of life and the universe but those listed above will suffice for the purposes of this chapter.

2. Behaviours Rewarded by Life

One vitally important fact is missing from the above list: humans are not the whole of life. With the meta-purpose we have chosen, it is our relationship to life itself that determines "moral" behaviour. Thus, we must carefully examine what this relationship entails.

Humans are just one species, one twig of a giant tree, and this places us in a rather precarious position. As a twig, we are not only beset by the storms and upheavals that continuously affect and change our physical environment, we are further subjected to the demands that the tree itself places upon us.

Life is our father and mother. Life produced us. It nurtures us, and it will absorb us once we die. Life creates and maintains our support system, and structures much of our playground. Life itself is the totality[2] to which we owe allegiance, and to which we should be paying most attention. Living life—not some imaginary after-death life—is our true supersystem.

Knowing this, I ask myself what subsystem behaviours might such a supersystem[3] reward, and what might it punish?[4]

To my way of thinking, the following statements are self-evident in the context of the supersystem "Life." (The word "Life," although from our perspective is currently constrained to that which exists on our planet, has been capitalized in several places throughout the remainder of the book to signify that the context applies wherever life exists.)

- Subsystems (including humans) will be tolerated by their encompassing supersystem (Life) as long as they do not hinder its continuance. (For instance, plants will provide oxygen and convert sunlight into energy forms that we and other living entities can consume—as long as we do not eliminate them.)
- Life "punishes" entities that disrupt its existence or growth. (For instance, discharging pollutants diminishes the abundance and variety of food producers, eventually creating a future that becomes one of subsisting rather than of plenty.)
- Life "rewards" entities that foster its spread and development. (For instance, enlarging rain forest acreage increases the abundance and variety of food and other resources that it supplies.)

(To best appreciate these points, think of the long-term implications of any endeavour, human or otherwise, that impacts upon some part of the ecosystem, then imagine what might happen if the scope and depth of this impact were to be greatly increased. Projecting to the limit often clarifies what may well be happening, unnoticed, on a smaller scale or behind the scenes.)

There are likely several other truths about the relationship between humans (or any species) and our supersystem that deserve to be uncovered and discussed, but those stated above are sufficient to move to the next step.

3. Behaviours that Enhance Life

When I consider our relationship to the supersystem Life as we experience it on Earth, I find that Life is actually behaving very much in a traditional "god-like" manner. It is effectively "judging" what its subsystems—including humans—do, and it subsequently rewards or punishes their behaviour. These rewards and punishments are meted out continuously, in various forms and locations, over short and long time-spans. Humans are learning to recognize these repercussions, but we still have a long way to go before we learn to respect—or even to expect—Life's judgements.

However, we can choose to behave in a manner that allows us to benefit from our relationship to our supersystem Life. For instance, we can reduce the harm we inflict on our supersystem by ensuring our discharges are benign. This would precipitate the reward of having more resources—food and oxygen, for instance—made available as greater diversity (and numbers) of other life forms survive and thrive. Or, as another example, we can increase rather than decrease the world's rain forest coverage, thus increasing the variety and number of benefits-to-life that accompany biological diversity. We can choose to behave in such ways (and many of us do), but the activities of numerous others, some for profit some simply to survive, are hastening the demise of significant portions of Life's supersystem.[5]

The reasons humans do not all act in ways that benefit Life are many and varied, but two are particularly significant to our discussions. First, as previously stated, we are only just recognizing, and do not yet fully comprehend, the fact that humans are simply a processing subsystem, subordinate to and dependant upon, a larger system. Second, failing to recognize our dependency, few of us value it appropriately.

There are also degrees of valuing. We can give a wary nod to an idea, or we can embrace it wholeheartedly. Thus, we could pay lip-service to the idea of Life being our supersystem and say, "sure, I think this idea is important," but carry on as before—and nothing changes. Or we could say, "yes, the ecosystem is very important; I'll be careful not to pollute," and start, for example, participating in the community's recycling program—producing a little change. Or we could say, "let me consider more fully this relationship between humans and Life," then seek others already active in this area to investigate what can be done. In the latter situation, actions having greater impact might result. The degree to which we value the relationship between ourselves and Life affects the future that all life (not just our descendants) will experience on this planet. And while our effects on life's future are typically minimal, the ramifications of humanity's actions are increasingly far-reaching.

Well, let's think about what insights might be gained were we to recognize that our supersystem's journey toward eventual possession of omnipotent abilities is the very same journey that all species as subsystems are undertaking, albeit that each will travel only an infinitesimal part of the way.

If we were to regard Life's continued evolution as an activity well worth supporting, and, particularly, if we were to use this "meta-purpose" to define the universal purpose that guides our moral decision making, then a whole new range of behaviours would become valued. We can use the ideas listed in section two above to educe what these behaviours would be. We can even make moral judgements and infer what types of activities should be considered "right" and which should be considered "wrong" within the confines of such a value system.

When I attempt this, I find the following.

- It is right to learn, to support others' learning, to try to understand how and why the universe and its contents are the way they are—because Life lives and advances by learning and by putting this knowledge to use.
- It is right to pass on this knowledge, to store it for future generations, to link knowledge together in theories, to find new avenues of thought—because Life has evolved intelligence as a helping mechanism, and knowledge is the food that nurtures capacity, intelligence and understanding.
- It is right to make use of this knowledge, to expand our limits, our control and our ability to exploit—because Life lives, grows, reproduces and becomes richer in every aspect, by using the energy and resources it has learned to extract from its environment.
- But it is equally right, and necessary, to control excessive exploitations—because these harm Life's future. Determining where to draw the line between helpful exploitation and harmful

excesses is, and always will be, a difficult undertaking, but one which must be made a priority if civilization is to continue.
- And, it is right to help other humans and other life forms—because Life's progress may benefit from the contributions of others as much as, or even more than, it does from ours.

These behaviours (and many others, of course) would be "right" for any living entity in this universe to practice, simply because actions of this kind help Life to actualize its potential. In response, the supersystem "rewards" subsystems for supporting its operations. That such actions are also "right" for humans to practice because they help each of us attain our own potential is likely to be secondary to Life's progress (although it usually is very important to our personal well-being). That which helps Life, helps us. The order of importance must be this way around, not the other, because humans are a subordinate system. What are to be considered "right" actions, in the logical system of morals we are developing, must always be determined by putting Life's advancement, not human advancement, first.

With this process of reasoning in place, new behavioural boundaries (i.e., rights and wrongs) might be established. Some of those newly "recognized" above as being "right" to practice have been ignored or even discouraged within traditional religions, although others have always been important. For instance, before now there has not been a rational explanation of why teaching and learning are so important, such "right" functions.[6] Furthermore, just as we can now clearly judge learning to be right, we can now immediately state why it is wrong to restrict knowledge, to burn books, to tell lies, to spread hatred, to prevent or limit the development of other life forms.

If, as a community, we were to adopt the practice of rationally deducing moral behaviour from the purpose we elect to support, we would, after sustained effort, eventually be able to justify our morality to any intelligent being (including those beyond our planet). Our existing moral systems would probably become subsumed within the rational one, and some components of the former might in due time simply fade away.[7]

Any rational being can deduce a moral code from a statement of desired purpose together with knowledge of the environment containing the criteria a successful solution must meet. If enough of humanity chose to value the living environment more than any possible dead one, then we could combine efforts to logically educe what behaviours should be called "morally wrong" or "morally right." Given enough time, we should be able to formulate a set of moral statements, each element of which would be traceable back to its origins. This latter feature is important, as it ensures that each assertion is adjustable should new information or understanding make correction necessary.[8] And we would know what is to be gained, both immediately and in the distant future, by acting in accordance with these values.

Until we reach this stage, our beliefs regarding which behaviours are "right" or "wrong" stem only from what we have been taught by our parents, teachers, or religion's authorities. That is, until we embrace logically deduced moralities, there is no rational way to independently verify the truth of such statements, and no straight-forward method to incorporate changes resulting from improved knowledge. (Christians, for instance, accept the authority of the Commandments on faith. These cannot be modified even if circumstances should so merit.)

With a guiding universal purpose statement and its derived set of moral codes in place, it would no longer be necessary to separate religious thought from rational or scientific thought. Causal links and logical deductions could be made in both domains, with the two becoming inter-dependent and mutually supporting. The data, their sources, the need to inquire, and the methods used when investigating, would become identical for science and religion, unifying these two great endeavours. Effectively, they become one and the same search for reality's truth.

Moreover, we would know that any intelligent living entity, anywhere in the universe, would be able to uncover rational reasons to value and support Life reaching its full potential, and thus develop the same ethical standards as we support. Rationality provides the means to develop a truly universal religion.

4. Determining Moral Behaviour

Even these first few steps in our exploration of a possible future morality move us far enough along to begin an examination of some of the contentious moral problems we are facing in the world today. I will try to illustrate how rational connections might be made between a few current ethical issues and a desire to support Life's continued evolution. The examples I have chosen to discuss include killing, some aspects of personal freedom, and genetic manipulation.

But, before we can begin, several cautionary points need be made. First, possessing the "potential to contribute" to Life's advancement needs much careful consideration when exploring moral positions. It is possible to state that all living things have this, and that their potential to contribute should never be limited. But this creates an impossible situation—eating kills what is consumed and moving crushes entities underfoot. Any kind of exploitation reduces potential in exploited arenas (raising it in others), but, as discussed, life and exploitation cannot be separated. In like vein, it could be argued that no individual's action should be curtailed[9] because any action may hold the future possibility of "contributing" to Life's advancement. "Potentiality" is clearly a very important concept, and the meaning, scope and depth of this term need defining and limiting before any significant work on moral behaviour can be advanced. I have mostly ignored the importance of any "potential" contribution in the following subsections (largely because I have not the ability nor inclination to examine such a difficult issue) and leave it as a task that others might perform.

Second, the discussions that follow attempt to show how a code of moral behaviour that relates to human interactions might be developed. It does not explore how humans might appropriately behave towards animals, plants, or other non-human life forms. Certainly, any moral code that proposes supporting Life's evolutionary journey should detail appropriate behaviour toward any and all kinds of life—more work left for others to consider.

Third, accepting Life's possible evolution to become oB as the meta-purpose we support (made useful by sculpting from it a definition of a universal purpose) means that decisions would be made toward furthering the attainment of that meta-purpose. We would value new discoveries, new knowledge, new understandings, and the increased ability to control each might bring, because each paves tiny sections of the highway to Life's future. Currently, we all "contribute" to helping life achieve its "meta-purpose," and we do so never learning the ultimate significance of our contribution. (In fact, any lengthy periods during which we do not contribute, may, in some of us, create the feeling that our lives were becoming meaningless.) But once we had decided to use the meta-purpose to guide our morality, our "moral duty" becomes much clearer; we would know we were acting irresponsibly whenever we behaved in a manner that undermined its attainment.

Thus it would appear that one takes on certain responsibilities when adopting Life's meta-purpose as one's own.[10] The notions of "responsibility" and "contributing" lie at the heart of our attempt to define a moral code and I will be referring to them from time to time below. However, these terms should also be carefully defined—another difficult task that perhaps others might undertake.

Lastly, teams of experts working jointly on individual issues would be needed to develop rational connections and useable codes of behaviour once a universal purpose had been defined; the subsections below are simply the product of my mind's undeniably biased constructs. They are included to demonstrate how a desire to support the attainment of some purpose might be used to determine "right" (and therefore also "wrong") behaviour. It is clear that this determination must be possible, as everyone of us does exactly this each time we decide how to act to solve problems standing in the way of completing our daily tasks. However, it will likely soon be equally clear that I am not the person to join any of those hypothetical teams!

Now to the examples.

4.1. Killing

The rationale for stating that it would be wrong to kill an individual is easy to state: any individual's actions may contribute to the objective of supporting Life's continued evolution, thus each life is valuable and should be preserved. Killing an individual prevents that individual from contributing (discounting the body's store of nutrients and energy that inevitably recycle and do contribute). However, this seemingly simple premise hides a few surprises, the first stemming from how we define an individual.

Two separate cells, the sperm and ovum, before joining to form a zygote do not constitute an individual. They each contain part of the potential to form an individual,[11] but they have not yet become an individual. Our new morality would therefore likely state that there is nothing "wrong" in killing these cells. And life routinely does exactly that—our bodies produce many more sperm and ova than are needed or used.

An embryo, then a fetus before birth, is also a "potential" individual, not yet able to contribute directly to Life's evolution (although it may very well be inspiration for some of the contributions made by its parents). Thus, our rational new religion would probably rule that it is not wrong to kill developing embryos at any stage.[12]

This may be its rational declaration, but human emotions would most often have it otherwise. Few parents would want to harm or kill their children-to-be. It would feel emotionally wrong to do so.

Our new religion may even come to the same conclusion about killing infants, as well as those individuals that no longer possess the ability to contribute, by arguing along the following lines.

Newborns are potential individuals, not individuals as we typically understand fully developed adults to be. Newly born babies exist as separate beings, having wonderfully formed bodies but relatively empty minds. Empty, that is, of most of the stored memories, links and thoughts that will rapidly form to produce an individual in its own right. Our new rational religion would likely not call a physical body, mostly empty of mind, an individual, and would probably not state that it is "wrong" to kill such an entity. But, of course, we do state that it is wrong.

We denounce killing newborns for emotional, cultural, and legal reasons. It feels wrong to kill children of any age, and the law in recognition of this usually declares that newborns become individuals at birth. Clearly we will continue to state that killing newborns is wrong, but it is possible that our new religion may not actually state that it is "morally wrong" to do so (for instance, if "potential to contribute" is given minimal weight by the religion's developers).

A similar argument applies to the way we regard mature individuals. In the grand view of Life's endeavour, the individual is everything and nothing. It is everything while it is contributing to Life's journey; it is nothing when it has made its contribution. During our lifetime, we all, knowingly or unknowingly, strive to support Life's journey. We all do our best to learn, to grow, to create, to procreate, to feel that we are living a productive and meaningful life. These are innate behaviours that are carried out daily—part and parcel of being a living entity. We may even accept them as responsibilities. But, as we end our days, with our physical and mental powers deteriorating, we become free of this duty to contribute. Our new moral code is likely to state that at this stage, those who so choose have every right to seek death when they are ready for it, be it self-awarded or assisted.

The same contention might well apply when a person's brain becomes damaged or debilitated by disease or accident. As long as there is the slightest chance that the individual will recover, to be able to contribute once more, then our new moral system would probably rule that it is wrong to kill or to sanction suicide for that individual. But this ruling could change as conditions worsen, as death becomes imminent, or as living becomes unbearably painful. For such individuals who will never be further able to contribute, our new religion would probably state that euthanasia is not morally wrong. However, as we may know, even under such circumstances it is next to impossible to kill someone we love. Our emotions (quite apart from our laws) make it very hard to hasten their death. But our new religion would now possibly offer consolation, not condemnation, were we to do so.

Using similar arguments, our new religion would probably tell us that it is irrational to simply declare abortion or euthanasia wrong, and also that there are times when we may morally allow compassion to rule.

Thus we begin to see that morality would likely differ from what it is now. Our new religion would clearly separate rational, emotional and legal arguments, allowing us to frankly examine the contribution each makes. It would open the way for our old, sometimes simplistic, sometimes cruel, laws to be reconsidered, and perhaps, if thought necessary, eventually modified. (Indeed, its construction would force us to reassess our understanding of what it is to be a thinking human).

On the surface, our new religion may seem hard and cold, ruling by logic first, and only allowing emotions to be considered second. But our proposed religion must be so constructed because the universe is so constructed, and because life evolves in obedience to the laws of physics that govern and define the universe and all its contents. While animal behaviour is largely emotionally governed—animalistic—because it has no other option, humans have gained the ability to be objective. Humans, in following their minds' attempts to think rationally, also try to behave rationally, and the two foremost dimensions of humanity, emotion and logic, are often at war in the effort. Our new religion, if developed rationally, should allow us to separate, then balance, emotion and reason, giving us tools to assess both before making any decision. We would no longer be commanded by dogma, emotions or beliefs, but by logical rationality. Surely, this is what our modern minds are asking us to institute when they react against the occasional religious (or parental, legal, employment, or other) requirement that seems irrational.

There are other "wrongs" to reconsider, for instance, the rationale for stating that birth control is morally wrong. If circumstances dictate that additional progeny will harm, rather than help, Life's continued evolution on this planet, then birth control would necessarily be considered by our new religion sensible and "right." What value to Life would there be in saturating an overpopulated environment with individuals if nothing remains for them but an arduous search for nutrients and niches where precious few are to be found? When would such individuals ever find the time, or develop the ability, to contribute? Of course, there will always be many outstanding individuals who will do exactly that in any population. Perhaps one percent, or, say, five, would surmount their disadvantageous surrounding conditions. Birth control, some might contend, would have denied Life their contributions. But that argument ignores the possibility that, if this world was less densely and more equitably populated, then a great many more than one or five percent would be in a position to contribute. Of course, it is not simply a matter of quantity, it is more one of quality. But, again, there are many more opportunities for quality to emerge in an educated and liberated environment than there are in a poverty-stricken or hopelessly overcrowded one.

(The overwhelming need for world population controls is one of the implications of a report written by Mathis Wackernagel et al.[13] This report discusses the compilation and findings of human "ecological footprint" statistics [the planetary acreage needed to sustain human life at its current rate of resource usage]. Two of its findings are particularly relevant to this discussion. First, that humans, on average, expend thirty per cent more than nature is able to sustain (and this figure is increasing rather than decreasing). And, second, that the resources of five more Earths would be needed for everyone to live at the average current North American rate. Clearly, the majority can never live as North Americans now live. But all could, should they so desire, were there fewer for the planet to nourish. One billion people is about this planet's limit, if the North American way of life is universally accorded. However, the world's population is currently over six billion, and could reach ten billion in thirty years.[14])

Another issue to contemplate is capital punishment. As above, the criteria used to weigh the merits of this practice would need to be reconsidered. Under the rationality of our new religion, anyone able to "contribute" should be allowed to live. While we may want retribution for heinous crimes committed, this is an emotional, not reasoned, reaction. However, if an individual was clearly unable to "contribute," if serial killing (for example) was his or her sole motivating interest, then there may be no rational reason (nor religious, for our religion would be rational) to let that individual continue living. The problem then, as always, becomes one of judging whether or not enough is known to be certain about the true state of affairs.[15]

Our proposed new religion tells us why individuals are important—because each individual has the potential to make a difference. He or she can uncover new facts, find new linkages and applications, discover new meanings, and perhaps augment Life's ability to control. This is why each and every individual matters. Embryos and fetuses before birth cannot contribute in this manner, infants in their first few months, and some individuals, perhaps in the closing days of their life or if criminally insane, cannot contribute. In these circumstances our new religion would likely tell us that killing is not morally wrong (although it is unlikely to decree that it is morally right). Our new doctrine would probably conclude that such individuals are of no relevance as they are and offer no guidance at all. (This, at least, would free us from religious censure if we choose to follow the dictates of our emotions.)

4.2. Personal Freedom

Individuals have to be free to explore and exploit their environment if they are to maximize their ability to contribute to Life. This suggests that the freedom of individuals should not be restricted in any way (provided their actions are not restricting the ability of others to contribute, of course). And this implies that individuals should be free to act in ways that might harm themselves.

The over-riding necessity for individual freedom affects how a rational religion might view private activities. For instance, individuals abusing drugs may be acting irrationally, and they may eventually suffer for doing so, but our new religion would likely not consider this action morally "wrong." Who knows what discoveries, what new insights and understandings, might be realized were a drug-induced state to open neural channels routinely by-passed in everyday thinking? (And there have been many instances when drugs have enhanced an artist's creativity, and others now reap benefits from that individual's experience.[16])

Many countries legislate against the recreational use of drugs. Clearly we need laws that protect immature individuals from harm but legislation itself will not accomplish this end. Declaring drug use to be illegal simply hands drug control (and its resulting profits) to criminal organizations.[17] Their activities simply make matters worse,[18] as prohibition tried to teach us.

Our new religion would state that individuals must have the freedom to experiment knowledgeably and to face the ensuing consequences. This is how every animal learns: they act, analyze the results of their action, then modify, cease, or repeat the action, learning and developing physical and mental skills as they do so. Education, not legislation, properly limits the harm that ill-considered experimentation can do. That occasionally people die through their own careless actions is distressing, but we cannot logically expect this to never happen, even were we able to foresee and forbid all possible harmful actions. We need to teach, for example, why wearing bicycle helmets and seat belts is important, not legislate then spend money, time and resources enforcing their use. Laws and their enforcement simply remove degrees of the self-responsibility that all individuals must possess if they are to mature.[19]

4.3. Genetic Manipulation

Under our new system of belief, all avenues of research would likely be inherently "good" and "right" because Life uses knowledge to gain control of needed resources, and control opens new avenues of development and leads to evolutionary enhancements. Of course, new knowledge carries with it the potential for doing wrong, just as every iota of understanding has always done. But it also carries with it an equal and opposite potential for doing right.

Genes control almost everything in nature, from behaviour (fidelity, for instance, has been transferred from prairie voles to mice by gene manipulations at Emory University), to longevity (the average lifespan of a fruit fly has been doubled, from 37 to 70 days, with no apparent diminishment of life quality, by rearranging genes). Since many genes that perform basic functions are identical across different species (including between plants and animals) it will not be long before scientists will be able to manipulate human genes towards progeny exhibiting almost any trait desired.[20]

Governments are grappling with where to draw the line when it comes to conducting genetic research. Some state that, for example, organs such as replacement ears or hearts may be grown from embryonic stem cells otherwise destined never to develop; others decry this. Most are inclined to say that embryonic cells should not be deliberately grown to obtain stem cells,[21] presumably because they do not want to be forced to decide exactly when human life begins, or to reopen debates related to abortion.[22] Querying the universal purpose definition should advise us how to proceed.

Almost all countries, at the moment, seem to contend that cloning humans is wrong, but I do not understand why. We have never hesitated to clone other animals and plants; how, precisely, are humans different? The desire to support the attainment of a universal purpose should help societies determine the most appropriate standpoint to take. And, as has been pointed out earlier, if a single global law is needed to simplify enforcement, then our best chance of defining one that might be respected has to be through the development of a supported universal purpose.

Xenotransplantation (i.e., transferring cells or tissues from one species to another) will probably be considered dangerous for many years to come, on practical rather than moral grounds. Viral fragments from one species can combine with genes in another and have devastating consequences. For example, tissues preserved in Alaskan permafrost of a woman who died from the Spanish flu epidemic (which killed over forty million people in 1918-19) showed when analyzed that the flu was a virus formed when sections of two genes, one normally occurring in humans, the other normally occurring only in pigs, somehow became spliced together.

Another issue that currently presents moral challenges is gene patenting. Universities and organizations conducting biological research have been patenting gene-altered plants and animals for decades.[23] Clearly, private investors and venture capitalists would generally not fund research if there were no prospects of financial gain. Sales of any resulting products or technologies return funds to investors, pay for past and future research, buy needed equipment, etc., but only while patents protect a company's proprietary rights. This money comes from those who can afford to buy the product, and therein lies the rub. Drugs that help AIDS sufferers, for example, are expensive to create, and this effectively restricts their distribution and use to wealthy countries. This places two organizing systems, an economic one and a moral one, in direct conflict.

The world's economic decisions are made to realize economic goals; the world's moral decisions are made to realize religious goals. This dichotomy prompts demonstrations of protest when monetary policy conferences or the like are held. Much discord and conflict would be avoided if the two value systems could be integrated.

Economic goals are simple to understand and usually simple to compute—the bottom line says it all. Religious goals, on the other hand, are many, complex and varied. They also fight each other, vying for precedence. If our various religious objectives could be united to present one overarching goal (perhaps under the banner of a universal religion), then its priority versus the priority of an economic goal might be more readily assessed. Clearly no unification of moral and economic goals can be achieved while the current situation prevails.

Summary

Please keep in mind that my thoughts have been sketched here simply to demonstrate how a value system might be later deduced from the desire to support Life's continued evolution. Let me be the first to say that the logic I display above is likely weak, and probably non-productively biased by personal constructs. Such deliberations should properly be carried out by experts, wise representatives of a variety of disciplines and communities, not just a single neophyte like myself.

Early theologians spent much time thinking about moral problems and formulating faith-based solutions. These satisfied the needs of the less-rational societies that existed in times past. Computer-driven cultures (that are beginning to dominate the world) crave a more logical moral code.

Developing a rational moral code of behaviour is clearly very difficult, but it is not impossible. Development can begin just as soon as a single supreme universal purpose has been defined and adopted.

I do not expect widespread acceptance of, nor even interest in, the idea that the world is ripe for a different kind of religion. But I do anticipate some level of interest, because discussions of a number of matters related to the theme of this book are common throughout the media today. My hope is that a few individuals, a small but critical mass,[24] will act or react in a way that benefits civilization.

A few ways they might do so are discussed in the next chapter.

Chapter Fourteen

A Universal Religion

From meta-purpose, to universal purpose, to a universal religion: what a train of thought!

Our meta-purpose remains just an undefined vision of what Life might eventually become. "Supporting Life's journey to become oB" may well be an emotionally appealing activity worth adopting when considering behavioural alternatives. However, it will not serve as the guiding purpose the world needs to craft legislation of use in international courts of law. For that a well-defined "universal purpose" is needed.

A universal purpose is also required if a nation-guiding moral code is to be developed. Such a code would provide the moral authority international bodies need if they are to serve humanity well as we move into a very uncertain future.

This chapter suggests steps that might be taken to build a universal religion from the yet-to-be-developed universal purpose. Some might consider that a powerfully worded and valued purpose should suffice to guide collective global decision making, but this is not how I contend the mind operates. As we saw in Part Two, the mental Construct that a belief develops can preclude alternative ways of thinking, thus all true believers of any doctrine will always claim that the commandments of their faith override any national or international law. Something labelled a "universal religion" may come to be regarded as worthy of being equally obeyed. My hope is that some day members of all religions might take the time to consider what was being said, if it were being expressed by a sufficient number of well-respected and influential people all claiming to follow a "universal religion."

Again, the "universal religion" being proposed here is not something to be force fed to anyone. It should be seen as a companion to other religions, concerned about and dealing with the welfare of community and life, but having nothing to say about any individual after-life beliefs. Eventually, however, I do think that the rationality of the proposed universal religion will lead it to replace the less objective religions that we have inherited, because humankind is itself becoming more rational. Perhaps this transition will occur sometime in the future, however, not in this century, I suspect.

Elements of this chapter trouble me. Section two seems to be promoting disorder, although that is not my intent. Yet this whole book would lose some of its possible value if it did not suggest ways to turn its abstract ideas into concrete results. I temper my anxieties by remembering that there are many who know much more than I about promoting a cause in a sensible manner; they would be the ones to consult when action is sought, not me.

1. Characteristics of a Universal Religion

In order to help solve problems of the kind noted earlier, our new religion must possess certain features.

- The religion has to be suited to our times. Real and relevant issues must be recognized and addressed in a practical manner.
- The religion must be rationally based. Modern-day living is founded upon knowledge discovered by rational thinking; to begin irrational speculation when developing a religion would simply not be sensible. In crafting our definition of a universal purpose to guide development of a new religion, the definition must assume as little as possible, be as logical as possible, and be based upon the best of current knowledge.
- Our choice of religious purpose must satisfy the same criteria that all religious purposes must fulfill—universality and timelessness. To have ubiquitous appeal it must be universally meaningful and applicable. To survive and guide our way into the future it must be soundly based and have longevity. It must, in effect, apply to and connect not just humanity, but all organisms living at any time and in any galaxy, just as some existing religions intimate their ideologies apply.
- Our new religion must embrace and support our emotional needs as well as our rational needs. We are creatures of both worlds, responding to feelings and concepts of spirituality that our body's emotions generate, as well as to the logic upon which our minds operate and thrive. Our religion's vision needs aspects of both dimensions—music, art, feelings, emotions, awe and wonder must heighten and colour, and coexist with, rational truth.[1]
- The guidelines and teachings of the new religion must be logically derivable from its purpose. If, to guide our moral

decision making, a universal purpose is indeed formulated from Life's "meta-purpose," then the guidelines we later develop must all emanate from the desire to achieve this purpose. Thus, we cannot, for example, simply proclaim an unfounded "it-is-wrong-to-xxxxx" commandment. An analysis of the links between the consequences of any particular action and the religion's overall purpose must clearly and logically show why each behaviour is deemed "wrong" or "right." We are developing an abstract environment which increasingly rational minds in the future will explore to its limits; if not rationally built, then this environment will collapse.

- Our new religion cannot be developed by only one individual—there is too much to construct and too much at stake. Its development must be crafted by many, particularly those who possess relevant knowledge: theologians and scientists, managers and workers, people who practice many disciplines, those who tread many lands, and members of many cultures. It must begin as it must continue, involving all who want to contribute to the future welfare of the supersystem Life that supports us.
- The religion's development cannot end. Being knowledge-based and rationally structured, its tenets must continuously be amended as our knowledge base enlarges. Only our assumed meta-purpose, if properly composed, should resist the need for change. It should be a statement that lasts forever.
- Ways must be found to separate religious power from legislated power, and legislated power must take precedence. The mental constructs that religions build may overrule logic in the minds of some and create fanatics; it must be made impossible for such individuals to seize control. (And legislated power should be refereed by the electorate, for it is individuals who contribute to Life's continuation and evolution, not the state.) When disputes arise, such as the economic vs. moral dilemma that patent laws create, the populace must decide how they wish to proceed if democracy is to be preserved.[2]
- The new religion, for reasons that apply to all institutions, must incorporate defences against being exploited. Open debate and welcomed questioning, transparency, frequent internal and external audits, auditors that change every few years, leaders that are regularly replaced, and precautionary measures of many other kinds must be developed and maintained. The power commanded by a position within the hierarchy serving the needs of a universal religion will always attract some who would position personal gain over Life's gain.

- The envisaged universal religion would not replace or usurp existing religions. It is proposed as an umbrella doctrine, developed to cover gaps that existing faiths may leave open. (The religion most closely resembles a universal "Hippocratic Oath." This oath does not prevent any one in the medical profession from being Christian, Muslim, Hindu or otherwise. It says nothing about the afterlife and little about God, but it does say much of what needs to be said about how to conduct oneself in an ethical manner.)
- A universal religion would not unite the world to form one nation, just as other religions do not unite individuals to form one entity. There is as great a need for singularity among nations as there is for individuality among individuals. Life's advancement is fostered by diversity; uniformity merely sustains life in between advances. (For this reason, any universal religion must accept the existence of other "universal religions." But that is another story—there are no others at the moment, and the future will take care of that need, when the time arises!)

Doubtlessly our new religion could have many other characteristics, but the above list should suffice for our purposes.

2. Developing a Universal Religion

Some individuals are likely more ready than others to help found a new religion. Possibly those who have already drifted away from their god, but feel the loss. Or, perhaps, those who may think that a God exists or existed, but one that intends Life to fend for itself. Or people who think that no such Being exists, yet are distressed by life's apparent meaninglessness. Or even those who think that their religion lacks the criteria they need to make some of today's moral choices and seek something supplemental or an alternative. This section suggests how such individuals might work together to fill some of these gaps.

Again, please keep in mind that I am not trying to overthrow any existing religion. This discussion that follows is simply to explore whether people of the world see any need for the kind of religion this book is proposing. One day, perhaps in the not-too-distant future, some kind of rational religion might become appealing, but I suspect that the time may not yet be ripe. Fertilizing humanity's mental soil in the hope that something might eventually grow is all that might occur if some of what follows were to be attempted. This alone, I think, is worth the effort.

Before continuing, let's recall why I think a new religion may one day be needed. Significant problems periodically threaten world affairs, and current institutions seem inadequate to address them.

Some likely solutions will eventually require expropriating national autonomy, subordinating it to world-wide authority, but there is currently no substantial authority of this kind. A massive blow, such as that dealt to the United States by the terrorist actions on September 11th, 2001, is needed before nations feel they have the moral authority to unite to counter further threats. This feeling soon evaporates, however, for only the recipients of the blow carry the loss constantly in their minds. And, as Chapter Twelve noted, many other threats, current and potential, practical but often moral, need some degree of global consensus to be effectively countered. An international court might be given the legal authority to enforce international laws, but there are likely to be many situations (population control, embryonic stem cell use, or euthanasia, perhaps) where some degree of additional moral authority would be needed. If developed, a universal religion of the kind discussed in this book might make such moral authority permanently available, thus legitimizing the early examination of such problems and perhaps preventing them from becoming pandemic.

Keep in mind that, while the premise of this universal religion is simple, the process of developing it is certainly not. Indeed, the endeavour will be fraught with challenges, distractions and setbacks (not the least of which will come from those who oppose such a new tenet).[3] Every stage of its development will therefore require tremendous dedication, perseverance, patience and altruism.

The remainder of this section assumes, based upon the reasoning given in earlier chapters, that acting to "support Life's continued evolution toward becoming a god-like entity or oB" is the most appropriate meta-purpose for rational people to adopt and transform into a universal purpose. Given this, perhaps something like the following "hierarchy of action" might feasibly lead to the eventually realization of a universal religion.

Individuals: May have read this book or may already be thinking along similar lines. Want to correct problems that impact upon our future, and will probably already be in contact and working with others of like mind. May already be working in organizations to achieve related ends.[4] Probably know other individuals active in parallel endeavours who will unite in support if one common purpose can be found. Already using websites and the internet to share ideas and to influence others.

Realize that the magnitude and number of significant world problems necessitates a proportionally large and long-term effort towards change. May be discussing the need to unite with other groups and individuals. May be drafting meta- or universal purpose statements and seeking consensus using Delphi survey methods[5] or equivalents. May act as website masters, developing, linking and maintaining relevant sites, chat groups, bulletin boards, etc.

Working groups: Would want to educate one another. Would need to formulate sub-purposes to guide joint efforts. Would want to unite like-minded regional, national and international groups and efforts. Would need the support of people with vision, passion and ideas, as well as energy, money and influence. Would seek the cooperation of any and all organizations, particularly religions and those currently involved in formulating or promoting universally applicable moral standards or ethical principles.

Would constantly strive to educate the public and new members. Would finalize the definition of the universal purpose and draft statements of moral codes and ethical principles derived from this purpose. Would refine these statements as groups in different nations (particularly those of different cultures and faiths) seek to meld.

Would utilize the best analytic and strategic techniques. Would outline desired scenarios for years ahead as guides to develop strategies, plans and tactics; such descriptions would also convey to all a vision of the kind of future being anticipated, so inviting discussion, feedback and revision. (See "Multi-year Targets," a postscript to this chapter, for speculations about possible long-term goals.) Would attempt to foresee possible setbacks and develop contingency plans, etc. Would provide intelligent guidance to the whole movement, yet remain particularly close to the grassroots level by ensuring a steady exchange of personnel, and by limiting how long any one person may serve in any role.

Action groups: Would use their influence to educate the populace, and formulate approaches that would gain the support of organizations and governments in all of the world's nations. Would find ways to respect and work within existing laws; would reject and help to prosecute those who harm others or damage property under the guise of participating in the larger cause. Would counter establishments' efforts to derail this work using the meta-purpose-conjured vision to obtain popular support. Would enlist the support of like-minded organizations, and exploit the media's need for news to gain national and international exposure, understanding, credibility, respect and active support. Would attempt to work with organizations that oppose the universal purpose's ideals, to minimize harm done by such organizations. Would eventually have enough support to influence multinational organizations of every kind.

World directorate: Would be structured to be accountable to the world's population, by ensuring free and unrestricted media access, and by setting up and maintaining all manner of web and internet interactions, including mechanisms that facilitate active debate of the pros and cons of the universal religion's various statements and activities. Would have secure referendum and web-voting facilities to involve the world populace. Must have many built-in safeguards and a variety of audit mechanisms to prevent subversion by those desiring to exploit the world using this kind of organization.

Would eventually direct mechanisms able to ensure the compliance of individuals, organizations and nations, in the one area of their mandate—that is, to ensure the continued development of life (or as otherwise more comprehensively and precisely defined). Would have no power to restrict non-related human activities, such as benign global commerce or freedom of religious expression. May resemble the United Nations.[6]

This endeavour is not intended to produce a totalitarian world. It is not intended to usurp any nation's authority or power to govern as that nation sees fit, except in its one, world-mandated, area of responsibility. It is not intended to replace or deny any religion, nor is it intended to remove any individual's right to freedom of thought, word or deed.

But it is intended to curb these behaviours whenever the activities of one or some threaten to jeopardize the future of life on this planet (and, later, wherever else life is found). Managing life's exploitive nature necessitates also developing the means to control its destructive excesses when they occur. Most nations have already developed ways to lawfully control individuals and organizations within their boundaries; we must develop lawful ways to do the same at an international level. A carefully designed universal religion would provide the rationale, moral authority and foundation for such laws to exist.

Above all, the universal religion should construct and maintain the environment that contains a new code of behaviour, a new morality, a new wisdom; one which will guide our decision making as we explore the many marvellous medical, technological, cosmological and other pathways opening up before us—routes to a life that the developers of our traditional religions never dreamed could exist.

Summary

Our new universal religion, should one come to be, must be founded upon, and headed by, a purpose whose truth, simplicity, utility and appeal are unmistakable. It must be easy to understand, clear in intent, and suited to guide us all, collectively, to a better way of living. Should peace between nations be our sole desire, then our selection of purpose is much less critical—any that brings unification will serve. However, if we seek more, if we value a long and healthy future for our descendants and for Life, for centuries and millennia to come, then our selection of purpose becomes extremely critical. We must choose one consistent with and respectful of the reality thrust upon us by this universe, simply because we must formulate a guide to living in this universe, not to living in an afterlife. Thus, the behavioural creeds we author must be rationally constructed with this reality in mind. Our new religion must be founded upon what we know—rather than what we invent—about ourselves, our cosmos, our origins, and our future possibilities.

Only the meta-purpose we adopt must be an assumption, for the universe itself cannot be shown to be directed toward a purpose, and this actuality thus applies to all within. Once this single assumption is accepted, then only truth and logic must be used to deduce the behaviour required to attain our chosen endpoint—thus constructing exemplary commandments. Circumstances may be forcing us to repeat doctrinal steps originally taken many hundreds of years ago, however today we have a better grasp of reality, and can use confirmed facts in many places where our forefathers could only conjecture.

To become an influential factor in controlling exploitive excesses, our universal religion must become an incontrovertible part of everyone's mind—perhaps, eventually, the mind's most cherished Construct. A constant awareness that no act should harm Life's continued evolution may be all that is needed. It may be enough for every child and adult to know that this responsibility is everyone's responsibility, and that it pre-empts all other purposes and duties.[7] Individual lives may come and go, but our hard-gained wisdom must continue. Our lives, and those of our ancestors, lose all meaning if our accumulated knowledge and understanding is not benefited from, built upon, and bequeathed forward.

(A postscript to this chapter titled "Multi-Year Targets" is to be found commencing page 234.)

Conclusion to Part Four

*Rational practical behaviour is purpose directed:
religions exist so that moral behaviour may also be this way.*

The world is in labour to produce a second renaissance. Like the first, this reconstruction results from a growth in knowledge and understanding about the real nature of life, the universe and ourselves. Unlike the first, this renaissance will grow very quickly, spread and fed by electronic media, sought and bought by the needs of a globalizing world. Unification of ideas, ideals, desires and, eventually, morality will inevitably force the development of a global religion of some kind.

Which course will humanity choose? Will we continue to view morality as an ordained given? Will we refuse to unify and continue to support a million or so different faiths, defend the need to have a multifaceted view of morality, carry on squabbling and never reach a collective agreement when international situations demand one? Or will we succumb to some new visionary who is revitalizing one of the old god-headed myths, and unite to create the needed global religion in this manner? Or will we choose to develop one that can be forward-looking and reality-based?

All we need to set out on this journey is a single meta-purpose to act as a beacon. Used to frame a universal purpose and an associated set of behaviours, we would have laid the foundation of a religion that would be rational and practical, moral and just, timeless and universal. Our descendents would then have the right to speak with confidence, proud of their beliefs and actions, certain about the behaviours they practiced, ready, willing and able to join, with heads held high, all the other great civilizations of the universe.

None of this will come to pass in the next few generations. But equally, none seems impossible to bring about, given the will and enduring effort of many who care.

Ah! If only we might return after death, to see what has come to pass. To see heaven on Earth—what an afterlife for us to witness, and what a legacy for us to bequeath!

Chapter Postscripts

Postscript to Chapter One

Consciousness and Conscience

What is the *"me"* that makes one think in a manner that is peculiar to only oneself?

The total *"me"* is easy to imagine; it must be the accumulation of events and understandings that one has experienced during one's life, added to the genetically inherited abilities and aptitudes present in one's brain.[1] As we have noted, molecular memories and the understandings they represent are stored as linked paths and networks of greater or lesser significance through everyone's brain—the whole constituting the "mind," just part of it forming the "me" concept.[2] This collection, together with the biochemical activities and emissions of the cells of one's body, makes the *"me"* think and act the particular way that one does. As Descartes said, *cogito, ergo sum* ("I think, therefore, I am").

Second-level thinking, i.e., when animals analyze situations and recognize their implications, then act upon (or dismiss) what they have understood, may or may not involve consciousness of self. If the situation is totally independent of their own individuality (for example, for an antelope when a lion walks nearby) then an awareness of their own unique identity is not called for (only the need to include the knowledge of such things as their proximity to the lion, wind direction, etc., in their analysis). But, if, in order to correctly assess a situation, an animal needs to separate its identity from that of others (for example, when in a family or grooming group, where knowing one's social standing, and how others act and react toward one's presence and actions), then a degree of consciousness of self must be present.

The recognition of personal identity, a separate self or *me* would have occurred very early in the development of third-level thinking ability. Cassirer knew this when he stated, "it is language that makes his existence in a community possible; and only in society, in relation to a 'Thee,' can his subjectivity assert itself as a 'Me.' "[3]

Third-level thinking, using words and languages, provides the consciousness we are familiar with, where thoughts can be consciously directed and where moral questions are formulated. This is the detached self that can examine (with some difficulty) what is happening at the second level.

As we have discussed, everything we "know" is built, held and maintained as second-level constructs—developed by second-level thinking that builds neural networks which form and link the memories. These give us the mental images of objects, events and ideas that we carry in our mind's eye; they are our own Platonic cave-wall shadows. It is the mental construct of one's own body that one "sees" when experiencing an out-of-body sensation (that of looking down upon oneself). Out-of-body sensations occur as the conscious third level of thought is (semi-consciously) drawn by prevailing circumstances[4] to picture mind images of one's body as though they were separate and distinct (i.e., disconnected) from the mental networks that denote self.

It was third-level thinking that made some early scientists postulate that there was an imp, or homunculus, directing mental traffic within the brain; the imp turns out to be the mind's second-level activities.

Consciousness, then, amounts to an awareness of the existence of an assemblage of thoughts and memories within the brain, and of the particular significance that these have to the possessor. The awareness occurs at the third level, and it is the presence of mental constructs that creates the sense of permanency to one's concept of self. Consciousness is aware of second-level activities, but their rapidity and subconscious independence make them hard to analyze. Second and third-level activities block ready access to first-level consciousness; training and practice aimed at decreasing third and second-level thinking activities (meditation, for instance) may occasionally allow first-level awareness to make itself known (as an experience, not as a detailed representation of the external environment).[5]

Research demonstrates that subconscious biochemical and electrical flows occur before we become consciously aware of them. (We should expect this because mental images must first form subconsciously to be recognized and analyzed for relative significance; only then can those of importance be selected and fed to our conscious third-level thinking where, finally, they may be put into words.) This is why the semi-consciousness we are occasionally aware of seems to have a life of its own. It does. Thoughts at the second level run their own course before we become aware of them. This effectively detaches them from our third-level thinking, and makes them seem to exist as an independent body of thought within our minds.[6]

Conscience is an entirely different issue. In essence, exercising one's conscience amounts to expressing one's concept of truth. This, therefore, represents both the highest and the most fundamental level of life's activities: the highest, because life survives by determining the true nature of its environment; the most fundamental, because life does this to most effectively exploit its resources in order to live. Unfortunately, the true nature of things is readily distorted; by one's sensors and one's understanding of signals received by them, and by the words and mental constructs we and others use. Truth, to the extent that it exists, is often costly to obtain; finding it requires openness to the widest possible range of experiences, facts and ideas, then a constant debate over their meaning, with oneself and with others.

Conscience is often associated with morality—knowing "right" from "wrong," and behaving accordingly. In that morality is always relative to its time and circumstances, it is a lesser concept than the concept of conscience. Most theologies recognize this, some going as far as saying that one's conscience is God-given and must be followed, even if it contradicts religious teachings.

Most biologists dismiss any discussion of an animal conscience. For example, Hauser, in *Wild Minds*, states categorically (page 253) that animals have no moral system. But I think that advanced animals may possess a conscience of some degree because they do seek to understand the true nature of their environment, and they can separate a knowledge of "self" from that of another. Animal altruistic behaviour, which has not infrequently been observed, may demonstrate the operation of a conscience and of animal morality.[7]

Postscript to Chapter Three

Purpose and Meaning

There is an important difference between asking, "what is life's purpose?" and asking, "what is life's meaning?"

The first question is by far the most important, for we seek an answer that must be universally and permanently true. All of life, wherever it is and in whatever form it exists, is expected to be subsumed within the answer to the question about life's purpose. "To do God's will" might be the reply of many to this question, giving an answer that, they would claim, applies to all things and all creatures for all time. The point to note is that, although the chosen "life's purpose" might vary from one person to another, every choice selected must meet the criteria of universality and timelessness.

The second question, asking life's meaning, is clearly of less significance, because subjective and multiple answers are acceptable and even expected. Everyone is quite willing to accept different replies from the same person for we fully recognize that "life's meaning" can change from day to day. "Life's purpose" has no such freedom.

The answer to the question of life's purpose turns out to be the key that unlocks the puzzle of life's meaning. We can be sure of this, because whenever someone says that life has meaning for them, we always find that they are expressing a feeling that stems from acting to achieve one or more purposes they deem to be important.

Many do not recognize that they live their daily lives happily striving to attain a multitude of purposes. The desire to live comfortably, to provide for a family, to be without pain, to be emotionally satisfied, to enjoy life; all these and thousands of similar phrases are statements of purpose, all more or less distant from conscious thought, but all significant to our minds as they go about their task of making the decisions that guide our daily activities.

We sometimes consciously chose one or two purposes to have particular significance for us, and their achievement may then take primacy over others. Getting a degree, saving money to buy a house, or helping charitable organizations might be examples, and many of us spend much time and effort supporting the attainment of goals such as these. However, whether or not we recognize the fact, every one of our activities is directed toward the achievement of one purpose or another.

Of course, we often react to emotions and feelings as well. But these actions are taken to satisfy or alleviate the emotions or feelings that prompted them; thus acting to satisfy our emotions is also acting to achieve a purpose. The difference is that these are not purposes directed by conscious thoughts, they are responses to body chemicals. Thus, they are usually more primitive or animal-like in nature (although emotional responses to music probably pertain to relatively recent evolutionary developments).

The happy feeling that we are living a meaningful life, or that life possesses meaning for us, is a by-product of a mind that is doing its job well by directing its support system (the body) to meet a multitude of purposes. The feeling stems from the mind being able to work relatively stress-free, both consciously and subconsciously, because the tasks we perform, the thoughts we arrange, the decisions we make, are directed toward some worthwhile, i.e. purposeful, end.

It is pointless to directly seek the meaning of life. Feeling that life is meaningful is the normal state—a feeling of well-being, when the bloodstream is relatively free of stress-causing chemicals, because the mind is working efficiently and effectively, making purpose-directed decisions. Such a mind has no need to instruct the release of anxiety-causing chemicals.

There is no physical or biological requirement to feel that life has meaning. Living entities can eat, survive and reproduce, without any such feeling, as the daily lives of bacteria, plants and insects presumably affirm. In organisms capable of conscious thought, however, there is a definite requirement for such thought to be purpose-directed. Solving problems and making decisions rationally requires a desire to achieve some purpose—this systematizes conscious thought. Working rationally is the activity that makes the mind valuable to survival, thus ensuring its own survival.

People who lack valued purposes are susceptible to depression, when nothing seems worthwhile and life can feel meaningless. The cure is not to directly seek meaning, but to find a purpose worthy of being valued and sought, then use this purpose to make decisions and guide actions.

Postscript to Chapter Four

Rationality in Science and Religion

Science and mathematics reign supreme in our understanding of the universe because, as has been elsewhere noted, each scientific fact and theory, each mathematical statement, has been exhaustively tested for inconsistencies and illogic before being given membership among the hierarchy of theories and facts that make up the totality of these disciplines. Our underlying belief in the universe's causality requires this rigour, as any discrepancy, until resolved, threatens to demolish our whole understanding of the cosmos.

The mark of a true scientist is that he or she willingly investigates discrepancies. The hallmarks of scientific method are that its findings are repeatable, measurable, and universal in implication and relationship, yet simple in concept once understood. Although humans have uncovered a great deal about the universe, we have much to learn, and the meticulousness of the scientific method is the only sound approach.

Most religions, in contrast, do not tolerate such a questioning attitude and, consequently, many have become less and less in tune with reality.[1]

Religions fail us when they ignore our need to be rational. Of course, anyone can hold any belief or statement to be true. There is no necessity (other than the mind's own operational need for rationality) to demand a logical relationship between subordinate statements and apex belief in religion. Each statement could be taken at face value, true and absolute in itself. Indeed, many people (particularly those who follow their religion's fundamental text conscientiously) seem able to accept most, and sometimes all, of their religion's statements as absolutes, and require no interconnectivity between them. But this treats us all as though we were automaton, incapable of thought, simply being required to believe and to act as we are told.

(Preachers do not usually ignore the inter-relationships within their religion. In my limited experience, preachers spend much time attempting to show links between a belief in God and subordinate statements [such as the existence of Heaven and Hell], or between actions and consequences. Possibly this is because preachers are more rational than most of us, and have been drawn to religion because of the need to find an authority for the moral decisions their mental constructs require them to address. If this is even partially so, it is truly ironic to realize that it is the universe's very own rationality expressing itself within their minds that has induced them to become leaders in an arena where rationality has become subordinated to faith!)

As earlier stated, we can believe anything we choose. Our beliefs will cause us no harm, as long as they do not cause us to act in a way that reality will punish. Thus, we can believe, to use an extreme example, that the moon is made of green cheese, that the man-in-the-moon is our real father, and that we will all go to be with him after death. We can construct a subsystem of subordinate beliefs, all guiding us in our daily decision making, and all assuring us that we will be rewarded with an afterlife amid green cheese. And we can live more or less happily within this belief system and die content.

We can sustain these beliefs forever, provided we somehow filter and modify any incoming stimuli that fails to support them. For instance, we could believe in a cheesy moon as long as we did not spectrally analyze moon light, and we could continue to believe in moon heaven for as long as we did not physically visit the moon. Others could go, but they could not return to report its true nature and so challenge our beliefs, for it is clear that our green-cheese belief would become untenable after the return from a moon landing. (Of course, this is exactly why a belief in heaven or paradise can exist.)

All belief systems run the risk of unravelling when forced to confront reality. The only belief systems that survive close encounters with the real world are those that are based upon the rationality of the real world. The less our belief system agrees with reality, the more difficult following that belief becomes.[2] We can enjoy our beliefs for as long as we like, but reality will compel us to revise such beliefs as soon as they create situations which threaten our existence.[3]

We stand at this juncture in our current religions. Many of our traditional beliefs have become less convincing. Reality keeps pulling at the tangled skein of religious thought, attempting to correct false assumptions and misunderstandings. More and more, we become obligated to ask if current religions really are the best source of guidance in contemporary issues. Moral decisions are in danger of becoming little more than political trade-offs at the parish level. Matters relating to population control or gene manipulation, for example, that need a global consensus if such decisions are ever to amount to anything of significance, cannot even be raised at the international level for fear of the religious conflict this would create. Surely a global civilization can never be established until conditions like these are corrected.

Postscripts to Chapter Five

Creativity, Free Will, and a Revelation

1. Creativity

To be creative, our thoughts must stop following the well worn neural paths they are accustomed to travelling. Thus, we start the creative process when we (mentally) say "no." By saying "no" to any particular thought, we force our minds to conceive alternatives, to search for different neural routes among our existing store of memories, to look for new links. Let me provide a couple of examples.

Consider an artist who paints a picture that is appealing and sells well. He or she might churn out several paintings of like vein without thinking and live well. But, other than the first painting, this is being productive, not creative. To be creative, the artist must first say "no" to some aspect of his or her work. Some large or small part of it must not be produced by rote; it has to be produced as the result of a conscious effort to discover and present something new. A novel way of using titanium white, an insight into the nature of anything, a new way of presenting an emotional experience, a rational discovery, anything at all, as long as it produces an informing[1] entity that is unique. The refusal to repeat what has been done before, because there must be a better way, is the act that initiates creativity.[2]

Alternatively, consider a manager, heading a division within a factory producing widgets. There are opportunities galore to be creative; all such a person need do is think, "No, there must be a better way of doing this," then work out what that might be. On the other hand, the manager may not be faulted for thinking little and creating nothing, being paid for his efforts, and going home knowing that he has done his job, content. (But, somehow, perhaps, feeling a little incomplete, for he has simply managed an operation, not led. To lead others one must first be creative.)

Everyone can be creative. And we all are, some of the time. We have all created many things, suggested a different approach, changed a routine, come up with a new thought, improved upon the past. Each time, in a moment prior to each occasion, we would have, in effect, said "no," and this would have stopped us from repeating what we may have done many times before.

Routine living, simply repeating with minor, externally induced, variations what has been done before, is not being creative. No improvements—no increases in life's quality—are produced, and life stagnates. It is the creative acts of millions who have lived before that has given us everything we have that animals do not.

When we refuse to allow our thoughts to follow their usual pathways, the search for new neural associations begins. Finding them completes the act of creativity; new links are made, new memories laid down, our mind's store of constructs enlarges, and our future abilities increase. Creativity adds to oneself as well as gives to others.

2. Free Will

Chapter One noted that we discover how the universe and its contents operate by examining the cause-and-effect relationships that tie events together. It was emphasized that nothing happens in isolation; every object and every event is linked through a chain of causality to everything that existed before and to everything that exists currently. Not one iota can change without being brought about by some prior event happening.

But, if no change can occur without being caused by some prior event, which itself must have had a prior cause, and so on and so on, backwards in time to the universe's beginning, then how can free will exist? How can any individual have any thought that hasn't been pre-programmed into the cause-and-effect network that exists throughout the universe?

Moreover, if free will does not exist, how can anyone be responsible for their actions? And if no one can be held accountable, then no one should be disciplined for anything they do.

This problem has agitated theologians and philosophers for centuries, and has never been satisfactorily resolved.

Intuitively we feel that we do have free will. We all think that we are free to make any decision we like, and most of us expect to be held accountable for the decisions we make and the actions we carry out as a result of those decisions. So there is some explaining to be done—where does causality give way to allow free will?

Possibly the answer is simple. It may be that causality does not apply to single particle events.[3] What follows is an elaboration of what is meant by this statement, and some evidence supporting the premise.

We think of particles as discrete objects, having mass and able to move from place to place (factors that we can easily measure) because this is our direct experience of the (large and small) objects that we encounter everyday. However, if particles are small enough (about the size of an atom) scientists find that their true nature is not that simple.

One of the peculiarities we find, is that we can never know simultaneously the position and momentum[4] of single particles such as an atom or an electron. This is because any time we try to measure either of these properties, the act of measuring one changes the other. For example, light photons reflecting from a particle that, once detected, should tell us the information we seek, actually give the particle a backward kick as they bounce off. This shifts the particle's position in an unknown way. It's a bit like trying to find out what a falling feather is doing by poking at it with a stick. Heisenberg developed the Uncertainty Principle as a description of this problem in 1927. (It precipitated much free-will discussion among scientists and philosophers at the time.)

Another unexpected feature of particle behaviour is that, if we send a beam of them (or even shoot them, one at a time) through two thin parallel slits to make an image on a screen, rather than the expected two lines appearing on the screen, we see several parallel lines of varying density (called an interference pattern). Moreover, these lines are being drawn by a succession of many single hits. Now, on our everyday scale, objects like bullets can't produce interference patterns. But waves can, so our explanation of such occurrences is that particles show "duality"; they move as if they were waves, but hit targets as if they were bullets.

Quantum mechanics helps physicists solve conundrums like these. This discipline has determined that energy exists as waves of interacting energy fields and that matter is actually bunched-up packets of waves (or photons). (You will remember that Einstein showed that matter and energy were different forms of the same thing, so quantum mechanics and the Theory of Relativity support each other's explanations.) Since waves are spread-out entities, the position of the particle they represent[5] can only be calculated as a probability of being at any particular place. (For instance, a scientist might say, "If a photon were to hit this screen, it is 60% likely to hit at this spot.") This may be the first clue in resolving our free will enigma.

The existence and behaviour of "virtual particles" might be another clue that causality does not apply to particles. Myriads of virtual particles constantly flicker into and out of existence everywhere (obtaining the energy to do so from the "vacuum energy" of space, see Chapter Seven). They are called "virtual" because they cannot be directly detected. Their occurrence was predicted by Heisenberg, and they are found by looking for the real particles and antiparticles they create. (These created particles and antiparticles immediately destroy one another; it is the leftovers from this destruction that scientists observe.) The comings and goings of the unseen originating virtual particles are completely unpredictable from our point of view within the universe. Since the behaviour of these particles is unpredictable, the results they produce are also unpredictable. Causality seems not to come into play on very small events in our universe.

Observations such as these suggest that tiny particles,[6] virtual or real, possess properties that are somewhat different from those exhibited when the same particles form large conglomerations. The observations suggest that, at the grassroots level, only probabilities exist. These probabilities build to become statistical certainties as the particle groupings becomes bigger. Once large enough, their behaviours exhibit the causality upon which the laws of physics depend, and that allows scientists to explain so much. In short, predictable causality is not possible (and absolute certainty does not exist) for events involving objects of small dimensions.[7]

So much for causality. Now, for free will.

Thinking, as we have noted, can actually be observed occurring in the brain. Imaging scans reveal that electrically charged ions travel along neural axons and prompt chemical transmissions across synapses to neighbouring neurons. But ions, we remember from our school science class, are atoms or tiny groups of atoms that have lost or gained electrons. That is, they are very small particles.

Now we have all we need to allow free will to exist. We exercise free will when we first say "no."[8] (As stated in the postscript "Creativity," this is exactly what we do to start the creative process.) Subsequent, conscious, third-level thought, capped by a decision, completes the act. This process consciously overrules, or at least re-thinks, any decision that may have been made by prior thinking, including that done at the second-level subconscious in our mind.[9] We are able to do this, because causality does not force small particles (particularly chemical neurotransmitters travelling between synaptic gaps) to trace previously determined paths.

There we have it! We possess free will because small particles are not causally constrained; they obey probability laws which only become certainties when large numbers are involved. We can say "no," and be responsible for creating an original decision.

(For what it's worth, we might note that we exhibit no free will at all when we just "go with the flow." All flexibility and freedom disappears when multiple entities merge, be they particles, photons, ions travelling along existing neural pathways, or mobs of people.)

3. A Revelation

I experienced a "revelation" (from simply thinking that an idea [see the Conclusion to Part Three and various chapters for details of this idea] could be true, to believing that it is true) three decades ago. Its sudden, totally unexpected arrival; its mental fireworks and fascinating light trails; its prolonged accompanying feelings of certainty, exultation and joy; and its ability to direct my actions even now, are all, I have come to realize, a matter of natural biochemistry. With the loss of its original wonder, and the expectation of never again experiencing its magic, comes a degree of sadness. But, it also brings the knowledge that something similar, something fully explainable and rational, must have happened to many people, many times in the past. Each one of history's prophets and mystics who claimed to have received divine intervention, with its accompanying brightness and light, surely experienced a similar phenomenon. Scientists, perceiving a sudden solution to a problem that had long occupied their thoughts, have reported similar happenings, sometimes adding that it was as though the universe had spoken to them. These feelings, as noted in Chapter Five, do not emanate from some external consciousness, some universal spirit; they come from the individual's own second-level subconscious mental activities.

Is it sad to say goodbye to the notion that these exotic experiences are proof that a higher Being exists, that some divine force is slowly but certainly bringing enlightenment to us? I don't hold so, for this imposes a dependency and subordination that harks back to the days when superstition and fear ruled the human mind. The idea of being manipulated by a god apportioning ideas in this manner is quite distasteful to me. I do not like to think that any god worthy of its title would do this to any of its creations.

Is it distressing to know that our thinking is not being supported or even directed by stimuli received from a god—to know that we are acting all alone? No; not at all. To the contrary, to know that life, starting from scratch and with absolutely no outside help, is actually on a journey towards comprehending the entire universe is far from troubling—it is magnificent. It is inspiring to think that any single one of us might add another piece to the elucidation of the puzzle. It is exhilarating to know that, as infinitesimal as humans may be on the grand scale of things, they are nevertheless slowly unravelling the nature of the universe, and, through the understanding this brings, gaining some measure of power over fragments of the cosmos itself.

To think that some distant descendant of ours might someday control all! None of the religions I have read about give life and living such an overwhelming sense of purpose and destiny to me. They may have done so, to some people at one time, and they may still do so, to other people today. But not to me. What makes my life meaningful to me is the thought that some of my actions might, through the later efforts of others, contribute morsels toward the eventual evolution of oB.

Postscripts to Chapter Seven

Gödel's Theorem, General Systems Theory, and The Conservation Laws

1. Gödel's Theorem

Kurt Gödel, in a paper published in 1931, proved that any mathematical system that includes the natural numbers (1, 2, 3, and so on) contains questions whose answers can neither be proved nor disproved using the axioms to be found within that system. This is now known as Gödel's Incompleteness Theorem. It implies that there are many mathematical truths that can never be proved, and, by extension, that any system will contain questions that cannot be answered from within that system. Since any meaningful questions that we might ask about the nature of any possible supersystem will inevitably involve use of the natural numbers, there are questions we will never be able to answer. Asking if our universe was "designed to meet some kind of purpose," is just one such question.

Another way of using Gödel's theorem to address why one is unable to understand everything from within a system, is as follows. A system is complete when all statements (or their negations) can be proved from within that system. Systems can be proved to be consistent, i.e. free from contradictions, but only by involving a larger frame of reference, which then requires an even larger system to prove its consistency, and so on. In short, we require information that is only available from outside of our universe to determine the accuracy of any answer to any question that can be raised within the universe. In other words, we can never know the answers to questions like, "does God exist?" or, "what is the universe's purpose in existing?" because we cannot obtain information about what exists beyond the boundaries of our universe.

In effect, Gödel is saying that we can never know anything fully and completely. Thus, even the very best of our scientific understanding is ultimately unverifiable.

Some might say that if this is true, then what is the point of doing anything. Why bother to develop a universal religion, for instance? The answer, of course, is that we need one just as much as we need an understanding of how things work, because both improve the quality of our lives. Time enough to stop doing our best after we are dead!

2. General Systems Theory

The basic concepts underlying General Systems Theory[1] are simple, once the terms employed are recognized and their meaning understood. The theory's power stems from its generalizability, for all systems (whether living or non-living, small or large) demonstrate the same principles.

General Systems Theory can be summarized as follows.

A system is a processing complex of interrelated parts that acquires supplies and turns them into something else. Thus, a person can be called a system, for each individual takes in oxygen, nutrients and water, processes them, and turns out movement, growth, and bodily waste. A factory can be called a system, for it takes in raw materials and energy, carries out operations, and turns out manufactured goods and waste.

Physical and biological systems exist everywhere; they range in scale and form from primitive Archaean life to galactic clusters, and the same systems terminology applies to all.

No system within our universe is "closed." In other words, there is no system within the universe whose boundary is impermeable to everything. For example, the Earth receives and processes energy from the Sun; the Sun was formed from earlier Milky Way galactic dust, and radiates energy that interacts with the galaxy's particles; all galaxies exert gravitational pulls upon one another (so their motions are interdependent), and so on. An alternative way of expressing this property is to state that all systems are "open."

Thus, all systems (except, possibly, the universe itself) are subsystems of larger supersystems, and, in particular, the biological system is a subset of the physical system. In other words, life is a subsystem of the universe.

We cannot tell if our universe is a subsystem of a larger universe. If there is no linkage to anything external, if the universe is entirely self-contained, and neither takes in nor gives out any form of material, then it is closed. If our universe is somehow related to (i.e., exchanges information, energy and/or matter with) a larger Universe, then it is open.

Systems are dependent upon, and thus controlled by, their various supersystems. This fact becomes readily apparent when a system can no longer obtain needed resources from its environment (its supersystem) and shuts down. It is also demonstrated when a system's outputs are so excessive or aggravating that its supersystem (its environment) can accept no more, and the resulting back-pressure (a.k.a. feedback) shuts down the system's operations.

The criteria that determine what we can do, or what we are able to produce, are all to be found in the way our supersystems react to our behaviour. Our supersystems can reject (partially or fully) or accept (partially or fully) our outputs. (For example, a rejection by family, friends, employer or society can soon effect our welfare.) Conversely, supersystem acceptance creates the demand for more of the same output and thus encourages more of the same processing activity.

General Systems Theory terminology can be used to increase our understanding of the problem-solving and decision-making processes described in chapters two and three. Thus, the supersystem (earlier termed the environment) provides the criteria that determine the success or failure of its subsystems' behaviours. Physically existing supersystems exhibit and enforce many real criteria, and we make practical decisions successfully by knowing and respecting these. Similarly, mentally existing supersystems (i.e. major constructs) exhibit and enforce many abstract criteria, and we make moral decisions successfully by knowing and respecting these.

3. The Conservation Laws

As the Conservation Laws have been referred to several times in the text, it might be useful to say a little more about them.

Conservation Laws state that, amid all the changes that occur throughout the universe, certain quantities and qualities (for instance, the total amount of energy/mass, momentum, charge, spin, parity, etc.) are always conserved. The value of each (although not necessarily the form) after an interaction is always the same as the value of each before. These laws explain why, for instance, a perpetual motion machine cannot be built. (Interacting system-parts generate heat which is lost to the surrounding environment. Thus the machine loses energy and eventually stops.) Conservation laws explain why there is a property we call inertia. (We feel a force termed inertia when, for instance, we push an object to start it moving. Accelerating an object in this way changes its velocity, and this means we have added to its momentum. Since momentum must be conserved, it must be taken from somewhere; in this case from our hand and body, and, ultimately, from the Earth, reducing its spin (i.e., its angular momentum) a tiny fraction. The inertial force we feel is our body's reaction [Newton's Third Law of Motion] to the force that transfers momentum from the Earth to the object.)

The several Conservation Laws are likely to be sub-manifestations of one comprehensive law that we have not yet discovered. Superstring theory may soon be able to tell us more, not only about the Conservation Laws, but also about why certain physical constants are just right for our universe to exist and to create and nourish life. Superstring theory, in Witten and Townsend's M-theory version, can now account for the existence of the known forces (gravity, electromagnetic, strong and weak nuclear), showing that they may all be derivatives of minute vibrating strings 10^{-35} meters or less in length, and existing in either 10- or 26-dimensional hyperspace. Superstring theory exercises the minds of many physicists and cosmologists (the first group, because it may be the elusive TOE/GUT [Theory Of Everything or Grand Unified Theory] long searched for, and cosmologists, because it predicts and allows for the existence of other universes.)

Some seemingly inexplicable phenomena (such as the behaviour of virtual particles, or the instantaneous transmission of quantum states, as well as time-travel and teleportation [both recently demonstrated to exist[2]]) might represent a window through which we may glean a little knowledge about the possible existence of any such super-universes.

Our universe may be just an adjunct of a larger Universe, with the larger Universe retaining ultimate control. Control by a super-Universe could be rigid, creating nothing more than a fully deterministic sub-universe if the connections between the two were entirely inflexible. However, this seems not to be the case. Wave/particle duality and the laws of conservation allow minuscule events unlimited freedom to act, as long as conglomerate activities obey the conservation constraints (see also the earlier discussion on free will).[3]

Alternatively, our universe's existence could be simply a manifestation of nothing, just as branches of mathematics can be created from definitions rather from actuality. All that is needed is for the whole to sum to zero, and that sum to be maintained regardless of how its parts manifest or become manipulated (a condition maintained by causality and described by the Conservation Laws).

Postscript to Chapter Eight

Origin Theory Modifications

Theories related to life's creation and its evolution are still being proposed. In the 1960's Francis Crick, Leslie Orgel and Carl Woese independently proposed that RNA preceded proteins in evolution, and introduced the idea of an early "RNA world." In 1983, Thomas Cech and Sidney Altman found evidence that RNA can act as a catalyst, so supporting the RNA world theory.[1]

Current thinking posits that early RNA exchanges occurred laterally (within a commune of different cells), rather than generationally (from parents to offspring), as DNA now replicates. The former may have facilitated many primitive evolutionary developments, and has been found to occur in bacteria.

An alternative theory, put forward by Graham Cairns-Smith, suggests that an inorganic genetic system is likely to have existed before the RNA world, possibly one involving the irregular distribution of cations since found in clays.

Ideas and findings such as these may help us to replicate possible early life forms in the laboratory. That we will create life from scratch one day is not much doubted by any biologist (although some prefer that we never make the attempt). However, the methodology we use to succeed may not be the way that life started (on this planet or elsewhere in the universe), because there are likely to be many ways that life could begin. We will probably use water as its basic ingredient,[2] and we already know the other elements and molecules from which Earthly life is constructed. However, it is not a matter of which ingredients to use, the problem is how to assemble these to form a self-contained processing system.

A web search for articles relating to the creation of life or the discovery of extraterrestrial life forms will yield many other interesting details. Chapter Ten adds a further note to this discussion of life's beginning.

Postscript to Chapter Fourteen

Multi-year Targets

Anything and everything is possible when fantasizing about the future. Everyone has their own views, and the great majority, we know, will turn out to be wrong. For what little they might be worth, here are some of my conjectures concerning the possible development of a universal religion.

- *25-year achievements:* A suitable meta-purpose is envisioned, and its legal definition as a universal purpose is agreed upon. Public awareness programs are developed and initiated. Political, financial, and religious support is being sought. National and international groups are being formed. Media and public relations units are active. Possible administration, legal, accountability, and other organizational structures necessary for the continuance of the universal purpose project are being discussed.
- *50-year achievements:* The universal purpose is used by 20% of the world's governments to guide their decision making in such areas as law, genetics, population, pollution, world aid, trade, and exploitation-control.
- *100-year achievements:* The universal purpose has been adopted by 25% of the world's population, and varieties of a universal religion, headed by this purpose, are being used by them to make moral decisions in arenas where their personal religion provides no answers.
- *250-year achievements:* Self-sustaining, off-world colonies have been built on several of the sun's planets or their moons and are supplying Earth with rare minerals; the continuation of any indigenous life forms found there is protected by the tenets of the (now commonly accepted) universal religion. Colony ships are on their way to several hospitable exoplanets.
- *500-year achievements:* Information exchanges between humans and intelligent alien life are becoming common occurrences. The possible need to reformulate our meta-purpose, universal

purpose and universal religion (and its moral codes) is debated in light of what we learn.
- *1000-year achievements:* Interchanges between numerous other-world species are facilitated by the adoption of a universal meta-purpose that guides the manner by which life's continuing evolution is supported.

Clearly many other targets have to be met, if any of this is to come to pass. But, look back the same number of years into our past: what changes have humans wrought during that short span. Then look ahead. All might become reality—if we take courage and act upon our dreams.

Chapter and Postscript Endnotes

Endnotes to Chapter One

[1] Breaks in the DNA strands of a sperm, ovum or zygote (caused by such factors as carcinogens, naturally occurring free-radical oxidation within cells, energetic electromagnetic radiation such as ultra-violet and X-rays, radon gas, and so on) are, to a large extent, repaired. The few that may not be repaired (or are incorrectly rebuilt) are called mutations; these become reproduced, as are all DNA molecules, in all of the cells formed from the zygote—including those of future generations. Since DNA controls cell formation and growth by affecting protein synthesis and the sequence in which sets of genes are turned on, these mutations can have various wide-ranging effects, from insignificant to fatal.

[2] A later different mutation in the same gene caused a fly to nap in the heat of the afternoon, which must also have contributed to that fly's survival, and to the survival of many descendants, for this behaviour has also become inherited by the majority of fruit flies.

[3] Read Jonathan Weiner, *Time, Love, Memory* (New York: Vintage Books, 1999) for an eloquent description of some of the experiments with fruit flies and mice that proved that instinctive behaviour can be genetically inherited.

[4] The use of computers and a variety of instruments has greatly expanded our knowledge of the brain in the past few decades. Magnetic Resonance Imaging (MRI) provides detailed, thin, cross-sectional images. (This technology, which uses high frequency radio waves and strong magnetic fields, can also detect chemical changes that occur in the brain during various behaviours.) Functional Magnetic Resonance Imaging (fMRI) maps changes in oxygen concentration and shows localized neural activity. (For instance, an analysis of fMRI patterns can tell researchers, to an 85% accuracy,

which particular picture, from a selection of several different pictures, subjects were viewing while being scanned.) Positron Emission Tomography (PET), using radioactive tracer chemicals, shows the formation of neurotransmitters as signals disseminate from neuron to neuron. Electroencephalography (EEG) and minute wire probes detect chemical and electrical changes occurring within single neurons. Voltage sensitive dyes show groups of neurons lighting up in sequence following sensory stimulation. Advanced Magnetoencephalography (MEG) scanners show that visual recognition and decision making processes within the brain move from the visual cortex, through memory and speech (i.e., subvocalization) regions, to the right parietal cortex, where decisions are consciously made.

New ways of investigating the brain's functioning are continually being introduced, and undoubtedly our understanding of what is occurring will grow rapidly over the next few years. (MEG scanners, which use an array of super-conducting quantum interference devices bathed in liquid helium, are one such recent introduction.)

[5] Axon fanouts can have between one and ten thousand branches.

[6] Synapses have been photographed growing in rats following stimulation of the optic nerve. New knobs take about an hour to grow.

[7] The development of the brain from its simplest beginnings to its current complexity in human beings is ably discussed by John Morgan Allman in *Evolving Brains* (New York: Scientific American Library, 1999).

See also John H. Holland, *Emergence: from Chaos to Order* (Reading, Massachusetts: Helix Books, Addison-Wesley Publishing Company, Inc., 1998). Larry R. Squire and Eric R. Kandel, *Memory: From Mind to Molecules* (New York: Scientific American Library, 1999) provide a different perspective.

[8] Neurons transmit data from body sensors to the brain, and from the brain to body muscles, as well as within the brain itself.

[9] Studies have shown that stimuli from the retina move successively through the lateral gemiculate nuclei (which respond to changes of brightness or colour), to the primary visual cortex (which can detect motion and its direction), then on to well over twenty other cortical regions (which detect shapes), and eventually on to more specialized regions such as the inferior temporal cortex (which can recognize objects and identify their form).

The sequential detection of optical stimulation shows how vision has evolved over time to become what it is today. Many hundreds of millions of years ago one or more genetic mutations occurred, producing a slight cellular sensitivity to light. Helping the entity to survive, the altered genes were passed on to descendants. Subsequent mutations, perhaps forming several light-sensitive patches, and probably occurring many generations later, gave additional survival benefits, and these were also passed on. Gradually, after many thousands of genetic modifications (the majority of which would not have helped survival, and whose possessors would not have had a greater chance of surviving to reproduce), primitive eyes and the associated decoding memory networks in the brain, would exist. All organisms' body tissues and systems have been constructed in this manner, with non-lethal modifications being passed to descendants as additions to those already present.

[10] One of these memories would likely be its name, for animals having language abilities. See section three of this chapter for more details.

[11] Magnetic Resonance Imaging (MRI) is able to show brain activity when mental tasks are performed. When a subject is shown pictures of places visited, memories of those places cause particular brain areas to activate. Pictures of places not visited do not elicit such a response. The techniques which detect this mental behaviour can be used to examine people suspected of taking part in criminal activities. This creates an interesting moral problem: should such a technology be developed? See Brad Evenson, "The guilty mind," *National Post*, February 8, 2003, A1 and A6.

[12] Brains of rats raised in stimulating environments possess many more synaptic knobs, are heavier, and have a better blood supply than the brains of rats raised in uninteresting conditions. See Susan Greenfield, *The Private Life of the Brain: Emotions, Consciousness, and the Secret of the Self* (New York: John Wiley & Sons, Inc., 2000). Rats (and mice) raised in enriched environments also learn better. See page 42 of "New nerve cells for the adult brain," in *The Hidden Mind*, a special edition of the *Scientific American*, May 2002, 38-44.

[13] Plants also do this; for instance, gravity orients stem growth upwards, roots develop toward nutrients, and branches shape so that their leaves gather maximum sunlight.

[14] William H. Calvin, in *The Ascent of Mind: Ice Age Climates and the Evolution of Intelligence* (Bantam Books, 1990) discusses this topic in a straight-forward manner. He explains reflex actions as due

to "sensory schemas" being firmly linked to "movement programs" (see page 39 of his book). Computers can be programmed to carry out similar functions, i.e., to oversee and care for the well-being of machines, vehicles and factories. Although many expect computers to eventually be able to think, these care-giving electronic chips certainly do not.

The parallels between the human brain and a computer have been interestingly developed in Chapter Seven, "The Evolution of Consciousness," of Daniel C. Dennett's book, *Consciousness Explained* (Boston: Little, Brown and Company, 1991).

[15] See Andrew Whiten and Christophe Boesch, "The Cultures of Chimpanzees," *Scientific American*, January 2001, 61-67, for intriguing descriptions of chimpanzee behaviour. Neighbouring communities of chimps apparently occasionally battle each other to the death. (Ah! Perhaps we can blame a common ancestor for contributing the same trait to us.)

[16] Crows in the New Caledonian rain forest are as advanced in their ability to use tools as were Stone Age humans. The birds strip bark from a twig, cut the twig just below an offshoot to create a hook, and then insert this hook into tree cavities to remove insects and larvae. They also use a barbed type of leaf which they peck into a tapered point for similar functions (showing a left-handed preference when tailoring pine needles). They make several different types of tools, each for its own specific purpose, and even produce tools in assembly line fashion—that is, they finish a number of tools before using any of them. Man did not reach this stage until the Lower Palaeolithic era, 2.5 million to 200,000 years ago.

Readers with an interest in the intelligence of birds, crows in particular, will enjoy Bernd Heinrich's book, *Mind of the Raven: Investigations and Adventures with Wolf-Birds* (New York: Harper Collins, 1999).

[17] Marc D. Hauser, *Wild Minds: What Animals Really Think* (New York: Henry Holt and Company, 2000), 209.

[18] Hauser, 257.

[19] Calvin, *The Ascent of Mind*, 24.

[20] However, Wilder Penfield, in his experiments that electrically stimulated points within the brain, may have been close to finding out. (This kind of investigative work is considered unethical and is not practiced today.)

[21] It may help some to use the word "consciousness" instead of the word "thinking" when reading this section. I have chosen to use "thinking" because I wish to emphasize differences ("levels" of thinking) that are harder to separate when using the word

"consciousness." (Consciousness is further, although briefly, discussed in a postscript to this chapter.)

[22] Ernst Cassirer, *Language and Myth*, translated by Susanne K. Langer (New York: Dover Publications, Inc., 1953), 57.

[23] Savants (see later) are likely exceptions to this generalization; many explanations of their exceptional capabilities depend upon their being able to access an almost perfect memory of things seen or heard.

[24] It also occurs as a stress-relieving activity, as will be discussed later.

[25] This is why information from the eyes is first routed to pass through networks that check for changes—see this chapter, endnote 9.

[26] Penfield, more than seventy years ago, noted that electrically stimulating tiny areas of the temporal lobes of a patient produced sensations of different smells, accompanied by associated memories and feelings.

[27] Stimuli propagate in two ways: as electrically charged ions, which flow along and between neurons; and as chemical discharges (e.g., the release of adrenaline or endorphin) which move about in body fluids. Neural transmissions are relatively fast, and some of them may give rise to feelings (e.g., pain). Chemical transmissions are relatively slow to act and take longer to fade; they may give rise to the longer-lasting emotions (e.g., happiness).

Emotional responses are considered to be inherited from ancient learned responses. Animals employing such devices have inherited them from ancestors who first developed these as solutions to survival or reproductive threats. Thus human males react emotionally (particularly in early adulthood) to other males entering their territory or attempting to usurp females. Overt emotional displays act as warnings, and may obviate the need to use potentially self-harmful force.

For a well-organized and informative discussion of the mind's psychological development and functioning, see David M. Buss, *Evolutionary Psychology: The New Science of the Mind* (Boston: Allyn and Bacon, 1999).

[28] Robin Dunbar, *Grooming, Gossip, and the Evolution of Language* (Cambridge, Massachusetts: Harvard University Press, 1996), 25.

[29] Temporary ion-flow loop formation is similar to storing data in random access memory (RAM) in computers; this information is retained only as long as its supporting medium is energized. Permanent link storage, on the other hand, is similar to

storing data on a computer's hard disk, where it remains even after the power is switched off. (This suggests that it may be possible, one day, to retrieve the long term memories stored in a "dead" brain.)

[30] However, additional synaptic knobs may form, lessening the neural pathway's resistance to future ion flows and thus somewhat increasing the probability that this path will be chosen above neighbouring others.

[31] The brain enlarges rapidly in volume, from about 350 cc (cubic centimetres) at birth to double that at six months, doubling again to approximately adult size (some 1400 cc) at four years old. (See Susan Greenfield, *The Human Brain: A Guided Tour* [New York: Basic Books, 1997].) Dendrites form most rapidly after this neuronal growth has occurred—from four to ten years of age. The majority of association-forming neural connections are made during these early years.

Newborns and very young infants initially experience stimuli devoid of context. Stimuli produce feelings and emotions—pleasure, pain, satisfaction, rejection, joy, anger, and so on—with initially no understanding that a link between stimuli and emotion, or between past cause and future effect, exists. Understanding only begins to arrive after experiences have become stored as memories, when neural links between them, or between them and new stimuli, can be made.

(Although the retrieval and use of some of the information already held in the mind is often under rational control, the storage of information coming to our brains from our body's sensors is usually not. However, when we want to sure we will remember something of importance, we can consciously direct our minds in the way it stores thoughts. Thus, for example, as a reminder to telephone Bill early tomorrow, we can picture ourselves drinking a breakfast mug of coffee, then picking up the phone. The next morning this task comes to mind while coffee drinking, just as desired. We remember to call because we have associated or linked it to another action, an action that needs no reminder to occur. Mnemonics, used in memory training, employ the same trick.)

[32] Christian de Duve, *Vital Dust: Life as a Cosmic Imperative* (New York: Basic Books, 1995), 241.

[33] Memory-building in infants must progress from knowing nothing, to becoming vaguely aware of a shape, noise, or other sensation, then on to storing this as an unrecognized neural pattern that seems to have some significance. Subsequent detection of similar stimuli, because it is of a comparable nature, follows the now-existing neural pathway and thus reaches the first neural

patterns stored. Any extra information brought in by the new stimuli may then be stored as additional neural patterns linked to (i.e., associated with) the earlier stored patterns. In this way, memories slowly build in complexity and data completeness, until they become what adolescents and adults experience—full-blown mental representations of objects and events that have existed (or exist) in the outside world.

(It is because many repetitions of an event must occur before it can be meaningfully linked to create an understanding, that fully one-third of all blind-from-birth adults, whose ability to see has abruptly been restored, revert initially to closing their eyes to navigate and generally make sense of the world.)

[34] We must again differentiate between simply recalling memories and second-level thought. The example of European blue tits all over England opening tinfoil caps on milk bottles to obtain the cream is widely known. But only the first bird to discover this was "thinking"; the others simply copied what they saw another bird do. (The first bird associated or linked memories of cream at the top of bottles and memories of pecking to make holes; it was "thinking." Birds copying this behaviour were simply demonstrating "learned" behaviour, or memory recall, not original thinking.)

A related observation involves Imo, a macaque monkey, who discovered the benefits of washing sweet potatoes in the sea before eating them. This could have been due to second-level thinking (for instance, if Imo had associated memories of eating sweet potatoes found in the sea and sensory perceptions that these potatoes lacked grit or were saltier, etc., and were more enjoyable to eat). The many other macaques who later adopted this practice did so because they had seen and memorized, then recalled and imitated, what Imo did. Thinking was not involved in these subsequent behaviours. (Similarly, much of what any animal does, including humans, does not require conscious thought.)

(Note that each of these behaviours have come into common use, and thus might be considered to have become part of the animal's culture, to be passed through repetition from generation to generation, and to die out when their practice is recognized as being no longer beneficial. Human cultures build in exactly the same way.)

[35] Plants, also, react to changes in their environment. For example, stomata close in dry weather, rootlets grow toward nourishment, flowers typically open in sunlight, etc. Although no one would claim that plants are thinking when they respond to changes in the environment, this kind of behaviour is genetically encoded, and was probably passed on to animals when they later

evolved. Thus, plant reaction to environmental variations may be regarded as being a precursor to animal responsiveness and even to human thinking.

[36] Much more than this may have been needed. For instance, recent research suggests that the gene FOXP2 mutated some 100,000 years ago, giving humans a genetic sequence that differs from apes in this area. In humans, a deficiency in this gene severely affects how language is both expressed and understood. See Wolfgang Enard et al., "Molecular evolution of FOXP2, a gene involved in speech and language," *Nature*, 418, 869-872.

[37] For example, a 14-year old bonobo chimpanzee called Panbanisha, first refused, then "granted" and participated in, an interview with a reporter.[37] Panbanisha lives at Georgia State University, and has been taught the meaning of about 3,000 words by scientists at the university's Language Research Centre.

Another chimp, Washoe, living at Central Washington University, has a working vocabulary of 240 signs and has taught other chimpanzees to sign.

[38] Robin Dunbar, in *Grooming, Gossip, and the Evolution of Language*, postulated that ape and monkey groups are necessarily limited in size to less than about 150 animals because they socialize through grooming. He extended this theory to state that languages developed to permit larger groups to bond via social gossip. I favour a different explanation. Group bonding requires intelligence to observe, analyze (i.e., associate relevant memories) or recognize behaviours that promote bonding rather than distancing. In other words, social intelligence incorporates the results of a great number of problem-solving activities. Thus problem solving predates bonding. In my opinion, languages developed to facilitate problem solving.

[39] We are not the only hominids to possess the low-lying larynxes required to form a full range of sounds: 200,000 year old Neandertal bones show that they also possessed such an anatomical feature.

[40] Cassirer, *Language and Myth*, 28.

[41] Klaus Zuberbüler, of the Max Planck Institute for Evolutionary Anthropology in Germany, may have found monkey-communication syntax. If so, then some monkey tribes may have developed relatively advanced linguistic abilities. (See James Randerson, "Call of the wild?" *New Scientist*, 30 March, 2002, 10.)

This issue of the *New Scientist* also contains an article that describes how robots, programmed only with "goals, agendas and the desire to form relationships" developed languages employing around 8,000 words. See Helen Phillips, "First Words," pages 24-27.

[42] William H. Calvin, *The River that Flows Uphill: A Journey from the Big Bang to the Big Brain* (New York: MacMillan Publishing Company, 1986). This very readable book interlaces a fact-filled description of the evolution of life and the universe with anecdotes about a trip down the Colorado River.

[43] This, if valid, nicely illustrates how a skill that evolved due to its survival value in one area can be put to use in quite a different area. Another, perhaps better known, example of this phenomenon (termed "exaptation") is the transition of feathers, which are thought to have first evolved as light-weight insulating material to keep the body warm.

Animal bodies have been built from, and consist of, numerous adaptations. Their convoluted origins frequently cause them to be more cumbersome and less efficient than those an intelligent being might design from scratch. The retina of most animal species, for instance, receives photons of light only after they have been filtered through several layers of non-active cells. Contrast this with the eyes of molluscs—light falls immediately upon the retina of an octopus, for example, a much more efficient and sensitive arrangement. Generally, body organs are effective, but probably all might be modified and made more efficient—something scientists have deliberated, and are beginning to attempt.

[44] Richard Rudgley, *The Lost Civilizations of the Stone Age* (New York: The Free Press, 1999), 224-233.

[45] Merritt Ruhlen, *The Origin of Language: Tracing the Evolution of the Mother Tongue* (New York: John Wiley, 1994).

[46] Johanna Nichols, *Linguistic Diversity in Space and Time* (University of Chicago Press, 1999).

[47] Ian Tattersall and Jay H. Matternes, "Once We Were Not Alone," *Scientific American*, January 2000, 62.

For a slightly more recent discussion of the significance of language, read Ian Tattersall, "How We Came to be Human," *Scientific American*, December 2001, 56-63.

[48] Cassirer, *Language and Myth*, 38.

[49] For instance, when the connection between the inferior temporal cortex (which handles the signals that allow us to recognize faces) and the limbic system (which deals with emotions) is severed, familiar faces (relatives, for instance) can be recognized, but this recollection is devoid of all emotional associations, making it impossible for affected persons to decide how to appropriately greet an approaching visitor.

[50] Magnetic resonance imaging provides evidence suggesting that emotions play a part in every decision made, even decisions that might be considered to be entirely based upon reason. (These emotions may be arising from the role our personal or private goals play in all decision making—see Chapter Three, section one.)

[51] The reason why this kind of subconscious activity takes place is explored more fully in section four of Chapter Five.

[52] E. MacPhail, "Vertebrate Intelligence: The Null Hypothesis," in the *Philosophical Transactions of the Royal Society of London*, 1985, B308:37-51, declares that language is the "big step" to becoming intelligent. I disagree, for "intelligence," to me, includes that which animals demonstrate when challenged by a problem of concern to them. (For example, tool-invention by animals or barrier-circumvention by squirrels demonstrates intelligence.) Intelligence (see section seven of this chapter) and second-level thinking are one and the same thing; neither requires language. However, language greatly improves the ability to associate findings and ideas; thus language use increases the ability to solve problems, and so acts to increase intelligence.

[53] Reality differs from person to person, and greatly depends upon the accuracy of each person's sensory perceptions. This is unquestionably demonstrated by people suffering from synesthesia (who often see black letters, words, and numerals as coloured differently, or as coloured symbols, or who may experience loud noises as bright lights, and so on). See Vilayanur S. Ramachandran and Edward M. Hubbard, "Hearing Colors, Tasting Shapes," *Scientific American*, May 2003, 52-59.

[54] The concept of "truth" is convoluted and personalized precisely because each of us uses our own experiences to interpret what different words mean. And as Ullian (W. V. Quine and J. S. Ullian, *The Web of Belief* [Random House, 1970]) argued, everything we think we know about the universe is subject to revision. Mathematics comes closest to being the "truth" (as we shall see in Chapter Two) and religion frequently claims to be absolute, but both give way in light of new knowledge (mathematics more readily than religion). Try as we may, our mental deliberations and verbal expositions can never represent the whole, real, or perfect truth because we can never know it, and because we can never find words precise enough to think or express it. Furthermore, different people will always interpret their personal experiences of the same event in different ways. The "pure and simple truth" can never be expressed.

Quine pointed out that no statement is necessarily true except those we ourselves decide to be true. In fact, extending the discussions presented in earlier sections of this chapter, since the words we use must necessarily be selected from our own mental dictionary of meanings, each one of us defines our own truth. This truth can never be conveyed to another. The best anyone else can do is to try to assimilate the general idea, then, using their own frame of reference, guess at what is meant.

It is interesting to note that a "Theory Of Everything" (see "The Conservation Laws," a postscript to Chapter Seven), if ever formulated, is expected to be only expressible mathematically. It would be impossible to sufficiently define words to represent all that this theory would be capable of telling us. A Theory of Everything would devolve to other less-comprehensive theories (e.g., quantum mechanics or a theory of gravity), which could be more or less understood through defining words, but the Theory of Everything itself could not be linguistically defined.

[55] For a discussion of consciousness see the postscript to this chapter.

[56] This is why we expect our religions and their teachings to be rational and are disappointed when they appear to be irrational. (More about this in later chapters.)

[57] Steven Pinker, *The Language Instinct: How the Mind Creates Language* (New York: William Morrow and Company, 1994).

[58] *Webster's New Collegiate Dictionary,* John P. Bethal, General Editor (Springfield, Mass.: G. & C. Merriam Co., 1959).

Endnotes to Chapter Two

[1] Steven Pinker, *How the Mind Works* (New York: W. W. Norton and Company, 1997), 21.

[2] And perhaps by the same formula—something like: the universe's underlying causality enforces its rational behaviour, while mathematics underlying rationality enforces its causal interrelationships.

[3] Of course, mathematics must describe the real world because each of its many terms has been precisely defined using language, a language that has itself been constructed from our knowledge of the real world (as section six of Chapter One and the previous paragraph pointed out).

[4] See "The Conservation Laws," a postscript to Chapter Seven.

[5] A light-year is the distance that light travels through space in one year, about 9.5×10^{12} kilometres, or 5.9×10^{12} miles.

[6] There are many important branches of theoretical science, where specialists work with pen and paper (or, more often these

days, with computers) and do not work in laboratories or the field, but their work will always have its links to the real world. If it didn't, colleagues would probably start calling them mathematicians.

[7] W. E. K. Middleton, *The Scientific Revolution* (Toronto: C.B.C. Publications, 1963), 12.

[8] This is because the universe's various substructures (e.g., quarks, electrons, atoms, etc.) are very small.

[9] They both probably knew that Aristarchus of Samos had discussed the idea of a sun-centred solar system in the third century BCE. (And was promptly accused of impiety for doing so.)

[10] When individuals judge people (or more accurately but perhaps less frequently, people's behaviour) to be "good" or "bad," they most commonly use criteria valued by their own society. (Note that these values always mirror those espoused by the nation's dominant religion; this is because religions gain their prominence by both guiding the state's evolution and by being reciprocally supported by the state as it grows.) Society and its intertwined institutions (families, schools, churches, governing bodies, powers-elite, laws, etc.) collectively, over time, determine what is considered "good" or "bad" within that society. And society's criteria provide adequate guidance for many, probably the majority, of us, for we often look no further when making a moral decision.

[11] These criteria reflect Kohlberg's six stages of moral judgement: from Self-Interest (Punishment and Reward) through Social Approval (Interpersonal Relations and Social Order) to Abstract Ideals (Social Contract and Universal Rights). See Lawrence Kohlberg, *The Meaning and Measurement of Moral Development* (Massachusetts: Clark University, 1981). Or see Lawrence Kohlberg, *Essays on Moral Development. Volume I. The Philosophy of Moral Development: Moral Stages and the Idea of Justice* (San Francisco: Harper & Row, 1981), 409-412.

Kohlberg, and others, have found that children generally operate at the first two stages (Punishment and Reward)—as do many in prison; that most adults work at stage four (Social Order); and very few are at stage five (Social Contract). No one has yet been found at stage six (Universal Rights).

[12] Social mores, of course, are necessarily trivial standards in this book's frame of reference because they are local and temporal. The criteria used to determine correct social behaviour vary from society to society and are constantly changing. (They can even be observed changing from moment to moment during emergencies.)

Endnotes to Chapter Three

[1] See Chapter Five for an elaboration of this term.

[2] According to Postman, individuals lacking a sense of purpose can fall into a state of psychic disorientation and become preoccupied by a frantic search for meaning. See Neil Postman, *Building a Bridge to the Eighteenth Century: How the Past Can Improve Our Future* (New York: Alfred A. Knopf, 2000), 10.

Postman subsequently postulates that we have no better choice than to search the past to find where to go in the future. I strongly disagree. We are where we are today because of our past thoughts and actions. While this has led to considerable human progress we have made mistakes. Surely we can do better—searching the past for ideas seems a prescription for repeating past mistakes. Moreover, all environments change over time, and historical environments no longer exist. To find where to go in the future, we must look in that direction. In fact, there may be a highly satisfactory beacon to be found in the future, one that does generate a sense of purpose and certainty. The outlook I have in mind will be discussed in Part Four; it is one that could only be determined using today's knowledge.

[3] See a postscript to this chapter for a discussion of the words "purpose" and "meaning."

[4] The metaphysical purpose adopted by many Westerners to guide their moral decision making is to do their best to ensure that they will continue living beyond death. A "soul" or equivalent is usually postulated to exist, since it is clearly not possible to continue living in a body that decays when dead.

In contrast, the metaphysical purpose adopted by many Easterners is to stop living beyond death. A series of progressive reincarnations is the accepted way to achieve this. (Features of major religions are outlined in Chapter Six.)

[5] The mind's prime requirement to think rationally about important issues accounts for the extreme lengths to which people may go in order to behave in accordance with such beliefs. More about this in Chapter Five.

Endnotes to Chapter Four

[1] Read Ruth Benedict, *Patterns of Culture* (Boston: Houghton Mifflin Company, 1934), for many insightful descriptions of how

religions have influenced cultures, and how cultures have influenced people's thoughts.

² Uncertainty is yet another consequence of the universe's causality. Since causality necessitates everything being related or connected (directly or indirectly) to everything else, we can never know absolutely all there is to know about all things and all events. Consequently we can never know all there is to be known about even the tiniest object or action.

³ A well written description of some of the many fascinating beliefs and rituals humans have conceived can be read in *Man's Religions*. See John B. Noss, *Man's Religions*, 5th ed. (New York: Macmillan Publishing Co., Inc., 1974).

⁴ Arrow-head-shaped sharpened stones, cutting knives, shaped piercing stones, and stores of red ochre have been found in South African coastal caves, in debris layers that are over 100,000 years old.

⁵ If such an afterlife did exist, it must certainly be rather crowded by now, for where is the line drawn on admittance? (And what a temporally and culturally wide and interesting mix of inhabitants we would encounter!)

⁶ See Noss, *Man's Religions*.

⁷ See Noss.

⁸ Or "Pious to Atom" (see Noss, *Man's Religions*, 44-45). Also known as Akhenaton and Akenaten (meaning the God Aten—or Light—is satisfied) see Naguib Mahfouz and Najib Mahfuz, *Akhenaten: Dweller in Truth*, translated by Tagreid Abu-Hassabo, (Doubleday and Company, 2000.)

⁹ China and Japan as recently as the past century, but also Ancient Egypt and several other cultures long ago, further believed that members of the ruling family were Earthly representatives of their God. This, no doubt, added considerably to the family's stature and power.

¹⁰ The assumption or belief that a god created the universe does not, of itself, also mean that the universe (or anything within it) exists for a reason, or to meet some purpose.

It is entirely possible to believe that the initiating god lives or lived outside of time, or inhabits a universe completely detached from ours—thoughts not at all foreign to some of our religions, nor to some scientists. Such a creator could have fabricated our universe from either of these positions and long since forgotten that he (read He, She, It, or even a multi-faceted Entity for "he") had done so. The originating god even may have decided long ago that he had nothing else to do, and ceased being.

Alternatively, he could have been acting whimsically at the time, and be quite unconcerned subsequently about what is happening within his creation. (This is one way to resolve the concern of some regarding how a benevolent god could permit the existence of evil, but an unacceptable explanation to many, particularly those who, for reasons of their own, want a judgmental god.) Or, he may be just sitting back, not interfering, observing how events in this universe play out, prior to deciding how to create an improved one. In other words, once we assume the existence of a god, with absolutely no factual knowledge about such an entity, we can attribute to it any properties we wish. Anything can be claimed to be god's will (as demonstrated by the innumerable, often incongruous, religious declarations sometimes proclaimed on television or the radio), and any action can be justified (as evidenced through statements made by some religious terrorists following their appalling actions).

The whole idea of a god seem rather pointless when viewed in this manner; furthermore this perspective completely misses the concept's major value: belief in a god-given purpose allows our minds to make moral decisions, and acting upon these decisions delivers meaning to our lives. Any other belief of equal or greater significance would do as much.

[11] It is important not to confuse administration and leadership. Administrators simply follow policies, conventions, and rules. They are told what to do, either by these statements or by other people. (Political heads of state, for example, are often more administrators than leaders; many rule by listening to what the majority are saying before acting.) Leaders, almost by definition, do not heed rules or other's instructions; they have their own internal guidance system and head where it dictates, fashioning the future as they proceed. Indeed, true leaders frequently feel that rules are made for others to follow, not them. (It might also be noted that leaders are invariably more creative than administrators—see "Creativity," a postscript to Chapter Five.)

[12] As monarchs generally live sheltered lives, few kings (or queens) have been leaders, although all possessed power enough to make their ideas bear fruit.

[13] The need to improve conditions is just one of many psychological needs that influence individual's thoughts and deeds. The need for power, the need to achieve, or the need to obtain or express love, are other well-known examples; any one or more of these may well have been the motivating factor that drove the cited individuals to behave as they did.

[14] Unless we believe that the universe has always existed, or that it is only a figment of our imagination.

[15] See Chapter Seven for a synopsis of this.

[16] The importance of being rational in both science and religion is discussed in a postscript to Chapter Four.

Endnotes to Chapter Five

[1] Recall that in Chapter One we defined memories to include such elements as facts, theories, opinions, personal experiences, emotions, past thoughts, ideas, etc.

[2] Something like the following was once said by an assembly-line worker: "Everyday I comes in, and I switches on the machine. Then I marries the Duke. . . ."

[3] Easier, but often less accurate. Over time, the accuracy and truth of any event held in memory can become unwittingly modified. Memories become erroneously linked (as witnesses' differing statements make obvious). What we think happened may not in fact have happened at all. A wished-for fantasy (for example, that the girl or boy next door had a crush on you) can later be remembered as reality, and is a disorder that has been called the False Memory Syndrome. (See Elizabeth Loftus & Katherine Ketcham, *The Myth of Repressed Memory: False Memories and Allegations of Sexual Abuse* [New York: St. Martin's Press, Inc., 1996] for a discussion of this syndrome.)

Severing the link between the left and right hemispheres of the brain can also cause false memories. The left hemisphere (which searches for and provides explanations of observations recorded primarily in the right hemisphere) when disconnected can be shown to invent reasons for witnessed events, because the mind needs to resolve the conundrum such unexplained events pose. See Michael S. Gazzaniga, "The Split Brain Revisited," in the July 1998 issue of *Scientific American*, 50–55.

[4] For example, any long-partnered individual can often predict how their companion will respond or behave, because many responses stem from a "hardwired" neural network chain.

[5] There is an even higher cost to holding constructs: they are never accurate. The reality-depicting constructs that we hold in our minds are always incomplete, and therefore somewhat false representations of the real world outside. Our senses, our interpretations of what they are telling us, and the way we rebuild in our mind what we imagine exists in the external world, all distort the accuracy of the mental constructs we hold.

Plato believed the reverse. He taught that our minds can comprehend the ideal, and that the real world is only a poor representation of this absolute. In fact, our minds comprehend a (not-too-poor) representation of the true reality that exists outside of the mind. (Plato's ideas gave rise to a science based upon religion and philosophy. This resulted in a millennium of science being used for little other than to "illustrate and interpret the scriptures." See Middleton, *The Scientific Revolution*, 34.)

Interestingly, numerous scientists and mathematicians currently suspect that the basis to reality is mathematical and therefore abstract rather than concrete.

[6] This, naturally, reduces our ability to be creative. (See "Creativity," a postscript to Chapter Five.)

[7] This implies that there are degrees of "valuing." (See also Chapter Thirteen.)

[8] Army "boot camps" regularly operate by enforcing a behavioural mode; after a while this becomes the soldier's mind-set. In time, such conditioning can even create belief. (Pompous "Colonel Blimp" personalities believe that their way of behaving is the one-and-only proper way to behave, and many children are brought up possessing beliefs inculcated in this manner.) The kind of "reformation" we are discussing in Chapter Five occurs in the reverse order. It starts within the mind with a changed way of thinking, and behavioural change follows later. Either sequence of events develops mental constructs.

[9] Much of what is being written here about religious conversions applies equally well to any kind of conversion (e.g., to fascism or communism).

[10] The work of Sunday school teachers and missionaries illustrates this point. Each describes the background, the stories, the key features of their religion, and explains the significance of their rituals to their listeners. They are painting a picture that attempts to convey the reality and relevance of a religious environment to those who lack such an environment.

Once some of these details have been absorbed, once a store of religious information exists to draw from, the pupil may be ready to take the next step. Neophytes are encouraged to value the attainment of some goal that the leader has in mind. The leader's zeal, obvious conviction, passion, and very presence as someone to emulate, all aid this process. What happens next depends upon how these ideas are perceived by the recipient. Often, in children, nothing visible occurs; the listener absorbs the speaker's intention, but does not feel impelled to do anything more. On occasion, in adults, when mental conditions (i.e., constructs created by past experiences and learnings) are receptive, something very dramatic happens: the listener experiences a "conversion."

[11] Western accounts not infrequently also report the appearance of white-cloaked, Christ-like figures.

[12] See later chapters (and the postscripts to Chapter Seven) for reasons why it is not possible to prove either that a god exists or does not exist.

[13] I am indebted to Timothy Ferris for this insight. See "The Interpreter," an essay in Ferris's interesting book, *The Mind's Sky: Human Intelligence in a Cosmic Context* (New York: Bantam Books, 1992).

[14] Animals also transfer mental activities performed consciously into the subconscious. Analysis of the neural firing patterns of Australian zebra finches when singing and when asleep indicate that the birds rehearse the song during their slumber. (See Daniel Margoliash in *Science*, 30 March, 2001.) Similarly, the neural firing patterns that rats produced while negotiating a maze were repeated exactly when these rats slept. (See Kenway Louie and Matthew A. Wilson, "Temporally Structured Replay of Awake Hippocampal Ensemble Activity during Rapid Eye Movement Sleep," in *Neuron*, January 2001, 145-156.) These subconscious activities may occur as synaptic knob growth transforms temporary memory loops into permanent neural networks, or they may be the brain's way of strengthening memories and constructs by repeatedly retracing mental routes taken earlier. Alternatively, the neural firing may be induced as the animal's mind attempts to reduce some kind of stress-causing primitive fear—fear of the consequences that might arise should they forget what has been learned, perhaps.

[15] Stored emotions, with their accompanying tensions, anxieties and stresses, drive many of our dreams. By dreaming, the mind reduces the amount of energy it would otherwise have to expend when awake to handle the by-products of these anxiety-causing emotions. Dreaming achieves this by activating possible stress-relieving (although not necessarily logical) alternative networks to those creating the stressful emotions. In other words, to determine if a dream has any significance, its emotional content must be sought and explored.

Discussing dreams reminds me that my wife, every year or so, dreams that she has lost her purse. These dream experiences, although stressful when occurring, perhaps act cathartically to relieve pressures accumulating from a possibly continual minor worry about the safe whereabouts of her purse. (This happens to be an example where the context as well as the emotion is relevant; dreams are not usually this easy to interpret.)

[16] Stress-produced chemicals may be released into the bloodstream during attempts to solve difficult problems; if so, then these might be the cause of "psychologically upset stomachs."

[17] To be read in a version edited by James R. Newman as a sidebar under the topic Creativity, in *Microsoft Encarta, DVD-ROM Reference Suite 99* (Microsoft Corporation, 1999) originally printed in the August 1948 edition of *Scientific American*.

[18] *The Ottawa Citizen*, February 26, 2001, B4.

[19] Poincaré, in his essay *Mathematical Creation*, reports two daytime instances when (after days of prior thought) solutions suddenly presented themselves to him.

[20] Robert Cooke, *Dr. Folkman's War: Angiogenesis & the Struggle to Defeat Cancer* (New York: Random House, 2001), 242-243.

[21] Adrian Desmond and James Moore, *Darwin, The Life of a Tormented Evolutionist* (New York: Warner Books, Inc., 1991), 419-420.

[22] A similar, but entirely unrelated, process is used by "data-mining" computer software. In this practice, vast amounts of information (for instance, the data banks of an insurance company, large retail outlet, or DNA-sequencing enterprise) are searched to find any qualitative or quantitative co-relationships or commonalties that may exist. By this method, even software that has been given absolutely no instructions about attributes to look for, can find new and often significant connections between various data. These new associations can then be used by forward-thinking individuals to develop new opportunities, products or lines of research.

[23] A temporary but powerful surge in ion flow could occur when tortuous and resistant neural pathways are suddenly replaced by new, free-flowing ones. This sudden increase in ion flow could be the trigger that precipitates a break-through, from subconscious to consciousness, of the newly found solution. Such a surge could also cause a release of emotion-creating chemicals, as well as excite portions of the visual network generating lights and other images.

[24] Mystical experiences are only mystical because we do not understand how they might be produced. Our understanding of such phenomena is progressing, however. Experiments that induce oxygen starvation of the brain (i.e., a biochemical event) can replicate similar perceptions. Subjects reported seeing bright lights, colours, landscapes and people; hearing noises ranging from roaring to screaming; having out-of-body sensations; and feeling emotions of

peace, detachment and pleasure—all of which made the subjects resist returning to consciousness, and all clearly fabricated within and by the brain or mind. (This investigation was carried out by doctors from the neurological department of the University Clinic Rudolf Virchow, Berlin, reported in 1994 in the British medical journal, *The Lancet* [and reviewed in *The Ottawa Citizen* on 24 September, 1994].)

M. A. Persinger and the Neuroscience Research Group at Laurentian University in Canada, have induced "near-death" and "mystical" experiences (with subjects reporting images of tunnels, lights, faces and figures) by subjecting volunteers to weak, transcerebral magnetic fields. As we learned in physics class, a changing magnetic field creates electrical currents in conductors, and neurons (which contain electrically charged chemical ions) act as electrical conductors. Thus, changing magnetic fields around the brain will induce random biochemical flows through neurons, activating stored memories but in distorted fashion. These are then interpreted by the mind to be the events as reported.

See also "A qualitative and quantitative study of the incidence, features and aetiology of near death experiences in cardiac arrest survivors," *Resuscitation*, Vol. 48 (2) (2001) 149-156, for a clinical discussion of experiences similar to those described above.

("Out-of-body" and other sensations formerly considered to be mystical, can also be repeatedly induced by electrically stimulating the right angular gyrus; see Olaf Blanke, et al., "Stimulating own-body perceptions," *Nature*, 419, 2002, 269-270.)

[25] The feeling of "being one with the universe," such as reported by some mystics, artists, scientists, religious persons, and individuals after meditating, also suggests that first-level impressions can be accessed at the conscious third-level of thought under suitable conditions. Cassirer, in *Language and Myth*, provides the clue. Pre-linguistic awareness, or mythic understanding, occurs when the brain receives stimuli from our senses with no interpretation. The whole appears just as it is, to the best of our senses' receiving capabilities. No pre-conceived, language-derived interpretations add to, or subtract from, the awareness. However, this un-analyzed impression hardly ever penetrates through to our consciousness, because we use words in third-level thinking, and words represent what we think to be true, not what is actually true (see Chapter One). When we feel "united" with the universe, we are actually united with our brain's impression of the universe (although even this is filtered through our senses and limited by their

sensibilities). Feelings of grandeur, exultation, immense joy and certainty are all likely to accompany this uncommon and profound experience. The conscious mind cannot in retrospect explain what happened, but it does perceive its significance. (Emotionally strong experiences are often extremely important, particularly those that re-route significant construct linkages.)

[26] I write from experience. See "A Revelation," a postscript to Chapter Five.

[27] The cone, pyramid, sphere, cube, cylinder and prism analyzed in a branch of mathematics known as solid geometry.

[28] Max Caspar, translated and edited by C. Doris Hellman, *Kepler* (London and New York: Abelard-Schumann, 1959), 65.

[29] A solution to any problem clearly cannot come to a mind not prepared to receive it. A prepared mind knows something about the problem's environment and is ready to notice that a problem exists. For example, a new scientific understanding can never be actualized by a non-scientific person, no matter how brilliant he or she may be, because, even if such a solution somehow did arise, the event would pass by unrecognized for what it was. For the same reason, an uninitiated member of an isolated tribe, for example, could never experience a conversion to a missionary's religion: whenever conversions occur, they follow, never precede, indoctrination.

[30] If belief can arrive only through an instance of surrendered rationality (see Chapter Three), then this explains why many intelligent men and women have trouble believing in a god or accepting the dogma of a religion. Intelligence and rationality are intimately linked, and the mind invariably resists onslaughts to its rationality.

This also suggests that many people professing "belief" must actually be relying upon "faith." Faith is weaker than belief because it can be shaken. In other words, the construct built by faith retains ties to the rational world, whereas the construct that harbours belief has severed all such ties. It is faith's ties to rationality that create the need for periodic boostings; true believers have no such requirement.

Endnotes to Chapter Six

[1] See Noss, *Man's Religions*.

[2] According to the *World Christian Encyclopaedia*, there are nineteen major world religions. These can be subdivided into 270 groups, which can be further subdivided into many others. (For instance, there are some 34,000 different Christian subgroups.)

David Barrett et al, Eds., *World Christian Encyclopaedia: A comparative survey of churches and religions – AD 30 to 2000* (Oxford: Oxford University Press, 2001).

[3] See Toby Lester, "Oh, Gods!" in *The Atlantic Monthly*, Vol. 289, No. 2, February, 2002, 37-45.

[4] A number of sources have been invaluable in researching this chapter: *Microsoft Encarta DVD-ROM Reference Suite 99.* Microsoft Corporation; Noss, *Man's Religions*; Chris Richards, general editor, *The Illustrated Encyclopedia of World Religions* (Shaftesbury, Dorset: Element Books Limited, 1997), and a variety of web sites. The statistics were taken from the *World Christian Encyclopaedia*. Another source for statistics is globalchristianity.org.

[5] See the Jesus Seminars (http://.religion.rutgers.edu or www.westarinstitute.org). Over two hundred biblical and religious scholars have met twice yearly for nearly two decades to discuss the accuracy of the words and deeds attributed to Jesus in the New Testament. In *The Five Gospels*, published in 1994, they state that Jesus did not claim to be the Messiah, and that he did not say at the Last Supper that the bread and wine represented his body and blood. In all, they reject over eighty percent of the words attributed to him. In *The Acts of Jesus*, published in 1998, these scholars further state that the resurrection did not happen, that Jesus did not change water into wine, did not raise Lazarus from the dead, did not feed the multitude with loaves and fishes, nor perform many other acts commonly ascribed to him. Indeed, little beyond the fact that Jesus was a first–century Jew who preached and was crucified by the Romans, is accepted to be historically accurate by these experts.

The strongest argument used by critics to refute such findings has been that the stories attributed to Jesus must be taken on faith and are not subject to rational debate such as that conducted by the members of the Jesus Seminars.

Akenson, an eminent scholar and Christian, rejects the Jesus Seminars' findings on the grounds that they frequently ignore Saul's letters. He points out that Saul's memoirs, written by a man who knew Jesus' brother Yacov (now called James the Less), are likely to be much more accurate than the writings attributed to the apostles Matthew, Mark, Luke and John. The Gospels, he shows, were actually written by anonymous authors following the Roman-Jewish war of 66-73 CE, and were intended to show Jesus not as a Jew, but as a Christian. However, Akenson too rejects the idea that Yeshua (Jesus) of Nazareth was anything more than a man of intense holiness. See Donald Harman Akenson, *Saint Saul: A*

Skeleton Key to the Historical Jesus (McGill-Queens University Press, 2000).

Akenson's findings echo those of David Flausser. (Flausser, together with Robert Lindsey, was instrumental in the founding of the Jerusalem School of Synoptic research.) Flausser's research indicates that Jesus was actually the leader of a messianic Jewish cult, and that this cult did not break away from Judaism (to become Christianity) until many years after Jesus died. The tales of Jesus' divinity began during those times.

Doubts about the veracity of all religious records exist. History is constantly being rewritten (by the victor, as the saying goes) and what really transpired in many ancient situations will never be known. An objective person might suggest that it is usually best to "take a grain of salt" with anything that seems completely at variance with common sense.

[6] A total of 124,000 prophets, starting with Adam, see *The Illustrated Encyclopedia of World Religions*, 154.

[7] *Ibid.* 151.

[8] Now considered to have lived from 448-368 BCE (formerly thought to be 563-483 BCE).

[9] One should bear in mind that archaeological findings to date fail to support, and often contradict, biblical accounts of the establishment of the Jewish people.

[10] The descriptions of Moses' exploits were written some 500 years after his death. Modern scholars consider the books of Moses to have had multiple authors, that their stories and the laws have been reworked and polished over many generations, and that Moses may not in fact have been a real person at all.

(Since so many learned scholars and theologians conclude that most bible stories are invented, one wonders why they do not revise the Bible. Surely using an inaccurate source only perpetuates misunderstandings.)

[11] Deists believe that a god was necessary to start the world, but afterwards does not intervene. Theists believe that God oversees and knows everything we do. (Theism is not a necessary part of religion, as Buddhism, with its many, non-divine gods, demonstrates.)

[12] Lucretius (circa 99-55 BCE) sought to show in his poem, *On the Nature of Things*, that gods have no interest or intervention in human affairs, that what is observed is always due to natural causes, and that therefore gods and death should not be feared.

[13] These theological arguments are as follows. Ontological: God, to be the greatest Being that can exist, must exist, for not to

exist lessens His greatness. Cosmological: only a God could bring the universe into existence from nothing. Teleological: the universe and life seem intelligent in design and therefore must have been designed to some purpose. Moral: virtue, the highest duty, must be attainable, therefore God must exist to have made it so.

[14] There are many reasons why more people prefer to believe a god exists rather than to not believe. First, our mind's rationality requires us to aim our decisions at accomplishing some purpose; for many, a belief that God demands certain behaviours provides all the purpose they need. Second, believing that "God is responsible for all" supplies a plausible explanation for everything unknown. For example, before our current understanding of nuclear physics (to trace the evolution of stars), or genetics (to draft an accurate depiction of life's evolution), or pathogens (to account for certain illnesses), a conceivable interpretation was that God was the creator of stars and people, or was driving out evil. "Explaining" significant unknowns by attributing them to the behaviour of a god is still the simplest, most readily understood, and in many cases, the most convenient, answer for the world's poorly educated majority. A third reason is that prominent and persuasive personalities, who may have a vested interest in the continuation of such beliefs, foster them. (Claiming to believe in God is considered to convey an image of being a caring, honest and respectable person in many societies—an image sometimes negated by the facts, but one which is nonetheless useful when seeking re-election, and vital when one's career lies within the church.)

Belief that God created all we see around us settles the question of how everything came into being, but it does not address the question of why the universe was created. This remains a mystery, to religions and to science.

To say that there was a creator is to make a statement purported to be factual. Any statement claiming to be factual opens itself up to scientific investigation. (This is the rationale for conducting the Jesus Seminars.) And science is valuable precisely because it rejects any supposition that has no way of being disproved. Beliefs, by definition, cannot be disproved in the minds of those who believe, and therefore cannot be scientific. (This is why Creationism is not a science.)

Religions are based upon beliefs—or upon faith when belief is non-existent—rather than facts. Rational arguments can never deconstruct a believer's mind, and there is nothing to be gained by embarking upon such an endeavour. However, rational arguments can shake faith (see Chapter Five, endnote 30). And knowledge, particularly scientific understanding, can reduce or destroy an individual's faith. Therein lies both danger (for purposeless minds are unhappy minds) and hope (for rationality's future).

[15] Turk al-Farabi, a tenth century Islamic philosopher, pointed out that philosophical truth was universal and must be superior to religious truth which varies. The following century, a Persian Islamic philosopher furthered this by stating that religion is philosophy made simple for the masses to understand. (This conflicts with my view. While believing in a god makes things simpler, religions seem excessively complex. I find their theologies impossible to unravel.)

[16] For what it's worth (given there are few true measures of "ethicality"), the following data on divorce rates might be interpreted to bear on the morality (if any) of this practice as carried out by members of different churches.

A 1999 survey conducted by the Barna Research Group in Ventura, California, interviewing close to four thousand adults in 48 American states, found that 30% of Jews, 29% of Baptists, 27% of born-again Christians, 25% of mainstream Protestants, 24% of Mormons, and 21% each of Catholics, Lutherans, atheists and agnostics, have been through a divorce. (Data source, *The Dallas Morning News*, 15 January, 2000, G4. This information may also be found at www.religioustolerance.org/chr_dira.htm)

Of course, one can conclude that data in this form is meaningless. On the other hand, one can think that, in as much as many religions promote the family unit, it may indicate something about the relative "morality" of followers of various religions compared to non-believers.

[17] Hinduism, being a compilation of ideas and beliefs, many of which are thousands of years old, cannot be traced back to one founder.

[18] Xenophanes, Herodotus, Julius Caesar, and Cornelius Tacitus all noted differences in religious beliefs, traditions and practices as they travelled from one country to another.

[19] See Benedict, *Patterns of Culture*, 254.

[20] Durkheim insisted that society itself makes religion important; that religion is neither a revelation from on high, nor the consequences of some misguided individual's beliefs and actions (see Emile Durkheim, *The Elementary Forms of Religious Life*, first published in 1915).

[21] Moral standards vary from culture to culture. Practices such as polygamy, infanticide, suicide, genocide, male dominance (including the power of life or death over wives), killing ancient

parents, genital mutilation, and torture, all formed part of past (and some current) cultures. A concept known as ethical relativism (see almost any text on anthropology) warns us against judging another culture's morality using standards drawn from our own.

Most ethicists argue that there must be some underlying moral principles that are universally "right." The trouble with this, as we now know, is that no one has found any such values, although some contend they have. The only single underlying principle, of any possible relevance, that I can think of, is the universe's causality. Perhaps we will be able to use this, some day, to determine moral righteousness.

[22] About three billion people (including Christians, Muslims, and Jews) can be said to be unified by their worship of one theistic God. Another billion people (Hindus) identify Brahman as the one eternal, absolute reality that is the universe, with all else being manifestations. And Buddhists endorse the impersonal cosmic order as being the ultimate reality. Thus, religions generally focus on the idea of one entity, God or otherwise, being of dominant importance.

[23] "Occam's Razor" is the name this rule is known by, because it has been adopted from William of Occam's twelfth century guiding principle, "what can be done with fewer (assumptions) is done in vain with more."

[24] Mary's immaculate conception, for instance, wasn't proclaimed Catholic dogma until 1854.

[25] See this chapter, endnote 5.

[26] Such behavioural differences between religions, whether western or eastern, have been the cause of many a war in the past, and remain so today. Does the God of each faith, or the one God of all, sanction such behaviour in His name? How can this be? And, how long must we continue to behave in this manner?

[27] This is so, simply because everything changes. Nothing is absolute; no entity remains the same for ever. This dictum holds true for the physical universe, and it also holds true for the metaphysical universe (an invention of minds constructed from, and manipulating data drawn from, the physical universe, and thus subject to the constraints that govern that universe). Everything is relative to its time and circumstance. If truth is the accurate description of what is, then truth, also, must be relative. So, too, are our morals. But this is precisely why we may change them—and why we *should* change them—when an improved awareness, changing times or circumstances, demand.

[28] The Vatican in 1992 apologized for arresting Galileo (359 years earlier), and in 1996 Pope John Paul II stated that evolution is

"more than a hypothesis" (formerly the church spoke out against Darwin's thesis).

At this millennium's beginning, the Pope sought forgiveness for the Catholic Church's many past errors. In doing this, he seemed to be implying that the church propagated mistakes. This leaves us wondering which of today's required behaviours may also be mistakes, and would therefore be best ignored.

[29] See "General Systems Theory," a postscript to Chapter Seven, for an explanation of this term.

[30] Thus, I argue, we do not need a god to obtain a list of moral injunctions. Humans can determine "right" behaviour by valuing the achievement of any "right" purpose. However, to guard against those purposes which mentally deranged individuals might call "right," our guiding purpose must be chosen with care and with the involvement of many. Part Four investigates how this might be done.

[31] A few years ago, we were told by the Vatican that heaven and hell do not actually exist—that their existence is best thought of as an afterlife state of existence, one within or without God's presence. I can only assume that this will become the normative belief for Catholics some time in the future. Nevertheless, the Devil must still exist, at least in the Vatican mind, for two priests, Father Gabriele Amorth and Father Giancarlo Gramolazzo attempted exorcism on a deranged girl early in September, 2000. Some state that Pope John Paul II, who had twice previously performed this rite, also participated. (Reported in *Il Messaggero,* and copied in *The Daily Telegraph,* then *The National Post* of September 11, 2000.)

The Anglican Church of England has recently published conflicting statements about hell. A report, "The Mystery of Salvation," approved by the General Synod in 1996, criticized the traditional notion that Hell was a place of eternal sulphurous fires. However, a 140-page report, "The Nature of Hell," released by the same institution in March, 2000, emphasizes that hell is punitive in nature, with torment and punishment awaiting those who reject the teachings of Christ. (Will this, I wonder, occasion mass conversions of Anglicans aware of alternative, more-lenient Catholic teachings?)

[32] I am not a vegetarian, nor am I against using animals to human benefit, but, surely, institutions that seek to provide moral guidance should have something to say about the indignities inflicted upon animals in some modern intensive-farming and animal-testing practices.

[33] The Bible, Genesis, Chapter 1, verses 27 and 28:

So God created man in his own image, in the image of God created he him: male and female created he them.
And God blessed them, and God said unto them, Be fruitful, and multiply, and replenish the earth, and subdue it: and have dominion over the fish of the sea, and over the fowl of the air, and over every living thing that moveth upon the earth

34 See Chapter Seven.

35 See Chapter One, endnote 4.

36 See Chapter Eight, endnote 33, on Creationism.

37 And because, in the past, education used to be restricted to an elite few who could use the authority and commandments derived from a religion to subdue "the masses." (This is still a significant factor in the less developed regions of the world.)

38 However, it may be that these statistics tell us more about the effect various social forces have on the assertions people make. There are many influences that might cause an individual to conceal their actual beliefs.

Writing this chapter reminds me that I not infrequently feel like the child in Hans Christian Andersen's fairy tale, *The Emperor's New Clothes,* must have felt—different from most other people, and wondering what all the fuss is about. I see none of the colourful raiments that others claim adorn the flesh of the religions that parade our world. Am I blind? How many others see as little of significance as I? (And, how many others also think that much of religion is simply wishful make-believe?)

But, worst of all, I sometimes think that we are all being deliberately misled by people in positions of influence who realize that the truth is not as they speak, but who gain by perpetuating falsehoods. What an evil that would be!

Endnotes to Chapter Seven

1 Aristotle, the Greek philosopher whose ideas influenced the whole of the western world for over two thousand years, proposed this arrangement circa 350 BCE.

2 Galileo is the Italian philosopher and scientist (1564-1642) who is also famous for dropping balls of different weights from the Tower of Pisa. (Thus again proving that Aristotle was wrong. Aristotle had stated that heavy objects fall faster than light ones.)

3 Galileo was lucky that nothing worse was ordered for him. A few decades before, in February 1600, an Italian philosopher-monk named Giordano Bruno was burned at the stake by the Catholic Church for saying that the Earth moved around the sun. (Bruno also

thought, as Epicurus did, that the universe must contain other planets that orbited distant stars.)

[4] About three-quarters of observed galaxies are spiral, with arms containing enormous quantities of dust (the birthplace and material of new stars). Spiral galaxies (and possibly all others) appear to contain an unknown dark matter (whose possible presence explains why stars in galaxies rotate faster than can be accounted for by the observable matter within their galaxies).

Current theories hold that dark matter constitutes about thirty percent of the total matter within the universe. Observations made using the Hubble telescope suggest that much of the dark matter associated with galaxies may be due to the presence of ancient white dwarfs (the burnt-out remnants of normal stars). Dark matter has been detected and mapped by observing its gravitational-lensing effects upon the shapes of some 200,000 distant galaxies; it appears to be distributed in a honey-comb-like manner throughout the universe.

[5] See "The Evolution of Galaxy Clusters," by J. Patrick Henry, Ulrich G. Briel and Hans Bohringer in *Scientific American*, December 1998, 52-57.

[6] Andromeda, a spiral galaxy just 2.2 million light-years away, is expected to collide with our galaxy in approximately two billion years time.

[7] Our sun is less than half this age.

[8] Newton (1642-1727) was the first to scientifically investigate why white light, when passed through a glass prism, splits into a rainbow-like band of colours (called a spectrum). His writings nicely demonstrate how much can be deduced from careful observation of a seemingly minor phenomenon. (This text can be read in a sidebar ("Newton on Light and Colors") under "Newton, Sir Isaac" in the *Encarta Reference Library 2002* (Microsoft Corporation).

[9] Spectra often show patterns of dark bands. These bands are caused by the absence (or presence) of chemical elements, either in the emitting source or along the path that the light has taken. This property is used by instruments called spectrometers to detect and measure the presence of minute traces of chemicals, and has applications in forensic, industrial, and research laboratories, as well as astronomical observatories.

[10] A shift toward the red end of the spectrum means that the wavelength of light has increased (i.e., has been stretched out) as its source moves away from us. We are all familiar with this as we hear its effects with sound waves. Sound from a police car siren or from the horn of a train, for example, is heard at a higher pitch as the

source moves toward us (because this forward movement compresses the sound waves and they arrive at our ears more closely spaced together); as the source passes by and moves away from us, the pitch rapidly drops to a lower frequency. Wave frequency change due to relative motion is called the Doppler effect.

11 Edwin Hubble (1889-1951) showed this in 1929 by graphing galactic red shift against their distance from the Milky Way. (The Hubble Space Telescope was so named to honour the discoverer of this very significant observation.)

12 See Fred Hoyle, *The Nature of the Universe* (Oxford: Basil Blackwell, 1950).

13 Gases cool when they expand and heat up when compressed (as is readily noted when using a hand pump to inflate a bicycle tire). Refrigerators exploit this property, using a pump to compress a gas outside the refrigerator (usually in tubes on the back, where excess heat dissipates into the environment) and allowing the gas to expand, and therefore cool, inside (usually in tubes surrounding the freezer box).

14 Since light from the most distant galaxies we can observe takes over thirteen billion years to reach us, the Big Bang must have occurred before then.

15 Matter and energy are different aspects of the same thing (as $E = mc^2$ informs us), and one can be turned into the other. (The symbols E, m, and c, stand for energy, mass, and the speed of light, respectively. Since c is so very large, and is multiplied by itself in this equation, a tiny piece of matter is equivalent to a very large amount of energy. Thus, it takes a very large amount of energy to produce a speck of matter.)

16 This radiation has since been accurately measured (by instruments on the COBE, or Cosmic Background Explorer, spacecraft) to be energy at three degrees above absolute zero. Calculations of the temperature changes which residual radiation would undergo over time following the Big Bang predict precisely this temperature.

Another COBE experiment mapped the universe's very early energy distribution, and found small ripples that could have been the variations that led to the formation of galaxies and galactic clusters. (If the originating Big Bang radiation was perfectly uniformly distributed, the specks of matter that formed from it [via $E = mc^2$, or rather, $m = E/c^2$] would also have been perfectly uniformly distributed, and gravitational pulls on each speck would have balanced on every side. In such a case, there would have been no gravitationally caused condensation, and therefore no stars, galaxies, planets, life, or us.)

Recent measurements of the polarization of cosmic background radiation provides additional evidence of the veracity of the Big Bang theory.

[17] Quasars are enormously bright objects located toward the edge of our universe, and look similar to stars (hence their name—"quasi-stella"). Quasars existed only within the first few billion years or so of our universe's formation. They depended upon the presence of supermassive black holes (gigantic agglomerations of matter about one hundred million times more massive than our sun). Each quasar emitted massive amounts of energy (the light we are seeing now, billions of years later—typically about three times more radiation than is currently emitted by the sum total of all of the stars in our galaxy). Electromagnetic radiations from quasars were produced by electrically charged matter (i.e., gases, stars, star clusters and even galaxies) spinning around the black hole before being swallowed. (Once inside a black hole's boundary—the "event horizon"—nothing can escape, not even light; hence the name, black hole.)

[18] One intriguing argument against the idea that the universe could have existed forever, as required by the Steady State theory, is that we have not been overrun by visiting aliens, either directly or by way of von Neumann probes. (These are devices that technologically competent life forms will be able to construct that explore planetary systems and use what they find to replicate themselves many-fold, before moving on again.) Of course, this argument fails if we are the only intelligent beings in the universe.

For more about self-replicating machines, see John von Neumann (A. W. Burks, ed.), *Theory of Self-Reproducing Automata* (Urbana: University of Illinois Press, 1966).

[19] See Donald Goldsmith, *The Runaway Universe: The Race to Find the Future of the Cosmos* (Perseus Publishing, 2000).

[20] Also known as "dark energy"—named (as is dark matter) because it cannot be seen.

Space is not a void as most assume; it is filled with a form of energy called dark or vacuum energy. This energy exerts a very weak negative gravitational force that builds in magnitude as the intervening space increases. Its weak nature explains why its repulsive force needs trans-universe distances to have any affect. Vacuum energy may owe its existence to a dynamical quantum field (similar to an electro-magnetic field) called "quintessence," or it may be an inert property of empty space (accounted for by the cosmological constant), a possibility first proposed by Einstein.

Dark energy accounts for about 65% of the universe's mass. Normal matter, of which we and everything we see are made, amounts to only 4%. Dark matter (see earlier) accounts for the rest.

[21] Inflation theory suggests that the energy contained within the universe's gravitational field exactly equals in amount, but opposes in type, the energy contained within all other constituents of the universe (photons and particles, etc.). Thus, since they balance out, the universe could have been created from nothing. This poses questions such as: "what existed to cause nothing to become something?" and, "are nothing and something one and the same thing, and if so, just what does that mean?"

[22] Theoretically, many inflation-causing bubbles could occur, each growing to contain a universe. Each universe would be discrete and unique, and each could perhaps be controlled by physical laws different from those that control events in our universe.

Current thoughts about the beginning of our universe (and the possibility that it could be only one of many) are presented by Martin Rees in "Exploring Our Universe and Others," in the December 1999 issue of *Scientific American,* 78-83. (This article also provides a pictorial summary of the evolution of our universe from its beginning to its possible ending.)

See also *Theories of Everything: The Quest for Ultimate Explanation* by John D. Barrow (New York: Oxford University Press. 1990). This thought-provoking book explores the significance of the initial conditions, laws, constants, and other critical factors, in the development of our understanding of what makes the universe behave the way we observe it behaving. Barrow makes a somewhat difficult subject enjoyable to readers as he describes the thinking of philosophers, mathematicians and scientists, from the early days of science to the quantum theories of the present.

[23] Our "gigantic" universe is mostly space. It has been calculated that, if all the space separating galaxies, stars, electrons from nuclei in atoms, etc., were removed, then the whole of the universe's matter would occupy a volume less than that enclosed by a sphere whose radius equalled the distance between our sun and Mars.

[24] This assumption may be incorrect. Recent measurements of the absorption spectra shown by light that passed less than a billion years after the Big Bang through gas clouds containing metallic atoms, suggest that the electronic charge at that time differed slightly from today's value. This does not mean that the laws of physics have changed, but it does warn us to be careful about the

assumptions we make: values thought to be constant, may not actually be so.

[25] 10^{-37} is shorthand for 1 divided by 10^{37}, a very tiny fraction of anything.

[26] In other words about one thousandth of a second, a relatively short period of time for what transpired. This "inflationary" period immediately followed the energy insertion we call the Big Bang. (The whole episode might be compared to the rapid inflation of an automobile air-bag that follows the detonation of its initiating charge.)

[27] This inflationary behaviour explains the homogeneity of the cosmos by showing that it could have resulted from the universe's initial uniformity being preserved by the rapidity of its expansion.

An excellent description of inflation is given in Michael White and John Gribbin's book, *Stephen Hawking: A Life in Science* (London: Penguin Books, 1992).

[28] This is because, to produce the amount of matter we observe in our universe today, the initial radiation energy density—and thus its temperature—must have been so high that any matter forming would have been immediately broken apart by radiation bombardment.

[29] Neutrons, protons, and other particles of matter, would have formed from little packets of energy much earlier, but they would have been immediately broken apart by collisions with highly energetic radiation quanta.

[30] Smoot and Davidson summarize existing theories about events during various time periods, particularly the initial seconds following the Big Bang, in two colourful plates (between pages 182-183) of their book. See George Smoot and Keay Davidson, *Wrinkles in Time: The Imprint of Creation* (Little, Brown and Company (U.K.) Ltd., 1993).

[31] The extremely high early temperatures forced hydrogen nuclei to fuse together and form helium. This early fusion stopped after expansion sufficiently lowered the temperature, and the universe was left with the 23-24% helium content we now find throughout space. (Although fusion continues in the centre of stars, next to none of the helium produced by this means escapes into space.)

[32] There are many millions of black holes in our galaxy alone. They range in size from small, just a few times larger than our sun, to supermassive. Supermassive black holes can contain millions or billions of times more matter than our sun.

The Chandra X-ray satellite telescope has determined (by analyzing radiations from objects twelve billion light-years distant from the Earth) that twelve billion years ago the universe teemed with billions of active supermassive black holes sucking up gas, stars, and debris. This same telescope has recently confirmed that our galaxy, the Milky Way, rotates around a supermassive black hole (this one some two and a half million times more massive than our sun). A different detection method (red-shift spectrography) has found more than thirty supermassive black holes in our neighbourhood, including one in Andromeda. Many (if not all) galaxies rotate around supermassive black holes, most of which have engulfed much of the matter in their vicinity and thus become dormant.

[33] See "The First Stars in the Universe," by Richard B. Larson and Volker Bromm, *Scientific American*, December 2001, 64-71, for an alternative, computer-generated, account of early star formation.

[34] Published in 1905, Einstein's $E = mc^2$ equation explains the origin of the large amounts of energy our sun and the stars release, although the particular sequence of events occurring in a star's core was not deduced until theoretical work was conducted leading to the atomic bomb in the 1940's.

[35] The power of an atomic bomb comes from atomic fission (splitting apart), whereas the vastly greater power of a hydrogen bomb comes from atomic fusion (joining together).

It is relatively simple to make atomic bombs using radioactive isotopes of uranium, because they are constantly splitting apart (with each split releasing energy, other emissions, and neutrons, which then bang into and split other atoms—producing the so-called chain reaction). All that's required is to drive together pieces of uranium (the more radioactive, "enriched" isotope U-235, is used). (The difficulty stems from finding a way to force the lumps together sufficiently quickly that many atoms split before the resultant energy release pushes everything too far apart [which stops the chain reaction]. This problem was solved by detonating a containing shell of conventional explosives.)

It is slightly more difficult to force enough hydrogen atoms together to make a hydrogen bomb. Physicists succeeded by exploding an atomic bomb and using the extremely high pressure this developed to compress surrounding tritium (an isotope of hydrogen that contains two, rather than one, neutrons in its nucleus). Squeezed tightly enough together, tritium atoms fuse to form slightly lighter atoms of helium; the small amount of extraneous matter is expelled in the form of large amounts of energy.

[36] The announcement that "cold fusion" was possible created much excitement a few years ago. Many thought, for a while, that everyone could one day have a little fusion reactor in their home, turning hydrogen gas into an unlimited amount of cheap energy. (Energy generated this way would be cheap because the hydrogen gas used as fuel can be produced by electrolytically splitting water—which requires significantly less energy than that released when hydrogen is fused to form helium.) Unfortunately, the experimental results could not be repeated: nuclear fusion cannot be achieved in the way proposed.

(This cost-benefit does not apply to hydrogen fuel cells. The amount of electrical energy required to produce the fuel hydrogen exceeds that released when it is later combined with oxygen in fuel cells. Automobile companies are gearing up to use fuel cells in transportation because fuel cell emissions are pollution-free [and because of government legislation], not because hydrogen provides low-cost energy.)

[37] Hydrogen was more plentiful earlier in the universe's life, and stars were generally bigger than they are today. Larger stars burn faster and have a shorter life.

[38] It was earlier proposed that hypernova, about a hundred times larger than the average supernova, could occur and be the source of extremely intense gamma-ray bursts (GRBs) of energy that have been detected, but GRBs are now thought to signal the birth of black holes.

[39] The remnants of a supernova recorded by Chinese astronomers as occurring July 4, 1054 CE, can still be seen in the Crab Nebula. When first observed, it remained bright enough to be visible during the day for more than three weeks. (Since the Crab Nebula is 6,300 light-years away, the supernova actually exploded 6,300 years before it was first observed on Earth.)

On February 24th, 1987, astronomers observed a star, known to have been about twenty times more massive than our sun, exploding as a supernova. The emissions from its remains are being carefully monitored to learn more about the processes involved.

[40] The visible universe is calculated to be approximately 13.7 billion years old.

[41] There are so many stars in the universe that modern telescopes would be able to detect supernovae occurring every minute, if they were aimed in the right direction.

[42] Most stars pair up to form binary (or larger) systems and orbit each other around a common centre of gravity. Single stars, like our sun, are the exception, rather than the rule. Binary systems

would produce complex effects on orbiting planets, and this might affect the number of planets supporting life forms.

[43] Part of Orion's sword, the Great Orion Nebula (about 1500 light-years distant from us) contains a star-forming region. About 700 young stars lie within the centre of this nebula, and some 150 of these are surrounded by rings of gas and dust particles that herald the future formation of planetary systems (see section five of this chapter).

[44] Asteroids are pieces of matter that have been left over from this process. Most of our sun's asteroids move in an elliptical orbit (the asteroid belt) between the orbits of Mars and Jupiter. Significantly more of the early dust from which our planetary system originated still orbits the sun as chunks of dust and ice outside Pluto (the Oort Belt). These lumps can be displaced from their orbits by passing stars, and some have taken up elliptical orbits around the sun, occasionally becoming visible as comets.

[45] However, some planets have been observed directly by telescopes (see http://www.eso.org/outreach/press-rel/pr-1998/pr-18-98.html).

[46] Two planets (with a strong likelihood of there being a third occupying a life-favourable position) have been found to orbit the star 55 Cancri, by this method.

[47] Light-bending was predicted by Einstein's General Theory of Relativity (published in 1916). When a solar eclipse occurred in 1919, a team of astronomers used the opportunity to check the theory's accuracy. As the moon blocked the sun's radiance, they were able to photograph light coming from stars located behind the sun. Since the sun itself lay on a straight line drawn between these stars and the Earth, this could only happen if the light from these stars bent, as predicted, as it travelled close to the sun.

[48] Some of the light from the star HD 209458 is periodically blocked by a planet that orbits it.

[49] The thousands of gaps in Saturn's rings are likely to have been created by satellites of various sizes. Saturn has about twenty confirmed moons, an additional dozen or so possible ones, plus millions of smaller chunks formed from frozen gas and water.

[50] The planet that orbits Boötis has been investigated in this manner.

[51] The same process (i.e., radioactive decay of elements such as plutonium) is used to provide heat (subsequently converted into electrical energy) in satellites sent to inspect planets that are too remote from the sun to allow effective use of solar panels.

It is conjectured that radioactive elements in the Earth's core created an atomic reactor that still operates, keeping the core molten even though heat is continually being lost through the Earth's mantle. See Brad Lemley, "Nuclear Planet," *Discover*, August 2002, 36-42. For information on naturally occurring nuclear reactors, see http://nuclearplanet.com.

[52] Calculations involving the rate of radioactive decay, as well as the amount and kind of decay products, give scientists one method of dating the Earth's beginning. For instance, analysis of the decay products of uranium isotopes found locked within zircon crystals from the Jack Hills section of north-western Australia, shows that these particular crystals are between 4.3 and 4.4 billion years old.

[53] Just a little cooler than the temperature at the sun's surface. (The temperature of the sun's core is very much hotter—about 16,000,000°C.)

[54] See "The Sound of One Rock Falling," *Discover*, February 2002, 18.

[55] A "purpose" of sorts can also be determined within open systems by examining the "feedback" received from their significant supersystem. Outputs that are accepted imply that the supersystem "wants" more of the same, thus providing a "purpose" or reason to continue their production. Outputs that are rejected by the supersystem cannot be exchanged for needed supplies so production must eventually cease. Thus, production of acceptable outputs (i.e., fulfilling the "purpose" of meeting the supersystem's requirements) is a necessity for continued existence. (However, we should note that large supersystems, such as our biosphere, can tolerate lengthy periods of non-productivity [and even negative contributions] from a portion of their subsystems, just as organizations can from a few of their employees. This buffering capacity can disguise the true state of affairs and "false purposes" may be followed for long periods of time before becoming apparent.)

See "General Systems Theory," a postscript to Chapter Seven for further elaboration of these concepts.

[56] This is not as surprising as it may at first seem, because, if superstring theory is correct, absolutely everything in existence is built from miniscule, vibrating, energy fields.

[57] In fact, if any religion placed God in this position and was content to have Him play no part in our affairs, then such a religion would survive any form of investigation or attack. (But then, such a God wouldn't meet our current psychological needs at all.)

⁵⁸ And surely any Designing God must have therefore also desired all to unfold exactly as it does. In such a case, it could be considered rather impertinent of us to ask Him to intervene to satisfy our own fleeting desires.

⁵⁹ If the universe is simply part of something that has always existed, then the reason it exists needs no explanation—the continued existence of something needs no more accounting for than the continued existence of nothing. Only changes of state need explaining (for example, where something exists which did not exist before).

Endnotes to Chapter Eight

¹ J. D. Bernal's book, *The Origin of Life* (London: Weidenfeld and Nicolson, 1967) provides a classic account and critical discussion of what was known in the 1960's about the origin of life.

Many books have been written about life's origin, more recently including:

David W. Deamer and Gail R. Fleischaker, *Origins of Life: The Central Concepts* (Sudbury, Massachusetts: Jones and Bartlett, 1994).

John H. Holland, *Emergence From Chaos to Order* (Helix Books, 1998).

Noam Lahav, *Biogenesis: Theories of Life's Origin* (Oxford: Oxford University Press, 1999).

² Miniscule microbes (about one thousandth of a millimetre in length) that possess membranes and DNA have also been found living in solid rock, at temperatures over 150° Centigrade, five kilometres underground. These probably developed from life forms that existed when the rocks formed. See "It's a small world after all," *Discover*, January 2001, 58.

³ Other theories relating to the origin of life are mentioned in the postscript to this chapter.

⁴ For more detail on this subject, see Michael Gross, *Life on the Edge: Amazing creatures thriving in extreme environments* (Perseus Publishing, 2001).

⁵ Meteorites are fragments of asteroids that did not become part of the solar system's planets, and they carry information that depicts what existed at the time of their formation. The Murchison meteorite was extensively examined in 1997 and found to contain an excess of left-handed amino acids—the same bias that life on Earth exhibits.

⁶ Amino acids in space show a slight predominance of left-handedness. (N.B. Miller-type experiments produce equal-handed amino acids.)

⁷ And may still be forming.

⁸ See "Life's Far-Flung Raw Materials" by Max. P. Bernstein, Scott A. Sandford and Louis J. Allamandola, in the July 1999 edition of *Scientific American*, 42-49.

Also see: David F. Blake and Peter Jenniskens, "The Ice of Life," *Scientific American*, August 2001, 44-51; Jason P. Dworkin et al, "Self-assembling amphiphilic molecules: Synthesis in simulated interstellar/precometary ices," *Proceedings of the National Academy of Science*, January 30, 2001. The SETI website (www.seti.org) also provides links to other information on this topic.

⁹ It should be noted that complex (i.e., multicellular) life forms could not have existed anywhere in our universe during the first third or so of its life. It takes several billion years for most stars to burn, then collapse, so producing the novae and supernovae that make and release the heavier chemical elements that partly constitute all planets and life as we know it. It has taken another four billion years for life on this planet to evolve into us. Complex life is a relative late-comer to the universe's party.

¹⁰ See Sarah Simpson, "Questioning the Oldest Signs of Life," *Scientific American*, April 2003, 70-77, for a recent review of this topic.

¹¹ Research carried out by some two hundred scientists from a dozen countries led them to recently state that there are at least five major kingdoms: animals, fungi, green plants, red plants, and brown plants. Their classification is based upon cladistics, a method that groups organisms according to evolutionary characteristics that are genetically shared with a common ancestor. (This contrasts with traditional classification methods whereby life forms are grouped according to the postulated relative importance of shared physical characteristics.)

Undeniably genetic tracing is the more accurate method. However, it is likely that the traditional classification system will continue to be used for many years to come—the scientific nomenclature that has developed over the centuries based upon these approaches is too vast to be revised very quickly.

The modern "family network" (rather than "family tree") is sketched in the article, "Deciphering the Code of Life" by Francis S. Collins and Karin G. Jegalian (*Scientific American,* December 1999, 90). It looks markedly different from those traditionally shown in school.

Ian Tattersall, in "Once We Were Not Alone," *Scientific American*, January 2000, diagrams (on page 60) the latest thinking about our own (the hominid) family tree. The essay is accompanied by two lovely illustrations of early life painted by Jay H. Matternes. The subsequent issue of this journal (February 2000) outlines the relationships between bacteria, Archaea and eukaryotes. (See in particular W. Ford Doolittle's article, "Uprooting the Tree of Life," 90-95.)

[12] Archaea have now been found to be living in many other environments—animal intestines, compost piles, and marshes, for instance.

[13] Hydrothermal vents are likely to exist on any planet having a hot core and water. (Possibly most planets possess these two features during their early years, with some retaining them for most of their lives). If so, primitive Archaea-type life forms may be abundant throughout the universe.

[14] Anaerobic: not requiring air or oxygen. Cyanobacteria still exist and can be found in water and soil, on trees and on rocks. Mats of floating cyanobacteria frequently form mound-like structures called stromatolites. Fossil stromatolites date from all ages, including back to 3.5 billion years ago.

[15] The transition from prokaryotic to eukaryotic cells is discussed by Christian de Duve in "The Birth of Complex Cells," *Scientific American*, April 1996, 50-57.

[16] Perhaps those that grew larger became more readily visible and excessively preyed upon.

[17] More than 98% of human genes are identical to those possessed by chimpanzees. (Thus we can effectively resuscitate the "missing links" any time we want—by way of the petri dish and molecular genetic techniques. The recipe would be: take one chimp zygote, replace those DNA portions that differ from ours with human DNA, return to the womb and wait. Turning one human race into another should be even easier: humans are over 99.9% genetically identical.)

[18] Via Earth's magnetic field reversal.

[19] Long before our species appeared, however, the brain pan size of early *Homo* ancestors began enlarging. This size change, occurring about two million years ago, could be related to the development of language, but, since complex languages probably did not develop until later (see Chapter One, section four), it is more likely that the increase was a result of the changes introduced by the onset of the ice ages. Having to cope in a frozen environment would have rapidly increased the number of life-threatening problems to be

addressed. Larger brain pans in and of themselves do not improve problem solving, but, if the genetic mutation that first brought them into existence also caused an increase in the number of neurons grown, this would. Greater problem-solving ability enhances survival, and the mutated genes that produced a larger brain pan (able to accommodate additional neurons) would have been passed on to subsequent generations.

(Several forces favour smaller heads [not the least being birth canal dimensions] and brain pans stopped enlarging about 200,000 years ago. Possibly word use [and the communal problem solving that third-level thinking and language use encourages] reduced the requirement for further enlargements.)

[20] The Vostok ice core from Antarctica contains records that date back to 420,000 years ago.

[21] More than a dozen intriguing photographs of insects entombed in fossilized resin are printed in "Captured in Amber," by David A. Grimaldi (*Scientific American*, April 1996, 84–91). DNA from plant and insect life preserved in amber for some 125 million years has been sequenced (i.e., the nucleotide order determined), adding to our understanding of evolution's pathways.

[22] See J. William Schopf, *Cradle of Life: The Discovery of Earth's Earliest Fossils* (Princeton: Princeton University Press, 1999) for a description of the beginnings and development of the science of precambrian paleobiology.

[23] Robert Francoeur, *Evolving World, Converging Man* (New York: Holt, Rinehart & Winston, 1970) provides a nice summary that, in less than twenty pages, describes life's gradual changes from its beginnings to the rise of man. By letting one day represent a fourteen million year time period, he compresses the more than 3.5 billion years of life's history on Earth into a one-year time-line. On this scale the Cambrian Period (when most of the major animal groups first appeared) corresponds to November 16–25, and the Jurassic (dinosaur) Age lasts from December 19–22. Early man does not appear until 6:30 p.m. on December 31 (the equivalent of 3 m.y.a. on this one-year time-line). Many similar accounts are in print.

[24] Every copy of Darwin's book was sold the first day it came out. It has been called "the book that shook the world."

For a readily accessible series of more recent discussions about Darwin and life's evolution, visit www.pbs.org and link to "evolution" at www.pbs.org/wgbh/evolution.

[25] Eukaryotic organisms (i.e., plants and animals) possess intracellular structures called mitochondria which process chemical

molecules obtained from food to release their energy. Mitochondria possess their own DNA (called mitochondrial DNA, or mDNA) which is passed directly from mother to child and does not vary between generations unless some random mutation occurs. The mutations that do occur can be used to trace a species' history, as well as relationships between different species. By this means, the progression from one original organism to subsequent divergent organisms can be uncovered.

[26] Scientists, for instance, have mapped the entire genome of the Archaean microbe known as *Methanococcus jannaschii*. This information, together with the genomes of representatives of the Prokarya and Eukarya kingdoms, may eventually allow us to find the genes common to all living things—that is, some of the genes possessed by the universal ancestor of life on this planet. It may only be a matter of time before a map can be drawn that will show definitive interconnections between all Earthly life forms. This will concurrently trace the major features of the full evolutionary route to *Homo sapiens*. (Genetic tracing becomes difficult in bacteria, however, because they are able to transfer genes laterally, i.e., directly from one to another. This suggests that we may have to be content with tracing life's ancestry back no further than bacteria.)

Scientists have already used mitochondrial DNA taken from five major ethnic groups which make up the current global human population to trace the ancestry of *Homo sapiens* back to a time between 140,000 and 290,000 years ago. We have all evolved from one or another of about one hundred or so woman, the "original Eves," who lived in Africa. (And we should really repaint any of our pictures involving Eve that do not show her having very dark skin.)

[27] Weiner, *Time, Love, Memory*, 184.

Surprisingly, the human genome contains around 30,000 genes, only about twice the number of genes possessed by a worm or a fruit fly. Several hundred of our genes turn out to be identical to those found in simple bacteria.

[28] Weiner, ibid, 206.

[29] de Duve, *Vital Dust*, 112.

[30] Human change today is likely to be occurring most rapidly in the mental, rather than the physical, arena. The most "mentally alert" individuals are the most likely to provide the broadest environment for their children to experience. These children will, as a consequence, likely learn more, in depth and variety, than their peers, thus becoming potentially better equipped for success in later life. Whether or not the descendants of the "most mentally alert" will create a sub-division that eventually becomes genetically built into

H. sapiens' future will depend upon the environment—it must continue to provide a niche where this behaviour is rewarded by reproductive success. For instance, if humans eventually move out into space, it is likely to be the most mentally able that are chosen to go. If these space colonizers do succeed and multiply, then this kind of speciation may become a wide-spread, potentially dominant, reality.

(Because social programs support the survival and reproduction of all, the genes of the "most mentally alert" individuals are unlikely to dominate on this planet in the foreseeable future [because individuals possessing such genes currently tend to have fewer children than others]. The fact that rational behaviour acts to eliminate the genes that result in this behaviour suggests that there is something irrational [possibly its sustainability] about the environment our current social programs create.)

[31] Natural selection states, essentially, that offspring are never identical, and that those possessing advantageous variations are more likely than their less-advantaged siblings or peers to survive and procreate. These advantages are thereby passed in greater numbers to the next generation, and this causes all species to change over time. There is not much to dispute about any of these postulates.

[32] We continue to call Einstein's masterpiece "The General Theory of Relativity," but few state that it is just a "theory," or that atomic bombs cannot exist.

"Laws," too, including the Conservation Laws of physics, can be overthrown if negating proof is discovered.

(Never knowing if any "fact" or theory is entirely correct is a consequence of living within a [presumably] closed system. See the postscripts to Chapter Seven for elaboration.)

[33] A certain amount of knowledge is needed to understand and appreciate what the theory of natural selection tells us about evolution. However, even those without such schooling still require some kind of explanation to account for life's beginning and the presence of humankind. Creationism was developed to offer an explanation of sorts. It is an ancient idea that attempts to explain the unknown in a simple way. (All religions, if they are to be taken seriously, must explain how and why things are as we find them to be.) Unfortunately, Creationism ignores or attempts to refute too many evolutionary facts to be credible to anyone with an educated and impartial mind. Moreover, a belief in Creationism (like all beliefs) installs the opinion that one knows just as much as (and, often, even

more than) is known by those who can call upon mountains of solid evidence that supports a different view.

That a few hold creationist views wouldn't particularly matter, if it were not for the fact that their belief forces them to influence what is taught to children. Currently, schools in the American states of Alabama, Kansas, Nebraska, New Hampshire, New Mexico, Ohio, Tennessee, Texas, and Washington must teach that evolution is deemed to be no more significant than the belief that Creationists hold to be true (in spite of the mountains of credible evidence that support the former, and none that supports the latter). Still other schools deliberately leave evolution entirely off the curriculum to avoid controversy; they resort to teaching facts alone, and say nothing about the simplifying and edifying explanation that makes the existence of all we see in nature so logical and understandable.

In our world so dependant upon scientific knowledge, Creationism is a capricious belief to support, and it is very likely to limit the future success of its believers. This may not matter to adults, but it hampers children, who have many years to live in a techno-medical society. Of course, in the long run, the fallacy is self-correcting—after all, we live in a universe where survival of the fittest gives preference to those whose actions fit the facts. Unfortunately, as noted in endnote 30 to this chapter, it can only confer preference to those who act rationally when the immediately controlling environment is a rational one. This appears not to be the situation in a number of U.S. school boards.

It may be necessary to articulate that science neither opposes nor supports religion—it simply tries to uncover and understand the facts as they are found to be. To refute the millions upon millions of pieces of evidence that reveal that life evolved (and that humans are just one consequence of this evolution) is foolhardy. Rational individuals might better ask themselves which is most likely to be the truth—that which was originally written by a few wishing to promote a particular belief, or that for which evidence can be found in tangible form, everywhere, by anyone who cares to look.

Read Robert T. Pennock, *Tower of Babel: The Evidence against the New Creationism* (Boston: MIT Press, 1999) for a scholarly refutation of creationist ideas.

[34] A single DNA change in a one-celled life form will have a more profound effect, more often, than a single change in a many-celled life form. Thus, although many mutations may be inconsequential and some may be fatal, the few that are neither can result in the rapid diversification and adaptation of simple life forms.

This is a common phenomenon in hospitals, where environments hostile to pathogens are routinely maintained—so this is where strains of bacteria able to resist the latest antibiotics keep cropping up.

[35] Darwin was ill at home and Wallace was collecting abroad at the time.

[36] See Jonathan Weiner, *The Beak of the Finch: A Story of Evolution in Our Time* (New York: Alfred A. Knopf, 1994). A lovely book for anyone to read.

[37] This chain of events is known as "punctuated equilibrium," and has been popularized by Stephen Jay Gould, an influential evolutionary biologist and widely read author of many books.

[38] The fallen rock perhaps forces a nourishing stream to forge a different channel. The fine dust thrown into the atmosphere from a volcanic eruption or a comet's impact might block sunlight for several years. Extensive ice sheets can prevent plant growth for centuries.

[39] Research suggests that biological recovery following any wide-spread ecological extinction takes an average of ten million years for complex animals, a relatively short period of time on the geological scale used to date fossils. (Recovery can be a matter of days, or even hours, for rapidly reproducing organisms such as bacteria.)

[40] Sediments formed around 245 m.y.a. have recently been found to hold carbon "buckyballs" that contain trapped helium and argon gases which are present in a ratio similar to that found in carbon-based meteorites. This adds support to the theory that the effects of a sizable comet or asteroid impact caused the massive extinction that wiped out over 90% of all extant species (and marks the Permian-Triassic Boundary). This extinction eliminated much competition and provided the niches that some lizards exploited during the following twenty million years as they slowly evolved into the earliest forms of dinosaurs.

Other environmental calamities may have occurred several times between 750 and 570 m.y.a. An analysis of carbon-12 to carbon-13 ratios in sedimentary layers formed in ancient oceans shows that life came to a standstill four times during that period (see the August 28, 1998 edition of *Science*). It is postulated that the Earth was entirely covered with ice during these times, resembling a planetary snowball. What subsequently happened may have been as follows. Life survived (as multicellular algae and seaweeds) in the small pockets that formed where volcanoes and hot springs maintained some warmth. Meanwhile, the same volcanoes continuously pumped carbon dioxide into the atmosphere, and a greenhouse environment slowly developed. After some tens of millions of years (during which time life in the warm pockets diversified as it variously adapted to each pocket's particular environment), the greenhouse gases triggered periods of planetary warming. About 565 m.y.a. most of the ice covering the Earth melted, and the pockets opened up. The life forms released from different zones would then have been able to cross-fertilize, and in the warm, nutritionally rich environment, with minimal competition, evolution would have run rampant. This could have spawned the broad diversity of ancestral multicellular plants and animals that we find in fossil form from this period, and begun the Cambrian Age.

[41] This type of formulation was first proposed in 1961 by Frank Drake, currently Chairman Emeritus of the SETI Institute. (SETI, the Search for Extra-Terrestrial Intelligence, is a project that has been running for over 25 years at University of California-Berkeley using radio telescopes.) Drake wished to guesstimate the possibility of being able to contact extra-terrestrial life, and made a calculation somewhat like the following:

> Number of technical civilizations in the Milky Way =
> *Number of stars in the Milky Way (say $2x10^{11}$) x*
> *Fraction of stars with planetary systems (say ½) x*
> *Number of planets per star (say 1) x*
> *Number of planets favourable to life (say 1/10) x*
> *Fraction eventually developing life (say 1/10) x*
> *Fraction with intelligent life (say 1/100) x*
> *Fraction at our technical stage of development (say 1/10,000).*

Multiplying these together we find that the number of planets with life at an "electronically-developed" stage in our galaxy could be around a thousand. Of course, the number likely to be at our stage of development, when communications over distances are carried out by AM, FM, or digitally encoded electro-magnetic waves, the kind of signals SETI's instruments have been looking for, is quite critical. More advanced beings may well be using a different form of communication—piped-optical for example, or some other method that our current instruments would not detect. SETI has also been conducting optical searches (without success) and has just begun looking for laser beacons (which, if narrowly focused, would only be detected if we happened to pass through their beam).

In our calculation, since we are only estimating the possibility that life exists elsewhere, we are not bothered about its intelligence or stage of development so can ignore the reduction these fractions would contribute. Moreover, we are discussing life's presence in the entire universe, not just our own galaxy.

[42] See Guillermo Gonzalez, Donald Brownlee and Peter D. Ward, "Refuges for Life in a Hostile Universe," *Scientific American*, October 2001, 60-67.

[43] Common understanding holds that, to be considered living, an entity must meet at least four criteria: consume energy, expel wastes, respond to its environment, and reproduce. But see Chapter Ten for an alternative definition.

[44] For a discussion on this topic see "Livable Planets: Calculations raise the odds for finding life in the cosmos," by Corey S. Powell in *Scientific American*, February 1993, 18-20.

The Earth may already possess a few samples of life from elsewhere in the cosmos, lying undiscovered on our ocean floors or hidden in rocks or crannies on our continents. Entities resembling a string of cells (and possibly being primitive life forms) have been discovered on a meteorite originating from Europa (one of Jupiter's moons). However the sample is not large enough to conclude whether any of the entities were once living.

Analyses of magnetic-field intensities along with various other measurements taken by satellites, indicate that Ganymede, Europa and Callisto (all moons of Jupiter) possess water. Some form of life may exist or have existed within this water, but this possibility remains to be explored. Probes, specifically equipped to test for water, may be sent to Europa within the next decade. Future Mars landers will be exploring areas where frozen reservoirs of water have been discovered, specifically looking for the presence of life. However, within our solar system, only our planet provides easy living; conditions on the other planets and moons are such that any life that might be found is bound to be primitive.

Astronomers occasionally search for distant signs of life using satellites and telescopes principally designed for other purposes. This will change in 2007, provided NASA's scheduled Kepler Mission satellite launches successfully. This mission will carry telescopes designed to locate and check the atmospheres of exoplanets for the presence of ozone. Ozone is a gas formed from free oxygen, and free oxygen can only be produced in lasting quantities by life. This is because methane, produced by bacterial decomposition of organic matter, constantly removes free oxygen by combining with it to form other compounds. If both methane and oxygen are found in exoplanet atmospheres, then life is almost certain to be producing a continuous supply of the oxygen.)

⁴⁵ This guess may be far too cautious. For reasons to be outlined in the next chapter, it is highly likely that life will always arise when circumstances permit (see also de Duve, *Vital Dust*, xv and 20).

⁴⁶ The pyramids, Nazca lines, Stonehenge, crop circles and other occurrences have all been suggested as being possible evidence of alien visitation. However, all can be more credibly explained as being due to human effort.

⁴⁷ Ian Crawford, "Where are they?" *Scientific American,* July 2000, 38-43.

See also Peter D. Ward and Donald Brownlee, *Rare Earth: Why Complex Life is Uncommon in the Universe* (New York: Copernicus, 2000).

For the opposite view, read Amir D. Aczel, *Probability 1: Why there must be Intelligent Life in the Universe* (New York: Harcourt Brace & Company, 1998).

⁴⁸ For an excellent review of life's evolution through its four billion years of development, read *Vital Dust* (op. cit.) by Christian de Duve, a Nobel Prize-winning biologist. de Duve traces life's four billion years of development on this planet from its chemical beginnings, through its RNA and DNA encodings, to its current status. His text contributes the kind of understanding that should be possessed by all who make decisions that bear upon life's future.

⁴⁹ In particular, the second law of thermodynamics. This law states that the total amount of disorder (also known as entropy or complexity) in a closed system (for example, the universe) can never decrease.

To understand entropy, it may help to consider a handful of black marbles shaken into a box containing a handful of white ones. The two mix, and the marbles become disordered, their arrangement "complex." It takes energy to separate the black and white marbles and return this "system" to "simplicity." Thus, the disorder of a complex system can be decreased but energy is required, and this energy must come from some larger system. In the example just given, the energy comes from the food eaten by the person separating the marbles. In turn, the energy in the food came from an even larger system—our sun (via photosynthesis), whose energy in turn came from that introduced at the universe's beginning (through the singularity that opened into the Big Bang).

But, the universe is the largest system we know. It is a closed system (as far as we can tell) and energy cannot be taken from "outside" (if such a place exists). So the universe becomes more and more disordered each second as innumerable events occur everywhere. It becomes more complex, its entropy is ever increasing, and it must forever continue to become so, because there is nowhere (again, as far as we know) from which can be taken the energy needed to order it again.

Subsystems within the universe can be made more ordered because they are open systems, and energy can therefore be taken from elsewhere in the universe's stock. Life does this organizing, for example when it changes complex food molecules into simpler ones before recombining them in ways useful to itself. Many other processes also reduce entropy, for example when sunlight or lightning break water into its constituent hydrogen and oxygen molecules. But the net result of any kind of organizing is always an increase in the universe's complexity, because the energy exchanges that are involved all release electromagnetic radiation (usually in the form of heat—think how hot a person would become were they to quickly sort ten thousand marbles, for instance). This energy release eventually heats (i.e., agitates) atoms somewhere, and adds disorder. In other words, with each exchange the total quality of the energy is irreversibly degraded, increasing the total complexity of the universe.

Life started simple and is becoming more and more complex through the addition of variations and adaptations to what existed earlier. In this manner, its evolution parallels that of the universe.

Endnotes to Chapter Nine

[1] This would still allow much variety. Control exerted solely by general laws of physics allows limitless unscripted scenarios to unfold between programmed birth and targeted death. (See "Free Will," a postscript to Chapter Five.)

[2] Mathematical physicists have shown that, if any of several physical constants (for example, the charge of an electron) were different by even the smallest fraction, then the resulting universe would be uninhabitable for life as we know it. Of course, this does not prove that a God existed. It does not mean that the universe was precisely designed to enable life to begin and eventually evolve to produce humans. The fact that we are here means only that we are here—as this universe developed, conditions arose that were and are right for life forms such as ours to evolve. If the universe existed in another form, then either our equivalents would exist in a different form, or no beings would be present asking questions such as these.

The most powerful argument against the proposition that the universe was designed solely to cause humanity to evolve, is that our universe might be only one of an infinite number of universes, many of which would have started with parameters that do not permit life to evolve, and just some, such as ours, that do. We do not know what exists outside of our own universe, and so cannot say whether or not this argument carries any weight.

[3] John D. Barrow and Frank J. Tipler, *The Anthropic Cosmological Principle* (Oxford: Clarendon Press, 1986).

[4] But see also the discussion on Free Will, a postscript to Chapter Five, for additional discussions on this point.

[5] Richard Dawkins, *The Blind Watchmaker* (New York: W. W. Norton & Company, 1986), 21. Dawkins evinces the same wonder about life as the Rev. William Paley expressed when he wrote that life's complexity proves that God exists. However, Dawkins repeatedly demonstrates that the much simpler explanation—mutations accompanying natural selection over time—is the correct elucidation, easily able to account for the existence of so many different and complex species developing (and becoming extinct) in such a long time span. The book provides a delightful romp through the nuances of evolutionary theory.

(The title of Paley's 1802 text was *Natural Theology*, an evocative combination of the two words.)

[6] Scientists at the State University of New York recently announced that they have built an active polio virus (that paralyses, then kills, mice) using ingredients obtainable from chemical supply houses. Viruses, although they possess DNA and can replicate under the right conditions, are not considered to be living (see Chapter Ten, endnote 8). Nevertheless, some see this as being another step toward creating life from scratch in the laboratory.

[7] See the previous chapter, endnote 43, for a "definition" of life.

[8] Pinker, *How the Mind Works*, 241.

[9] Usually in small steps, and through repeated trial-and-error effort, but, increasingly, with the more intelligent animals, by way of second-level, association-recognizing, thinking.

[10] Evolutionary Psychology, an important recent advance in understanding behaviour, argues that many inherited behaviours began as evolutionary adaptations to survival or reproduction problems. See David M. Buss, *Evolutionary Psychology: The New Science of the Mind*.

[11] Loyal Rue, professor of religion and philosophy at Luther College in Decorah, Iowa, states the same thing. He points out that living things make much use of deception, and that humans have always used myths to ward off nihilism and the angst that comes from realizing that the universe and life are without purpose or meaning. He calls for the invention of a "noble lie" to fill the void that

our loss of belief in God has produced. See Loyal D. Rue, *By the Grace of Guile: The Role of Deception in Natural History* (New York: Oxford University Press, 1994).

I could not agree more. However, it hardly needs saying that this artifice would have limited value if we knew the myth to be a lie. What I will be suggesting we should use is not a lie. It is an assumption, declared to be just that, right from the beginning. (A noble assumption, if you like.)

12 Physicists have been working on this for decades. Controlled fusion is still only possible for small periods of time, and energy input still greatly exceeds energy output, but progress is being made. The internationally funded Iter Project, based in Germany, intends to build a new research and development facility (see www.iter.org for their latest news), and it has the longer-term goal of constructing a prototype fusion power plant. (It has been recently shown that smaller fusion reactions can be controlled more easily than large. This may reduce the projected twelve billion dollar cost.)

13 Beam me up, Scotty! Star Trek, and similar programs, are more than just science fiction to many. They seem to be calling to, and resonating with, dormant feelings of human potentiality. However, the amount of energy required to construct the reassembling matter (or convert a supply into the form needed) will doubtlessly delay this achievement several millennia. Too far ahead for you or I to benefit, but not too far for humankind—if it survives.

14 Teilhard de Chardin had a similar idea. He held that all the universe's material and spiritual content would eventually converge into a super-consciousness that he named the "Omega Point." See *The Phenomenon of Man* (New York: Harper & Row, 1959). First published in French as *Le Phénomène Humain* (Paris: Editions du Seuil, 1955).

15 Omnipotent, because with knowledge comes power; omniscience would simply be a precondition to this final state.

16 *Webster* defines "meta" as follows:

> *Meta, prefix. "situated behind or beyond," "later or more highly organized or specialized form of," "more comprehensive: transcending . . . used with the name of a discipline to designate a new but related discipline designed to deal critically with the original one."*

Webster's Ninth New Collegiate Dictionary, Frederick C. Mish, Editor in Chief (Markham, Ontario: Thomas Allen & Son Limited, 1986).

Thus, the term "meta-purpose" is intended to convey the idea that its stature is greater than other purposes.

17 See "Free Will," a postscript to Chapter Five.

Endnotes to Chapter Ten

1 Darwin used the words "competition" and "competes" frequently in *On the Origin of Species*. He knew that life is assertive. Tennyson, too, knew what much of life was about, writing, "nature, red in tooth and claw," when penning *In Memoriam*.

2 Thomas Malthus, in *An Essay on the Principle of Population*, published in 1798, was among the first to write that life (although he limited his discussion to human life) would continue to grow in numbers unless prevented by external forces. Darwin's thoughts were influenced by that essay. This chapter takes for granted that Malthus' principles continue to operate, and apply to all forms of life.

3 Even we "modern" parents do not automatically limit the number of children we have. We use contraceptives only when we consider that additional progeny will curtail, endanger, or affect the quality of our life, or adversely affect the lives of others we care about, or when a restriction is imposed and enforced, such as in China where more than one child per couple is made illegal and penalized.

4 It is precisely because life's processes are basically chemical processes that we can treat illnesses with chemically synthesized drugs, and can chemically manipulate emotions and genes. (Indeed, genes themselves are simply chemical molecules—and not even very complex ones.)

5 Not all life on Earth depends directly upon sunlight, but all life requires an energy supply of some kind. As earlier noted, many simple life forms living near deep ocean hydrothermal vents or in subterranean rock crevices obtain their energy by chemosynthesis.

6 Attaching atoms to, or releasing atoms from, a molecular complex invariably results in the loss of some energy to the environment; thus the complex cannot simply reuse the same energy it has just released. (It would be a perpetual-motion machine were this not so.)

7 It is likely that this process is ongoing, continually occurring on Earth even today at sub-life levels in fluid environments of sufficient complexity. However, energy-enriched molecules, of any kind, living or dead, make excellent fodder for omnipresent bacteria and therefore would not survive very long.

8 Freeman Dyson, in *Origins of Life* (Cambridge: Cambridge University Press, 1999) hypothesized that life began twice; once as a

metabolic (or energy-processing) entity, and once as a replicating entity, with the two forms later uniting.

I cannot understand how an entity could replicate without an energy-processing mechanism being involved. (A virus is a replicating entity, but (in many people's opinion) it is not a living one. It has to control its host's energy-exploiting mechanisms before it might be said to be living.)

⁹ See page 20 of Richard P. Feynman's book, *Six Easy Pieces* (Reading Massachusetts: Addison-Wesley Publishing Company, 1995). Although based upon a series of lectures first presented in 1963, their originality still makes this book very enjoyable reading.

¹⁰ Of course, if the world was awash with food and there were few inhabitants, then competition need not be aggressive. Its denizens would still be "exploiting" the resources, but they would have no need to fight each other to gain a share of what is available, and the "less-able" would possibly survive and reproduce as often as the more-capable. This peaceful situation would change as the population sizes increased however, for life does not voluntarily restrict its own procreation.

¹¹ At first glance, this statement may appear to be too sweeping. Indeed, some life forms cooperate symbiotically, and many never come in contact with one another. But, I would argue, symbiotic relationships essentially create single organisms out of two—both are needed to survive. And those who never contact each other still draw upon resources that either directly or indirectly (through growth and spreading, or the distribution of waste products [via movements in the surrounding environments]) would otherwise eventually supply energy to those at a distance.

¹² This suggests a direct relationship between perceived population pressure and aggressive human behaviour.

¹³ I have searched many times for a better word than "exploit" to define what life does. Exploit is a harsh word, and conveys many negative images and feelings. But I can find no other word so descriptively accurate. (We will better understand why this is so as we continue.)

¹⁴ Dawkins, *The Blind Watchmaker*, 192-3.

¹⁵ Lawrence and Nohria, condensing work conducted by many into one comprehensive theory, state that humans are controlled by four drives: Acquire, Bond, Learn and Defend. This is too many, in my opinion. I think that just two drives can account for the behaviour of all species—Exploit and Reproduce. The compulsion to exploit, to me, contains Lawrence and Nohria's concepts of Acquire, Defend (what one has acquired), and much of

Learn (we learn to better exploit). The urge to reproduce is equivalent to their drive to Bond.

See Paul R. Lawrence and Nitin Nohria, *Driven: How Human Nature Shapes Our Choices* (San Francisco: Jossey-Bass. 2002).

[16] If it is life's basic nature to exploit, then we would be foolish to ignore or deny this fact. Recognizing that life lives through exploiting allows us to explain much, and facilitates the correction of excesses when they occur. We do ourselves no favour by refuting the nature of reality, regardless of how unpalatable it may seem.

[17] A billion years ago was near the end of the Proterozoic Eon, when bacteria, prokaryotes, eukaryotes and multicellular organisms existed in the oceans, but the lands were barren. See Chapter Eight for a little more detail.

[18] This is why, to quote Ernst Haeckel (a German biologist, 1834-1919), "ontogeny recapitulates phylogeny," i.e., fetal development restates evolutionary history. Presumably, research will show gene expression successively turning on stored instructions in the same sequence as evolution changed the species. (This also suggests that, sooner or later, body structures become so burdened by their out-grown history that radical change—evolutionary surgery—occurs, and gene expression is turned off.)

[19] The brain is a clear example of this. The cerebrum, considered the seat of intelligence where the brain's most complex functions (i.e. problem solving) are carried out, is outermost. The cerebellum (which co-ordinates movements) and the medulla (which helps to maintain respiration and other involuntary functions) lie underneath, on either side of the thalamus (which directs all sensory signals—except smell sensations—to and from the brain). The hypothalamus (which regulates many basic body functions such as temperature control, sexual and emotional behaviour, urges to eat and sleep, and so on) lies near the centre of the brain. And at the core, the central brain stem carries out the most basic and primitive tasks—those of regulating heart rate, blood pressure, regurgitation and respiration, as well as conducting electrical signals to and from the body's organs and systems. This construction demonstrates how one complex body structure, the brain, has been formed: modifications that proved useful to survival were outgrowths of earlier ones.

[20] Brain imaging provides physical evidence that this occurs. As different portions of the brain control different body functions, imaging its pattern of electrical activity reveals which functions are being called upon. Using this technique, it has been found, for example, that the brains of violinists grow unusually high numbers

of synaptic connections in the area which controls the finger movements of the left hand.

²¹ Applying new understanding may be as mundane as filling in a box on an IQ test sheet, as overlooked as recognizing a face in a crowd from an earlier chance meeting, or as practical as designing a bridge. Intelligence is expressed through actions that result from biochemical flows through neural links *consciously* formed by an animal.

²² And toward complexity, but its complexity will be that of the mind rather than that of the body. Humans are developing technology that will transform society, and this technology is becoming indispensable. Today we have instant messaging between places anywhere in the world. Tomorrow we will have the ability (via nanotechnology, and perhaps otherwise) to manipulate individual atoms and molecules. This will have immense consequences, affecting everything from genetics to space exploration. The tools and devices of the future will have to be created, used and maintained by minds well-versed in complex matters, a situation likely to create the conditions where mental complexity confers greater opportunities to survive and procreate.

Incorporating electronic circuits into the brain (already being performed to confer hearing and sight, with much more likely to take place within the next decade) will create a different, but possibly equally viable, kind of mental complexity.

²³ Barrow and Tipler, *The Anthropic Cosmological Principle*, 675 and 677.

²⁴ Gerald Feinberg, *The Prometheus Project: Mankind's search for long-range goals* (Garden City, New York: Doubleday & Company, Inc., 1969), 147.

²⁵ Ursula Goodenough, *The Sacred Depths of Nature* (New York: Oxford University Press, 1998), xv and 174.

Endnotes to Part Three Conclusion

¹ Tipler has written a book that might appear to state the same thing. His view is that life must, and therefore will, eventually convert the whole universe into a liveable habitat. See Frank J. Tipler, *The Physics of Immortality: Modern Cosmology, God and the Resurrection of the Dead* (New York: Doubleday, 1994), 57.

However Tipler's approach and conclusion differ from mine. Tipler uses physics in an attempt to prove that God grants eternal life (see page 7). I have a problem with this. If eternal life means to rejoin loved ones, as he suggests, consider what this might entail. Let's say that I wish to rejoin my wife, my children and grandchildren, my father, mother and sister. But (to make this short) my grandchildren might wish to rejoin their spouses and their children. So they will be elsewhere, surrounded by an entirely different set of people than those I know. In fact, in this scenario, the only others we would be with would be those that equally reciprocate our own love for them (a much smaller, if existent, subset). Therein lies another problem for me. I would not want to spend eternity being reminded that those who fully reciprocate my love are few and far between.

(Worse; what if we fell out? An eternity is an awfully long time to spend with someone you no longer like!)

No. I am very content to look forward to nothing after I die. Life is for the living, I think, not for re-living once we are dead.

Endnotes to Chapter Eleven

[1] There are many examples of this: funding gigantic dams or re-directing rivers with disastrous results, financing governments that promote genocide, supporting dictators who are politically astute but morally bankrupt, depleting fish stocks to provide temporary jobs, and so on.

[2] This may have already happened. It has been suggested that the AIDS virus may have been passed along in polio vaccines tested in central Africa in the late 1950's, because those vaccines were made from chimpanzee-kidney tissue which may have been contaminated with the chimpanzee precursor of the AIDS virus.

The human version of mad cow disease might be considered to be another example. It was once found only within sheep, but then diseased sheep were made into cattle feed. Other examples (for example, genetically transformed fish and plants that later escaped to proliferate in the wild) were mentioned earlier.

[3] This is a possible, if somewhat implausible, consequence of developing nanotechnological medical tools. Molecular-sized motors and circuits have been made in the laboratory. It is predicted that by the year 2020 we will have made machines a hundred times smaller than a pinhead, that can move within an animal's body correcting ills, possibly extracting the energy to do so from fat molecules. Nanotech machines can be designed to self-replicate, and may be used to seek and destroy cancer cells. What if they mutated, replicated, and started consuming other kinds of molecules? How could they be contained?

[4] The great library of Alexandria, for example, was deliberately burnt (on three occasions, by order of three different rulers, according to legend). Jewish relics were destroyed in Nazi

Germany, as were 1500 year old colossal Buddhas and other museum artifacts recently in Afghanistan (where Taliban rulers thought their existence "un-Islamic").

⁵ The amount of information our senses detect from the total available in the full electromagnetic spectrum (and discounting any other spectrum of information that might exist) is probably comparable to the fraction represented by one day out of a full year.

⁶ That the exact parameters necessary for life to arise and evolve within the universe were built into the universe at its beginnings has been postulated by many authors. Perhaps the most significant contribution to this discussion has been made by Barrow and Tipler in *The Anthropic Cosmological Principle*. They maintain that a life-giving factor had to have been designed into the origins of the universe. Their rationale is that none of the fundamental dimensionless constants of physics can be altered without resulting in a universe that could not support life.

This theory, of course, has been countered. The most significant rebuttal contends that this universe could be just one of an infinite number of universes, each somewhat different from the other. Those that provide conditions that allow life to exist, eventually develop life; those that do not, do not. By definition, we must exist within a life-developing universe, and the fact that its parameters cannot be changed without making it unable to support life proves nothing. Martin Rees has written an interesting and relatively short book that explores the significance of these universal constants, and prefers this latter explanation of our existence. (Martin Rees, *Just Six Numbers: The Deep Forces that Shape the Universe* [New York: Basic Books, 2000].) Superstring theory (see "The Conservation Laws," a postscript to Chapter Seven) actually predicts the existence of an infinite number of universes.

Barrow and Tipler conclude that we must be the only intelligent life to exist (which might be inferred from the title they chose for their publication). This is an unlikely possibility in most scientists' view, given the vast number of planets that must exist. Toward the end of their book Barrow and Tipler argue that, once begun, life must continue to evolve until it has "regulated" everything within all possible universes (pages 675 and 677). I agree, as the similar conclusion formed in this book indicates.

⁷ This is where the "life-becomes-god" scenario differs from the gods of old. Previous conceptions of god install him before the universe began; this book's vision sees a god-like entity emerging as the culmination of life's evolution, not existing until the universe has spawned life and life has developed to its full. In this scenario, either

the universe developed spontaneously from nothing (or vacuum energy, see Chapter Seven, endnote 20) or, as earlier noted, there was no beginning and no end, just an endless succession of universes, some generating life that evolves to possess god-like abilities.)

⁸ Although computers may be having an equal or greater effect on the way we think and act. Successful computer operation entails learning new concepts and methods to solve the many minor problems that inevitably turn up. Tackling these challenges trains the mind to think logically (since all software has been logically developed). Moreover, computers connect individuals and ideas—ideas that may be very different from one country to another. Different ideas in a logical mind need reconciling, and new mental constructs and behaviours may develop.

Endnotes to Chapter Twelve

¹ Where will all these people live? Not in my backyard, you say?

It is easy to view others outside of our immediate community as potential poachers, likely to take what we do not actively defend. We exhibit this kind of thought pattern when we erect trade barriers, restrict immigration, perpetuate or tolerate racial hatred, amass excessive wealth, or mouth obscenities in road-rage. As the world's population increases, we can expect this behaviour to increase in frequency and degree, because life acts in this manner when its survival is threatened. If such behaviour is already happening, it is not too hard to predict how another two or three billion people will affect the quality of life for all, no matter where this increased number of people live.

² Many organizations make efforts to educate the world's public and influence opinions and activities. The World Resources Institute, for example, "provides information, ideas, and solutions to global environmental problems." Its program advocates "knowledge to catalyze public and private action." Its goals centre upon the Earth's climate, its ecosystems, the environment, and use of materials. (See the WRI web site, www.wri.org.) The Worldwatch Institute has similar concerns that can also be read on the web (see its web site, www.worldwatch.org.)

³ Paul Hawken et al, in *Natural Capitalism* (Boston: Little, Brown and Company, 1999) estimates tens of thousands of groups.

⁴ It is even worse than this, if we are to believe statements made by some of the activist groups who routinely gather to protest at meetings of organizations such as the G8, the World Trade

Organization, the International Monetary Fund, and the World Bank, to name a few. The use of large sums of money to bring about global change is said to be doing more harm than good. Furthermore, these and other large multi-national organizations, they claim, are making the decisions that local and national governments should be making.

5 Although the organization's structure and machinery also have a bearing on this inaction.

6 This purpose guided decision making, and, it might be argued, victory was achieved because everyone, from the war-room to the trenches, kept the overall goal firmly in mind. (Perhaps too, the Axis were defeated in part because not everyone fully shared Hitler's vision.) This was responsible behaviour, and the goal-directed actions of everyone during those WWII years paid for the freedoms many of us now enjoy.

7 See "Creativity," a postscript to Chapter Five.

8 Individual freedom to exploit is the driving force behind capitalism, of course, and restriction of this freedom probably had much to do with the demise of communism.

Prosperity does not follow democracy, as has been claimed. It follows the freedom to exploit, and capitalism acknowledges this in the mechanisms it employs. Democracy is needed to curb capitalism's excesses, and so preserve civilization. Freedom (to exploit) must always take priority because living and exploiting are one and the same thing, as section four in Chapter Ten, explains.

9 The Magna Carta became law in England in 1215. It is the source of legal practices (such as the right to trial by jury) since adopted by countries around the world.

10 Communism, which eliminates competition and free markets, teaches us much about what not to do when running a country.

11 The West actively opposed the spread of communism (particularly in the last half of the twentieth century—overtly, as in Korea or Vietnam, or covertly, as in many other parts of the world) only because it felt threatened. The United States, through the UN, declared war in the Gulf in 1991, for the same reason.

12 Benefits the United Nations might bring are effectively neutered because nations hold their country's welfare to be more important than the world's welfare. This is surely because the world has no common vision of where its heading.

13 See "Is Economic Growth Good for Us?," a public lecture given by Professor Nick Crafts to the Royal Economic Society, December 4th, 2002.

For background material, see Nicholas Crafts, "UK Real National Income, 1950-1998: Some Grounds for Optimism," available at www.ise.ac.uk/Press/currentNews/crafts.pdf.

[14] In the meantime, companies conducting international business frequently opt to be governed by Vienna Sales Convention rules, rather than the often less-rigorous laws of their own country. Many claim that a comprehensive global trading standard is sorely needed.

[15] "Economic" refugees, much in the news of late, are just one example of what can result.

[16] Loyal Rue, *By the Grace of Guile*, 275.

[17] See Chapter Five, section two, for an elaboration of the term "construct."

[18] For example: algae, used in the biotechnology industry to produce food and dietary supplements, were formerly grown outdoors (because they needed sunlight to grow), where their ponds were readily contaminated. The harvest then had to be put through an expensive purification process. Today, through the addition of one (ex-human) gene, they can be grown in the dark, in sterile vats. Another example: silk (for textile and industrial use) used to be spun from spiders. Today, goats, cloned from gene-altered cells, produce milk from which large quantities of spider's silk can be extracted.

[19] Cloning animals is not yet a simple process and many clones die from developmental and genetic problems before birth. This may result from the fact that clones are usually produced from DNA taken from adult animals (of proven worth), and a number of these genes will have suffered mutations during their life within the donor cell. Mutations have little effect when involved in the reproduction of just one cell, as occurred before the genes were altered, but can affect the formation of whole organs, and produce malformed or non-functioning systems, when made to program an entire animal.

However, the science of cloning is rapidly improving. Ten or so years ago the success rate for cloning apparently healthy cattle was about one percent. At the time of writing, the success rate is about twelve percent. Further, the premature death of clones that survive birth is now less than twenty percent (normal death rate is about fifteen percent).

[20] For instance, a deaf lesbian couple in America recently chose a deaf male friend to father a child who, they were happy to discover, was born deaf. They explained that they wanted the child to enjoy the same experiences that they enjoyed. From their frame of

reference this may have merit, but many think that it was not the correct moral decision to make.

[21] We see such a global awareness in public reactions to the events of September 11, 2001. People everywhere are thinking more carefully about the consequences of terrorist actions. Terrorist organizations today, and the groups that support them, have less credibility and more to fear, than used to be the case. Much of this counterforce stems from the general public's new awareness, and the support it generates for the implementation of anti-terrorist actions.

Endnotes to Chapter Thirteen

[1] See introduction to Part Four for a distinction between these two terms.

[2] James Lovelock, in *The Ages of Gaia: A Biography of Our Living Earth* (New York: Bantam Books, 1990) shows that life modifies its environment, eventually reaching a state of equilibrium when energy consumption balances waste disposal. This results in an interdependency that can be considered to act as a single entity. Eventually, one supposes, this interdependency between living and non-living might encompass the whole of the universe.

[3] See "General Systems Theory," a postscript to Chapter Seven, for a background discussion of terms such as subsystem and supersystem.

[4] Forgive my personifying life by saying that it will "reward" and "punish" behaviours (here and in later sections). Doing so makes various points easier to express.

[5] In this book's scheme of things, what happens on Earth affects the larger supersystem of Life within the universe only as much or as little as it ultimately contributes to the formation and actions of oB. If descendants of humans will some day explore the universe to eradicate all living things, then destroying ourselves now to prevent such an occurrence might be the best contribution we could make.

[6] In fact, learning was made suspect in some western societies. The very roots of Christian theology warn against knowledge. The story of Adam and Eve declares that their innocence was lost when they ate fruit from the Tree of Knowledge of Good and Evil, and their punishment was the loss of immortality, for themselves and their descendants.

I have a personal experience to recount that relates to this matter. For a few months, almost five decades ago, I taught a class in a village elementary school in England. One day I asked the

Headmaster why it was always the same few children who stayed at home whenever they had the slightest sniffle. He replied, "Oh, they're Catholics, and they have a Catholic doctor. He tells them to stay at home. He doesn't believe in too much education." Of course, this might be just the Headmaster's bigotry showing through, and the doctor might have wanted to reduce the spread of infection. But, since medical training in England is secular, and non-Catholic doctors did not tell children in their care to stay at home whenever they had a sniffle, perhaps the Head had reason for his statements. He may have been basing his remark on his many past experiences with a variety of doctors. (On the other hand, one example proves nothing; this particular doctor may have been an exception. However, I have vague memories of reading other anecdotes that suggest he wasn't.)

The majority of religions have not valued learning for everyone, perhaps because to do so might teach that reality's truth—the practical kind that we use everyday—has been discovered by humans over centuries of hard inquiry into the nature of things. It is not "revealed" by some interceding god.

[7] Of course, rationality does not prevail where emotions, cultures, traditions, or any other such influences, dominate. Some, as we know, would say that their God has other intentions in mind, and that these should take priority over any man-made efforts—but we have already traced that contention to its source.

[8] "Correcting" views featured in existing religions pertaining to any moral issue (homosexuality, for instance) is often very difficult: it should be relatively simple in a rationally constructed religion.

[9] We are approaching this state in some "emancipated" parts of the world, where individual freedom and universal equality are becoming sacrosanct principles. The first is interpreted to mean that anything (not harming others) is permitted; the second equates to "what you have, I must be able to have." Combine both, and we end up with garbage-strewn streets that disgust visitors, and gay bishops that split religions.

[10] This is the mechanism that underlies religion's value in society: social tensions and disagreements are reduced when everyone values the same religious goal—because each undertakes the responsibility of following the same code of behaviour.

[11] Just as every other DNA-containing cell does, if cloning is included in our considerations.

[12] There may be numerous reasons why an abortion might be logically wise. Examples include: when the developing fetus puts the

mother at risk (the mother is contributing to Life, and so takes priority over a non-contributing fetus); when the fetus is abnormal to the point that it could not survive birth; or when conditions mean that a baby could not be fed or maintained, and so on. (The last example suggests that some pre-existing external factors are wrong.) Abortion, then, may not be a mortal sin in our developing system of morality (although actually having an abortion might well be emotionally impossible).

[13] To obtain the report, "Ecological Footprints of Nations," see www.ecouncil.ac.cr/rio/focus/report/english/footprint.

[14] For a statistical calculation of current and projected future world population numbers (as well as past figures), visit the website www.ibiblio.org/lunarbin/worldpop.

[15] This may soon cease to be a problem, if MRI screening is used to examine the brains of people suspected of having knowledge about criminal activities.

[16] For instance, *Confessions of an English Opium Eater* by Thomas De Quincey. Samuel Taylor Coleridge is said to have written the symbolic poem, *Kubla Khan*, in an opium-induced state. (He began taking opium to reduce his pain from rheumatism, but eventually became addicted.) See Marcus Boon, *The Road Of Excess: A History Of Writers On Drugs* (Boston: Harvard University Press, 2002) for many other examples.

[17] We can't even stop recreational drug use in our prisons. What does this say about the kind of controls that would have to be put in place (and, presumably, about the people who want to put them there) to completely stop drug use in the "free" world outside of prison?

[18] This topic has been the subject of an extensive, award-winning, inquiry by Dan Gardner. See "Losing the War on Drugs," at www.mapinc.org/gardner.htm (the Media Awareness Project website).

See also *Sensible Solutions to the Urban Drug Problem*, a series of policy papers released August 22, 2001 by the Fraser Institute, which claim that the war on drugs is lost. The series is retrievable by following links starting at http://www.fraserinstitute.ca/publications.

[19] The reason such laws are enacted, I suspect, has as much to do with reducing the nation's medical costs and retaining votes as it has to do with saving lives. Would it not be better to proportionately reduce—or even deny—insurance payments, medical treatments, and other benefits, to the degree individuals consciously contributed to their own injury? (Some doctors already do this: they

refuse to treat lung cancer sufferers who continue to smoke. And am I the only person who thinks that those whose wilful carelessness contributes to their own downfall deserve to some degree what they get?)

[20] Adam Nash, born in the United States in 2000, has been called the first designer baby. He was conceived specifically so that his six-year-old sister, who would otherwise die from Fanconi anemia, could be given stem cells from his umbilical cord. Several eight-cell embryos were screened and one that matched the sister's tissues but did not contain the disease-causing genes was implanted. (Geneticists find that 75% of all embryos screened for chromosomal disorders are abnormal; an explanation for why so many embryos abort spontaneously.)

[21] This debate may soon become unnecessary, because stem cells can now be grown from embryos created by parthenogenesis, whereby an egg cell is chemically induced to develop into an embryo (i.e., no sperm cell is required). Such embryos occur in nature but fail to live beyond a few divisions. Parthenogenetically created monkey stem cells have been used to grow functioning heart and brain cells.

[22] Politicians seldom like to discuss ethical or moral matters. I think this must be because they cannot predict how expressing possibly contentious views might turn voters' opinions in the next election.

[23] However, when the courts ruled that the Harvard Mouse (a genetically altered mouse much used in cancer research) was property, they were stating that companies can claim ownership of newly created living organisms, another potential moral minefield. Does a genetically altered human baby become a company's property now?

[24] Critical mass does not mean fifty percent or more of the world's population. It simply means the number of people needed to bring about a significant change. Very few, like-minded, influential individuals may be all that's required.

Endnotes to Chapter Fourteen

[1] A religion built rationally might more effectively be sold emotionally. Humans respond to both to varying degrees. But beware of loss of integrity, and let rationality be present and dominate at every stage of its presentation.

[2] Recall the triangular pyramid mentioned in section four of Chapter Twelve—democracy forms one corner of civilization's foundation. In a democracy, the direction in which civilization heads

is a matter for the population to decide. It also determines the apex, the purpose to be used when writing society's governing laws. The population, in democracies, has always placed religion in this position.

3 Opposition is likely to come mostly from those in the middle—organizational and institutional heads and managers who fear disruption of their niches. Leaders of many religious organizations are extremely likely to oppose the development of an alternative universal purpose. Heads of non-religious organizations and academia are less likely to oppose such an endeavour, because people in these positions must already realize that one globalized or universal religion is likely to create a more orderly world. This end is particularly desirable, from their point of view, because the value they have built during their time in the organization is best passed on in an orderly world. (Since Life advances through the efforts of those who exploit, this last benefit should not be decried.)

4 For example, the WFA (the World Federalist Association) "promotes the universal rule of law at the international level," and is just one of many activist-organizing associations. (See www.wfa.org.)

5 Such survey methods involve summarizing the results of a survey or poll and returning this summary to the respondents, who are asked to read it then respond to another survey. Repetition can clarify ideas, and may develop consensus.

6 There is currently no organization constituted or able to perform the functions we are discussing; something entirely new needs to be developed.

7 Eventually we may draft an international code of ethics, and its acceptance and subsequent honouring may become an important rite of passage, perhaps marking the transition from infancy to adulthood (or, even, from nationhood to inter-nationhood). Such a code is likely to be similar to those that many professional organizations develop to guide members' decision-making—the Hippocratic Oath, for example.

(This proposal would be similar to undertakings of the 8th and 9th centuries, when the Hadith was written to guide the behaviour of the many non-Arab converts to Islam. Coming from differing cultures, many did not know the accepted Arabic norms of behaviour, and needed some guidelines when the Koran was not sufficiently explicit.)

Endnotes to Chapter One Postscript

[1] Possessing particular body attributes (e.g., long muscular legs that might predispose one to be a runner) contribute to building the mind's "*me*" concept, of course.

[2] The same principles (i.e. networks of varying connective strengths and thresholds) have been used by David Fogel and Kumar Chellapilla in designing a computer program that evolves through survival and replication of successful variants as it competes with similar programs to play the game of checkers. The program can now beat an average human player. This achievement is important because the program was given only the rules of the game—it taught itself how to win. (This is radically different from the IBM computer program Deep Blue that defeated the chess champion Garry Kasparov in 1997. That computer was given a data-base of many thousands of possible moves and their consequences, and simply ran through them to determine the most advantageous move to make.)

The same has happened to us. Over the ages the universe has taught us how to win, and our memories, neural links, constructs, and the knowledge implicit in the words and language we use, sum up what we each understand of the rules of the game in the conglomerate we call our mind.

Computer programs that, once given a target and some parameters, recursively design to optimize their output, are now reality. In essence, these programs mimic the evolutionary process that life uses. See Steven Johnson, "Darwin in a Box," *Discover*, August 2003, 24-25.

[3] Cassirer, *Language and Myth*, 61.

[4] See Chapter Five, endnote 24, discussing oxygen starvation and other considerations.

[5] Interesting work that can be related to our understanding of consciousness has been conducted by two scientists, using a methodology suggested by Snyder. Young and Ridding used transcranial magnetic stimulation to inhibit frontotemporal neural activity in volunteers, so preventing language and concept manipulation and reducing the volunteers to a savant-like state (where skills demonstrated are always associated with the possession of an exceptional memory). Over a quarter of these volunteers then showed an improved ability to draw pictures and perform mental calculations (although not to the degree frequently demonstrated by some savants).

In our terms, what may have been demonstrated is that savants (and some of the volunteers) could be directly accessing aspects of their first-level consciousness that have been stored for some reason. It may be this (relatively perfect, i.e., unencumbered by second or third-level thought manipulations) memory that is being used by savants, to perform, apparently instantaneously, certain kinds of mathematical calculation and to accurately draw what may have been seen only once a long time ago.

See Douglas S. Fox, "The Inner Savant," in the February, 2002 edition of *Discover*, 44-49. Also Donald A. Treffert and Gregory L. Wallace, "Islands of Genius," in the June 2002 edition of *Scientific American*, 76-85.

[6] Much has been written about consciousness. For an excellent discussion, read Antonio R. Damasio, *The Feeling of What Happens: Body and Emotion in the Making of Consciousness* (New York: Harcourt Brace & Company, 1999). (N.B. Terminology differs between Damasio's text and mine. For instance, what I have termed "first-level thinking" Damasio describes as "core consciousness." Damasio, a research neurologist who maintains a clinical practice, describes patients' disorders to add weight to his hypotheses. He provides many references for further reading.)

[7] Frans de Waal, in *The Ape and the Sushi Master: Cultural Reflections of a Primatologist* (New York: Basic Books, 2001) shows how primates, particularly chimpanzees, develop complex social relationships, communicate, possess cultures and exhibit empathy and sympathy.

Endnotes to Chapter Four Postscript

[1] The Anglican bishop of Edinburgh, Scotland, said as much when he stated that the primary job of bishops has become that of preserving the church's existence by resisting change. This, he claimed, will lead to the death of the institution. (See John Allemang, "The blaspheming bishop," *The Globe and Mail*, March 16, 2002, F6.)

[2] We can believe, for instance, that the world will feed twice as many people as it supports now, or that chloroflorocarbons do not harm the ozone layer. But, if our beliefs are incorrect, then life for our descendants will not be as comfortable as it may be for us.

[3] Thus, for example, we no longer believe, as many of us once did, that radical Islamists can be ignored because they are simply harmless theologians.

Endnotes to Chapter Five Postscripts

[1] One thing it must have, in my opinion, is something to say. Meaningless daubs do not constitute art, no matter how original. The daubs should represent the artist's best attempt to convey a new understanding that he or she has discovered. This what distinguishes art from the inane.

[2] Of course, it takes a great deal more than this for the piece to have merit: here I'm just talking about the act of being creative.

[3] This solution has occurred to others, see White and Gribbin, *Stephen Hawking: A Life in Science*, (London: Penguin Books, 1992), 82.

[4] Momentum = mass x velocity, and velocity is a term that includes both speed and direction of movement.

[5] Remember, single particles travel as waves, but interact with matter—on hitting a screen, for instance—at only one point, thus appearing again as though it were a particle.

[6] Surprisingly, relatively large particles (e.g., atoms and even small molecules—including "buckyballs," geodesically configured, 60-atom, molecules of carbon) can exhibit wave behaviour.

[7] Because energy "waves" define a particle's position as a probability, any particle exists in innumerable possible (quantum) states. This property is being further explored in order to design "quantum computers," because possessing multiple states allows multiple computations to occur simultaneously. Calculations requiring hundreds of thousands of years to compute on today's computers could be carried out in less than a second using a quantum computer. See Michael A. Neilsen, "Rules for a Complex Quantum World," *Scientific American*, November 2002, 66-75.

[8] Although we may subsequently change our mind and say "yes." It is the act of not automatically following our routine (i.e., construct determined) behaviour without first thinking (be it physical or mental behaviour) that marks an act of free will. Free will activity requires a conscious assessment of the pros and cons of alternative behaviours before a decision or an action is taken.

[9] It is important to remember that subconscious second-level thinking always races ahead of conscious second-level realization. At any time, subconscious "summaries" may nudge into the conscious second-level of thought whereupon third-level thinking (where words are used) may take over. (At any point along this sequence of events, the body might be directed to act upon what is occurring within the brain/mind.)

A free will choice is a consciously made decision. It is the conscious acceptance or rejection of what the subconscious offers, made explicit when acted upon, spoken or written. The fortuitous occurrence of any stress-relieving, subconscious-thinking that hits upon a new answer, does not constitute an act of free will. Only if this new answer is subsequently recognized for what it is, and consciously analyzed, then accepted (or rejected), displacing existing answers (or lack of answers), does the act of free will occur.

Endnotes to Chapter Seven Postscripts

1 Ludwig von Bertalanffy, *General Systems Theory: Foundations, Development, Applications* (New York: George Braziller, 1968).

F. Kenneth Berrien, *General and Social Systems* (New Brunswick: Rutgers University Press, 1968).

2 Pairs of "entangled" photons (i.e., identical entities that share common origins and properties) have been separated and sent along optical fibres in opposite directions a distance of ten kilometres before being made to randomly choose and take one of several, equally possible, paths. The two photons always make identical decisions, even though the distance separating them when this decision is made greatly exceeds the distance any form of radiation could travel in the time available to make the choice. In fact, identical random decisions are apparently made instantaneously. (This behaviour is already being discussed as the possible basis for an uncrackable encryption code that the military or banks might use.) Although predicted by quantum mechanics, the phenomenon has yet to be understood. An external Universe might be just what's involved, with information that controls supposedly random behaviour being instantly passed through to our universe, in a way that makes this information appear to us as being in two places at once. If this is the case, then our universe is actually (although possibly restrictedly) open.

A team of Australian scientists have recently teleported a laser beam; that is, they destroyed it in one location then reconstructed its identical copy in a new location, one meter distant.

(Also see Anton Zeilinger, "Quantum Teleportation," in *Scientific American*, April 2000, 50-59.)

3 It is intriguing to recognize that causality and the Conservation Laws implies that our universe is always retaining the ability to return to any of its earlier forms.

Endnotes to Chapter Eight Postscript

[1] The ribonucleotides in RNA are more readily synthesized than the more complicated deoxyribonucleotides in DNA. Most importantly, RNA can replicate and store genetic information.

[2] Water is plentiful throughout space, but any fluid could be used because fluids readily transport energy-providing resources and molecules from place to place. Gases (and high temperature plasmas) are fluids, and life may have originated in such environments.

Selected Bibliography

Aczel, A. D. *Probability 1: Why there must be Intelligent Life in the Universe.* New York: Harcourt Brace & Company, 1998.

Akenson, D. H. *Saint Saul: A Skeleton Key to the Historical Jesus.* McGill-Queens University Press, 2000.

Allman, J. M. *Evolving Brains.* New York: Scientific American Library, 1999.

Barrett, D. et al, eds. *World Christian Encyclopaedia: A comparative survey of churches and religions – AD 30 to 2000.* Oxford: Oxford University Press, 2001.

Barrow, J. D. *Theories of Everything: The Quest for Ultimate Explanation.* New York: Oxford University Press, 1990.

------------ and F. J. Tipler. *The Anthropic Cosmological Principle.* Oxford: Clarendon Press, 1986.

Benedict, R. *Patterns of Culture.* Boston: Houton Mifflin Company, 1934.

Bernal, J. D. *The Origin of Life.* London: Weidenfeld and Nicolson, 1967.

Berrien, F. K. *General and Social Systems.* New Brunswick: Rutgers University Press, 1968.

Buss, D. M. *Evolutionary Psychology: The New Science of the Mind.* Boston: Allyn and Bacon, 1999.

Calvin, W. H. *The Ascent of Mind: Ice Age Climates and the Evolution of Intelligence.* New York: Bantam Books, 1990.

------------. *The River that Flows Uphill: A Journey from the Big Bang to the Big Brain.* New York: MacMillan Publishing Company, 1986.

Caspar, M., translated and edited by C. D. Hellman. *Kepler.* London & New York: Abelard-Schumann, 1959.

Cassirer, E., translated by S. K. Langer. *Language and Myth.* New York: Dover Publications, Inc., 1953.

Cooke, R. *Dr. Folkman's War: Angiogenesis & the Struggle to Defeat Cancer.* New York: Random House, 2001.

Damasio, A. R. *The Feeling of What Happens: Body and Emotion in the Making of Consciousness.* New York: Harcourt Brace & Company, 1999.

Dawkins, R. *The Blind Watchmaker.* New York: W. W. Norton & Company, 1986.

de Chardin, T. *The Phenomenon of Man.* New York: Harper & Row, 1959.

de Duve, C. *Vital Dust: Life as a Cosmic Imperative.* New York: Basic Books, 1995.

de Waal, F. *The Ape and the Sushi Master: Cultural Reflections of a Primatologist.* New York: Basic Books, 2001.

Deamer, D. W. and G. R Fleischaker. *Origins of Life: the Central Concepts.* Sudbury, Massachusetts: Jones and Bartlett, 1994.

Dennett, D. C. *Consciousness Explained.* Boston: Little, Brown and Company, 1991.

Desmond A. and J. Moore. *Darwin: The Life of a Tormented Evolutionist.* New York: Warner Books, Inc., 1991.

Dunbar, R. *Grooming, Gossip, and the Evolution of Language.* Cambridge, Massachusetts: Harvard University Press, 1996.

Durkheim, E. *The Elementary Forms of Religious Life.* First published in 1915.

Dyson, F. *Origins of Life.* Cambridge: Cambridge University Press, 1999.

Feinberg, G. *The Prometheus Project: Mankind's search for long-range goals.* Garden City, New York: Doubleday & Company, Inc., 1969.

Ferris, T. *The Mind's Sky: Human Intelligence in a Cosmic Context.* New York: Bantam Books, 1992.

Feynman, R. P. *Six Easy Pieces.* Reading Massachusetts: Addison-Wesley Publishing Company, 1995.

Francoeur, R. *Evolving World, Converging Man.* New York: Holt, Rinehart & Winston, 1970.

Goldsmith, D. *The Runaway Universe: The Race to Find the Future of the Cosmos.* Cambridge, Massachusetts: Perseus Publishing, 2000.

Goodenough, U. *The Sacred Depths of Nature.* New York: Oxford University Press, 1998.

Greenfield, S. *The Human Brain: A Guided Tour.* New York: Basic Books, 1997.

------------. *The Private Life of the Brain: Emotions, Consciousness, and the Secret of the Self.* New York: John Wiley & Sons, Inc., 2000.

Gross, M. *Life on the Edge: Amazing creatures thriving in extreme environments.* Cambridge, Massachusetts: Perseus Publishing, 2001.
Hauser, M. D. *Wild Minds: What Animals really Think.* New York: Henry Holt and Company, 2000.
Hawken, P. et al. *Natural Capitalism.* Boston: Little, Brown and Company, 1999.
Heinrich, B. *Mind of the Raven: Investigations and Adventures with Wolf-Birds.* New York: Harper Collins, 1999.
Holland, J. H. *Emergence: from Chaos to Order.* Reading, Massachusetts: Helix Books, Addison-Wesley Publishing Company, Inc., 1998.
Hoyle, F. *The Nature of the Universe.* Oxford: Basil Blackwell, 1950.
Kohlberg, L. *The Meaning and Measurement of Moral Development.* Massachusetts: Clark University, 1981.
------------. *Essays on Moral Development. Volume I. The Philosophy of Moral Development: Moral Stages and the Idea of Justice.* San Francisco: Harper & Row, 1981.
Lahav, N. *Biogenesis: Theories of Life's Origin.* Oxford: Oxford University Press, 1999.
Lawrence, P. R. and N. Nohria. *Driven: How Human Nature Shapes Our Choices.* San Francisco: Jossey-Bass, 2002.
Loftus, E. and K. Ketcham. *The Myth of Repressed Memory: False Memories and Allegations of Sexual Abuse.* New York: St. Martin's Press, Inc., 1996.
Lovelock, J. *The Ages of Gaia: A Biography of Our Living Earth.* New York: Bantam Books, 1990.
Mahfouz, N. and N. Mahfuz., translated by T. Abu-Hassabo. *Akhenaten: Dweller in Truth.* Doubleday and Company, 2000.
Middleton, W. E. K. *The Scientific Revolution.* Toronto: C.B.C. Publications, 1963.
Nichols, J. *Linguistic Diversity in Space and Time.* University of Chicago Press, 1999.
Noss, J. B. *Man's Religions*, 5th ed. New York: Macmillan Publishing Co., Inc., 1974.
Pennock, R. T. *Tower of Babel: The Evidence against the New Creationism.* Boston: MIT Press, 1999.
Pinker, S. *The Language Instinct: How the Mind Creates Language.* New York: William Morrow and Company, 1994.
------------. *How the Mind Works.* New York: W.W.Norton and Company, 1997.
Postman, N. *Building a Bridge to the Eighteenth Century: How the Past Can Improve Our Future.* New York: Alfred A. Knopf, 2000.

Quine, W. V. and J. S. Ullian. *The Web of Belief.* New York: Random House, 1970.

Rees, M. *Just Six Numbers: The Deep Forces that Shape the Universe.* New York: Basic Books, 2000.

Richards, Chris, ed. *The Illustrated Encyclopedia of World Religions.* Shaftesbury, Dorset: Element Books Limited, 1997.

Rudgley, R. *The Lost Civilizations of the Stone Age.* New York: The Free Press, 1999.

Rue, L. D. *By the Grace of Guile: The Role of Deception in Natural History.* New York: Oxford University Press, 1994.

Ruhlen, M. *The Origin of Language: Tracing the Evolution of the Mother Tongue.* New York: John Wiley, 1994.

Schopf, J. W. *Cradle of Life: The Discovery of Earth's Earliest Fossils.* Princeton: Princeton University Press, 1999.

Smoot, G. and K. Davidson. *Wrinkles in Time: The Imprint of Creation.* Little, Brown and Company (U.K.) Ltd., 1993.

Squire, L. R. and E. R. Kandel. *Memory: From Mind to Molecules.* New York: Scientific American Library, 1999.

Tipler, F. J. *The Physics of Immortality: Modern Cosmology, God and the Resurrection of the Dead.* New York: Doubleday, 1994.

von Bertalanffy, L. *General Systems Theory: Foundations, Development, Applications.* New York: George Braziller, 1968.

von Neumann, J., ed. A. W. Burks. *Theory of Self-Reproducing Automata.* Urbana: University of Illinois Press, 1966.

Ward, P. D. and D. Brownlee. *Rare Earth: Why Complex Life is Uncommon in the Universe.* New York: Copernicus, 2000.

Weiner, J. *The Beak of the Finch: A Story of Evolution in Our Time.* New York: Alfred A. Knopf, 1994.

------------. *Time, Love, Memory.* New York: Vintage Books, 1999.

White, M. and J. Gribbin. *Stephen Hawking: A Life in Science.* London: Penguin Books, 1992.

Index

A

abortion............ 44, 97, 195, 196, 200
activists
    action groups 208
    individuals 207
    working groups....................... 208
    world directorate..................... 208
afterlife, an91, 98, 141, 168, 206, 210, 211, 221
    belief in................................ 61, 62, 96
agnostics 91
Akhenatom..................................... 64
Amaenhotep IV 64
Archaean life 122
Aristotle.. 108
assumptions 63, 131, 134
    ancient 60
    and life after death 60, 62
    become beliefs..................... 63, 64
    every day 59
    existence of gods 62
    false 79, 98, 143
    practical applications for 63
    why made 60
atheists... 84
    and non-believers...................... 91

B

Barrow and Tipler 153
behaviour
    'morally right' 191-193
    'morally wrong'............... 192, 195
    and constructs 81
    animal 146, 197
    blind 67
    codes of 187
    collective 164
    'correct' 180
    credible 91
    degenerate................................ 179
    evolutionary............................. 136
    genetically controlled 200

behaviour (continued)
    herd... 128
    individual.................................. 163
    innate.. 196
    insect 146
    instinctive 17, 18
    irresponsible 176
    life's 145, 169
    moral 41, 192-194
    new moral................................. 191
    non-thinking 20, 22
    of gods 63
    of molecules 136, 150
    of supersystems 231
    of the universe 66
    parental..................................... 138
    plant.. 145
    rational....................................... 32
    religious..................................... 65
    virtual particle 225, 232
behavioural norms......................... 57
belief... 65
    a globalized 169
    above reason............................. 93
    and assumptions 61, 134
    and conviction 51, 66
    and human life........................... 98
    and ideas.................................... 61
    and knowledge......................... 199
    and non-believers 91
    and rationality............ 94, 197, 220
    and reality................................ 221
    and stress 69
    atheist 91
    Buddhist 88
    changing 63, 92
    Christian 84
    current 50
    harmless................................... 221
    Hindu... 86
    in a green-cheese moon 221
    in a meta-purpose 181

belief (continued)
  in causality 220
  in God 96, 221
  in many gods 64
  its source 59, 66, 69
  Jewish 89
  Muslim 85
  of scientists 102
  primitive 83
  unifying 57, 99
  why needed 15
Bible, the 59, 84, 91, 95, 125
Big Bang, the 94, 110-112, 117
  following 113
  theory 110, 111
birth control 197
Brahman 86
brain, the 17, 19, 20
  and constructs 71
  and information 152
  and the mind 79, 216
  and thinking 22
  its function 79
  neural patterns 22
  of animals 26
  training 138
Buddha 88, 89
Buddhism 88
Buddhist practices 88
burial rituals 61
  of Chinchorro 61
  of Cro-Magnon 60
  of Neanderthal 60

C

Calvin, William H. 22, 28
capital punishment 198
Cassirer, Ernst 22, 28, 29, 215
causality ...31, 34, 118, 188, 220, 226
  and free will 224, 226
  and language 32
  and single particle events 224
  and the universe 37, 80
  and thinking 32
  and virtual particles 226
cave drawings 61

Christian practices 84
Christianity 84
cloning humans 97, 200
complexity
  and evolution 141, 151, 155
  and intelligence 152
  and mental skills 152
  and neural networks 22
  life's 135
conscience 217, *See also* Postscript
    to Chapter One
  a global 184
  and morality 217
  and truth 217
  animal 217
consciousness215, *See also*
    Postscript to Chapter One
  a universal 153
  and Buddhism 88
  and Cassirer 29
  and constructs 216
  and language 31
  and second-level thinking 215, 227
  and third-level thinking 215
  definition of 216
Conservation Laws, the *See*
    Postscript to Chapter Seven
constructs48, 70, 77-81, 152, 153,
    171, 205, 221, 231
  and aging 71
  and creativity 71
  and reformations 72
  and second-level thinking 216
  and single mindedness 71
  and truth 217
  cost of holding 71
  minor adjustments to 72
  value of holding 71
conversions 49, 50, 72, 73
  and constructs 73
  and proselytizing 50
  and reformations 74
  externally induced 73
  religious 75, 81
  self-induced 73, 78
Copernicus, Nicolaus 37, 108

cosmology and physics 118
creativity 199
   and constructs 224
   artistic 223
   everyday 223

D

Darwin, Charles 38, 77, 125, 126, 151
Dawkins, Richard 135, 151
de Duve, Christian 25, 125
decision making 29
   and a universal religion 209
   and assumptions 60
   and constructs 81
   and private purpose 48
   and public purpose 48
   and purpose 161
   criteria 47
   environment 47
      religious 50, 65
   global 154
   moral 50, 51, 98, 139, 191, 205
   practical 51
Descartes, René 31, 215
direction 166
   and individuals 161
   divine 95, 227
   moral 95, 161
dreams 76
   and second-level thinking 76
   and stress 76
drug use 199
Dunbar, Robin 24

E

earth, the 116
   and Aristotle 108
   and Copernicus 108
   and the universe 110
   its resources 198
Einstein, Albert 36, 38, 225
energy exchanges 147
   in biological processes 148
   in chemical processes 147
eukaryotic life 123
euthanasia 196

evolution 38, 123, 125, 132, 135, 136, 143, 151
   active 137
   and intelligence 152
   and latent abilities 137
   and learning 137
   and punctuated equilibrium 128
   and survival 129
   as a fact 126
   as a theory 126
   evidence showing 125
   its end-point 140, 141
   its future 138
   its trend 153
   itself evolving 137
   life's 132, 142, 154, 163, 164, 167, 172, 191, 193, 197, 205, 207, 210, 233
   occuring in laboratories 126
   occuring in nature 127
   planned 139
   two-step 137
exoplanets 131
   detecting 115
exploiting 151, 177
   and international controls 209
   and life 184
   excessive 177
   controlling 180, 191, 209
extinctions 128
   specie 128, 129, 174
eye, the 19, 25, 138, 151

F

feedback *See* Postscript to Chapter Seven
Fermi Paradox, the 132
finches 127
Folkman, Judah 77
free will 143, 224, 226, *See also* Postscript to Chapter Five
   and accountability 224
   and probability 225, 226
   and saying 'No' 226
freedom 180, 226
   and constructs 71

freedom (continued)
    and self-responsibility 199
    life's 155
    of the press 177
    of thought 209
    personal 193, 199

G

galaxies 108-111, 113, 115, 118, 130, 230
    their formation 113
Galileo, Galilei 37, 107, 108
General Systems Theory 117, 230, *See also* Postscript to Chapter Seven
genes 35, 125, 128, 200
    and the future 183
    patenting 200
    the period gene 17
genetic manipulation 162, 172, 182, 183, 184, 193
    allowable 183, 200
    controlling 184
genetic mutations .... *See* mutations
genetics 37, 138, 182
    who benefits 183
global civilization 181
global consensus 207, 222
globalization 178, 179
    and international controls 180
    its effects 179
God's residence 118
Gödel, Kurt 117, *See also* Postscript to Chapter Seven
    the Incompleteness Theorem 229
Goodenough, Ursula 154
Grant, Peter and Rosemary .. 127, 150
Greeks early 62

H

Haldane, J.B.S. 120
Hausser, Marc D. 21
Heisenberg, Werner 225, 226
Hindu practices 87
Hinduism 86
hominoids 124

Homo sapiens 30, 124, 134
homunculus, the 216
human evolution 129
    directing 129
humans as subsystems 190, 192

I

ideals
    the meta-purpose's 208
    three 180
identity 87, 93, 168, 215
individuals, their importance 198
intelligence 33, 80, 152, 154, 155, 171, 188, 191
    as problem solving 152
    Neanderthal 124
    non-earthly 131
international regulations 181
Islam 85

J

Jesus 65, 84, 94
Jewish practices 90
Judaism 89

K

Kekulé von Stradonitz 76
Koran, the 85, 91

L

language . 24, 26, 33, 61, 80, 153, 215
    a proto- 28
    and causality 32
    and identity 215
    and morality 45, 49
    and Neanderthals 124
    and neural networks 30
    and problem solving 30
    early use of 28
    its development 27, 28, 30
    its possible origin 29
    mathematical 36
language use
    in animals 27
    precision in 31
leaders 57, 65, 75, 174, 176

Index

leaders (continued)
    and convictions 66
    in World War II 176
    religious 65, 66, 221
    with vision 161
learning .. 25, 137, 139, 148, 152, 191
    adult 26
    and complexity 22
    and control 139, 140, 152, 155, 163, 169, 188, 194, 198, 199, 227
    and evolution 138
    and life 169
    animal 138
    infant 25
    its importance 192
    its source 143
    to exploit 140
    to see 19, 138
life
    after death 60, 84
    ancient forms of 117
    and complexity 155
    and energy exchanges 147
    and evolution 34, 183
    and exploiting 150, 151, 155, 164, 188, *See also* exploiting and life
    and humans 142
    and mutations 137
    and reproduction 123, 149
    as a subsystem 230
    as a supersystem 189
    behaviours supported by 189
    behaviours that enhance 190
    complex 136
    conditions to support 130
    designed 134
    future 170
    hibernating 170
    human contributions to 168, 171, 172
    in balance 146
    its beginning 64, 92, 120, 136, 147, 149, *See also* Postscript to Chapter Eight
    and reproduction 149

life (continued)
    its beginning (continued)
        as methanogens 121
        in hot springs 120
        in the laboratory 120
    its behaviour 145, 189
    its direction 153
    its end-point 166, 169
    its evolution 155
    its existence elsewhere 130
    its future 98, 143, 164
    its meaning .... *See* meaning, life's
    its purpose 93, 135, 136, 139, 141, 153, 155, 161, 166, *See also* purpose of life
    its ultimate outcome 142
    its welfare 180
    living a moral 48
    past 170
    quality of 164, 177
    sitting in judgement 190
    the facts of 188
    without end 170
life on earth
    development of 122, 123
    early evidence of 122
    its future 165
    tracing its history 119

M

mammals 23, 124
mathematics 35, 38, 95, 220
    abstract 36, 38, 41, 45
    and problem solving 37
meaning 27, 29, 30, 32, 36, 45, 67, 78, 141, 162, 171, 172, 217
    life's 139, 206, 210, 218, 219
    personal 162
    search for 75
memories 19-21, 23, 30, 73, 78-80, 152, 171, 195, 215, 216, 223, 224, *See also* constructs
    and conversions 72
    comparing 28
    component parts of 21
    forming 25

memories (continued)
   infant 19, 24
   linking24, 25, 28, 30, 69, 71, 76, 77
   permanent links between............70
   religious....................................50
   transient links between...............69
meta-belief 211
meta-purpose 156, 160-162, 164, 173, 180, 191, 193, 194, 200, 201, 205, 208, 210, *See also* purpose
   a collective 168
   a surrogate 207
   an overarching..........................163
   and decision making.................162
   and extraterrestrial life 168
   and genetics..............................162
   and multi-year targets...............234
   and religious conflict................168
   and responsibilities...................194
   and zero-growth 164, 165
   rationale for proposed 164
Middleton, W. E. K..........................37
Milky Way, the 114, 122, 130, 230
Miller, Stanley...............................120
mind, the17, 20-23, 25, 29, 31, 32, 35, 40, 41, 45, 48, 49, 51, 53, 57, 66, 70, 71, 74-77, 79, 152, 171, 197, 205, 218, 219, 224
   in a quiescent state 21
   in an active state..........................21
   of a god 135
   training 138
molecular complexes............148, 150
   additions to...............................149
   living vs non-living 148
monotheism..............................64, 89
moral decisions 187, 201, 221
   a dilemma...................................49
   and purpose 49
   making15, 44, 48, 80, 164, 166, 167, 231
   the dilemma's resolution.............49
   their environment.................48, 50
moral direction 95
moral problems 41, 49, 200, 201

moral problems (continued)
   a dilemma...................................43
   and genocide 44
   criteria for solving......................41
   solving....................... 15, 35, 39, 42
   their environment........................41
      if lacking 43
   their source.................................45
morality15, 88, 93, 98, 184, 192, 194, 195, 211
   'Western' 86
   a different..................................196
   a new 209
   and a Universal Grammar 32
   and language 33
   rational 197
Muhammad......................................85
Muslim practices.............................85
mutations18, 51, 79, 128, 135, 137, 150, 188
   dormant 137
   in DNA nucleotides 137

N

natural selection125, 126, 132, 135, 137, 155
natural world, the 57, 150
Neanderthals 60, 62, 124
Neolithic Age...................................61
neural networks 18, 19, 21-23, 70, 79, 152, 216
   and constructs 70
   and creativity............................223
   and link formation......................24
neurons........................ 18, 25, 152, 226
   and neural loops 18
   and synaptic knobs...............18, 20
Newton, Isaac 36, 38, 231
Non Governmental Organizations175
nova and supernova 109, 112, 114

O

Ob 156, 166, 169, 170, 172, 194, 195, 207
   our contribution to 171
Oparin, Alexander........................120

P

Paley, William 135
particles 225, 226
  and waves 225
  virtual 225, 232
personal purpose 51
photosynthesis 147
Pinker, Steven 32, 35, 138
planets 79, 108, 114, 118, 121, 130, 139
  colonizing 172
  exoplanets 115, 116
    number of 130
  finding 115
  their formation 115
Poincaré, Henri 76
Postscript to Chapter Four
  Rationality in Science and
    Religion 220
Postscript to Chapter Fourteen
  Multi-year Targets 234
Postscript to Chapter One
  Consciousness and Concsience 215
Postscript to Chapter Three
  Purpose and Meaning 218
Postscripts to Chapter Seven
  Gödel's Theorem, General
    Systems Theory, and the
    Conservation Law 229
primordial soup, the 120
problem solving 30, 38, 47, 77, 188,
  See also intelligence
  and vision 177
  criteria 38-40
  environment 38, 40
    examples of 39
    external 39
    internal 40
    religious 80
  failures 176
  metaphysical 67
  subconscious 78
  successes 175
problems
  abstract 35
  mathematical 35

problems (continued)
  real 35
  scientific 37
  world 173, 184
    and genetics 183
    current 174
    excessive exploitation 178
    terrorism 182
Prokaryotic life 123
purpose 15, 16, 42, 45, 49, 64, 66,
  69, 73, 75, 80, 98, 139, 141, 167,
  172, 210, See also meta-purpose
  a collective 163
  a common 176
  a forward-looking 168
  a surrogate 105, 142, 143, 154, 166
  a universal 105
  and daily activities 218
  and depression 219
  and meaning 219, See also
    Postscript to Chapter Three
  and moral codes 187, 192, 205
  and survival 219
  and vision 173
  contriving a 141
  God's 67, 134, 135
  inventing a 139
  life's 49, 105, 135, 136, 139, 153, 218
  metaphysical 49, 50
  personal 51, 73
  private 48
  religious 66, 80, 93, 204
  the universe's 105, 133
Pythagoras 35, 36

Q

Quantum Mechanics 225

R

rationality 32, 45, 96, 171, 193, 198,
  220, 221, See also Postscript to
  Chapter Four
  in religion 220
  in science 220
reformations 72-74

religion, a universal 105
religions 15, 43-45, 48, 50, 57, 59,
    62, 63, 65, 69, 80, 83, 92-98, 134,
    139, 142, 156, 160, 161, 167, 179,
    184, 192, 204-209, 220, 221, 227
    and assumptions 98
    and causality 187
    and divine intervention 98
    common features of 92
    early Egyptian 62
    number of major 83
    number of followers 83
    personal problems with 94
renaissance, a second 211
revelation, a personal 227
revelations 49, 75, 80, 86, 91
    and accompanying emotions 75
    and the subconscious 78
    creating leaders 75
    erroneous 78
    non-religious 75
    religious and secular 227
    self-induced 78
    their source 75

S

science 92, 118, 220
    and causality 187
    and religion 101, 102
    its beginnings 37
scientific method, the 37, 220
SETI 131
shaman 57, 61
singularity
    a terminating 170
    an impenetrable 118
    the creating 112, 133
species 121, 126
    and Darwin 38
    behaviour 26, 145, 146, 150, 199
    convergence of 128
    development of 127, 128
    divergence of 128
    extinction 140
    interrelationships between 125
    number of 126

species (continued)
    the human 167, 189
spirituality 171, 204
stars .38, 108-110, 118, 122, 130, 131
    behaviour of 114, 115
    formation of 113
    the number of 115
Steady State Theory, the 110, 111
stress 49, 69, 75, 76
    and problem solving 77
    and second-level thinking 76
    freedom from 219
    relief of 78-80
subsystem*See* Postscript to Chapter
    Seven
superstring theory*See* Postscript to
    Chapter Seven
supersystem *See* Postscript to
    Chapter Seven
survival 23, 27, 69, 142, 155, 219
    and learning 20
    and problem solving 30, 219
    of the fittest 135
system*See* Postscript to Chapter
    Seven

T

Ten Commandments, the 90
Thales of Miletus 37
Theory of Everything, the*See*
    Postscript to Chapter Seven
Theory of Relativity, the 225
thinking 17, 22, 28, 30, 71, 226
    and belief 67
    and constructs 71, 72, 75, 81
    and control 34
    and conversions 72, 73
    and intelligence 33
    and problem solving 15
    and stress 76, 78, 80
    animal 21, 26
    definition of 21
    evolution of 22
    first vs second-level 24
    first-level 22, 23
        awareness of 216

Index

thinking (continued)
  first-level (continued)
    definition of 23
  language and intelligence 34
  modes 22
    relative speeds of 29
    order of 29
    patterns 45
  rational 24, 33, 34, 43, 45, 49, 51, 69
    incapacitated 49
  second-level 23, 25, 26, 28, 30, 76, 215, 216
    and causality 32
    and constructs 71
    conscious 24
      example of 25
    definition of 23
    subconscious 23
  third-level 26-29, 138, 215, 216
    and language use 29, 31
tool-making
  animal 21
  human 29, 124
Torah, the 90
truth, the 49, 50, 69, 79, 156, 190, 193, 204, 217
  and revelations 74
  personal definition of 31
  search for 193

U

umbrella religion, an 206
Uncertainty Principle, the 225
unifying science and religion 102, 193
United Nations, the 174, 175, 209
universal religion. 187, 206, 207, 209
  as an influential force 210
  characteristics of a 204
  developing a 206
  its intentions 209
  why needed 206
universe, the 30-32, 36-38, 69, 107, 109-111
  age of 109
the universe (continued)
  and causality 31, 32, 34, 51, 80, 188, 220, 224
  and change 111
  and God 118, 133, 170
  and life 130, 132, 136, 141, 155
  and morality 42
  and physics 134, 153
  and purpose 105, 133, 135
  and purpose-directed change ... 134
  initially designed 133, 135
  its beginning 64, 66, 92, 94, 101, 112, 117, 170
  its behaviour 102
  its end 111, 135, 169, 170
  its expansion 110, 111
  its future 112, 134
  its history 112
universes, other 112, 232

V

values 43, 181, 193
  religious 59, 86, 93
valuing 16, 80, 190
Vedas, the 86
vision 62, 65, 66, 69, 138, 141, 161, 167, 173, 176, 180, 181, 204, 208
  a collective 176
  and leadership 65
  and terrorism 182
von Neumann probes 132

W

Wallace, Alfred Russel .. 38, 125, 126
Weiner, Jonathan 18, 125
why bother? 159, 166, 172
  because we care 166
  to avoid irrationality 167
  to hand on to the future 167

X

xenotransplantation 200

Z

zero growth 164